D1210280

Architectronics

THE McGRAW-HILL DESIGNING WITH SYSTEMS SERIES
Eric Teicholz *Consulting Editor*

Stitt *Systems Drafting: Creative Reprographics for Architects and Engineers* (1980)

Stitt *Systems Graphics: Breakthroughs in Drawing Production and Project Management for Architects, Designers, and Engineers* (1984)

Teicholz *CAD/CAM Handbook* (1984)

Radford & Stevens *CADD Made Easy* (1986)

Winn *Architectronics: Revolutionary Technologies for Masterful Building Through Design* (1987)

Gerlach *Transition to CADD for Architects and Engineers* (1987)

Teicholz & Orr *Computer Integrated Manufacturing Handbook* (1987)

Architectronics

Revolutionary Technologies for Masterful Building through Design

Michael Winn

Illustrated by Martin Schaefer

McGraw-Hill Book Company

New York St. Louis San Francisco Auckland Bogotá
Hamburg Johannesburg London Madrid Mexico
Milan Montreal New Delhi Panama
Paris São Paulo Singapore
Sydney Tokyo Toronto

This book is lovingly dedicated to my father and mother from whom I learned that an act of love is an act of integrity.

Library of Congress Cataloging-in-Publication Data
Winn, Michael, date
Architectronics: revolutionary technologies for masterful building through design.
Bibliography: p.
1. Architecture design—Data processing.
2. Computer-aided design—Data processing.
3. Office buildings. I. Title.
NA2728.W5 1987 720'.28'5 86-18491
ISBN 0-07-071072-4

234567890 DOC/DOC 893210987

ISBN 0-07-071072-4

The editors for this book were Harold B. Crawford and Esther Gelatt, the designer was Naomi Auerbach, and the production supervisor was Teresa F. Leaden. It was set in Baskerville by Braun-Brumfield, Inc.

Printed and bound by R. R. Donnelley, Inc.

Contents

About the Author

Michael Winn is presently a telecommunications and information systems consultant in Del Mar, California. He received his Bachelor of Science degree in communications from California State University at Long Beach. Mr. Winn has conducted training seminars about integrated office information systems for developers, businesses, and telecommunications firms in California. He has also written a report on multitenant telecommunications services for the *Datapro Telecommunications Management Resource Book*.

Foreword

In *Architectronics*, Michael Winn attacks issues that lie at the heart of social progress and issues which affect every man, woman, and child in the urban community. And he poses an important question: What do we need to know to effectively manage development so that we produce communities that are free from such conditions as crime and juvenile delinquency, conditions which we seem to have resigned ourselves to living with, as if they were unresolvable? Winn embarks on a formidable task as he seeks in contemporary society the source of dramatically worsening statistics on drug abuse, alcoholism, juvenile crime, and terrorism. In this inquiry, he traces an interesting trail which relates our use of technologies to the growing sense of isolation experienced by residents in all urban areas.

To begin with, Winn views building development as a technology for providing various kinds of community resources. We do not usually think about building development in this way—as an arena in which to examine the social problems of our culture. Usually, the problem of crime is discussed as a police issue; poverty is thought of as a circumstance related to employment and education; and so on. Conversations about building development are conducted by investment planners and real estate entrepreneurs. The involvment of government in development is administrative rather than creative, having to do with the regulation of building codes and the planning of roads, highways, and other services.

Guiding the development of a city is an overwhelming task. For those of us who sit on legislative bodies in fast growing communities, the task becomes manageable when we have a conceptual view of the evolving technologies which are now an integral part of development. Very few of us have been schooled in the sciences of computers, engineering, telecommunications, or electronics, yet our responsibility to the public trust seems to make it obligatory for us to become knowledgeable in these areas. We are making decisions daily which commit vast expanses of land to development, affecting the way we live, work, and play for generations to come. The technology of development is determining the kinds of communities that will result from this development. Were we to examine the possibilities of making use of technology to create communities with decreasing crime statistics, for example, where might this kind of inquiry lead us? Perhaps we would place more emphasis on preserving open space and natural environments. We might be more committed to providing transportation and social facilities for youth and senior citizens who are not able to drive cars. We might put attention on providing child care for young families and dealing creatively with the frustrating dilemma which is the root cause of child neglect and abuse.

Through understanding the use of technologies, we may have a better opportunity to create the most enriching environment we can envision for future generations. The way we build, where we build, and what we build must be studied in conjunction with technologies for living and working, the procedures of which are already dominating all of our activities. Now more than ever, it is imperative that legislators, community activists, and students involved with planning, architecture, and development become aware of the effects of new technologies. These technologies exist only because they provide potent and reliable structures for managing complex tasks.

Councilman Mike Gotch
City of San Diego, California

Preface

Recently, I spent 3 days in a hospital in Phoenix, Arizona, where my father was ending his life. At the time, I was just starting to write this book and I could not help noticing the hospital personnel and the technologies they used in treating my father. I was also more aware of my own and my father's and family's reactions to the hospital and its technologies.

My father was a remarkable man. My brother said about him, at the funeral service, that he was a simple man, a man without deceit; that he was humble; that he loved people absolutely without regard for their personal situations, religious or political positions, or nationalities; that he expressed his love through action rather than words. Very simply, he was a man of his word. In his presence during his last moments, I was moved by my experience of the paradox of his nature: His humility and the simplicity of his nature seemed to free him from being subject to technology even when its presence seemed oppressive.

My father responded to technologies the way he responded to gravity. He managed them when necessary in order to keep his word. He had been raised on a farm in Iowa. When he was 15 years old, he left the farm and joined the navy, becoming a boiler technician responsible for the management of the ship's engines, drive, and control mechanisms. As a Chief Petty Officer, he was responsible for the lives of his crew—the mechanics, who worked in the engine and machine rooms of the ship. The sailors called him "Pappy." He was serving on the battleship *USS West Virginia* during the attack on Pearl Harbor in 1941. He was decorated on several occasions for saving the lives of his crew. He was on the deck of the battleship *USS Missouri* when the leaders of Japan officially surrendered, at the end of the war in the Pacific.

As I sat at the edge of my father's bed, I remembered these things about him. Looking out of the hospital room window at the Arizona desert, I reflected on the audacity of our civilization in creating the possibility for supporting life and abundance in this seemingly hostile, desert environment. As I watched, a turbojet-powered helicopter landed outside to deliver an emergency patient. I watched the whirling cyclone of its rotors subside until the blades seemed like gossamer wings of a dragonfly—a magician's trick. I thought about the things that had happened during my father's life—about the advent of travel into the solar system and the recognizable potential of our technologies. It occurred to me that, given the adventure that life could be, we have been wasting a lot of time by not solving the very petty problems through which most human misery is allowed to continue. And I thought about the satisfactions of life—what it is one can hope to accomplish in a lifetime.

I am speaking about these things because it became clear to me that the event of my father's death prepared me to look at things and to listen in a way different from the one I had been used to. From this new perspective, I examined what I see, hear, and know in relation to my life's purpose. In thinking about the book I was about to write, it seemed apparent that the commercial exploitation of technologies may be either a key to solving major issues of planetary ecology and human well-being or a factor that could keep us in the straits of confusion until we burn ourselves out of existence through the gradual mismanagement of our most important resource—the ecosystems of the planet Earth.

Technologies are a part of what man is. We are as much driven to be in certain ways by technologies as we are empowered to move the material universe around us. We are shaped today by our technologies perhaps more than anything else. They afford us the opportunity to manage economic and social development in a way that is responsible to the interests of all people. The simple availability of this opportunity changes the outlook, ambition, and potential of our young people. And what of the simple people like my father, who witnessed and participated in the struggles of Western civilization through the experiments of fascism, communism and war—people who have been so willing to give to those around them and whose faith in the value of life is unquestioning despite circumstances?

My father watched television a lot during his last few months, when he was confined to his house. He watched the C-Span network, which broadcasts congressional and local political hearings, and he was frequently upset and angry about what he heard. I felt I should apologize to him for this, on behalf of all of us who recognize our responsibility for community politics. More practically, I wanted to do something about it; to that purpose, I became dedicated to completing this book, in the wish that it be a contribution.

When I offered to write a book about technologies to assist those who develop commercial buildings, I was naive. I assumed that it would be easy to organize a discussion about computers in intelligent buildings and provide a reference for builders, real estate developers, and managers of businesses.

Working as a consultant, I have frequently answered questions about emerging technologies, their uses, and how they work. I have many critical opinions about land development and developers, and I sometimes have withheld the benefit of knowledge from individuals and companies whose practices I thought were sociopathic. I am of the opinion that it is dangerous to continue developing land as we have, and I feel that to export our development practices to developing nations is unbelievable folly. Our leadership in international political and economic systems is dangerous, given our record of land-use planning. Even our redevelopment projects have created problems of pollution, crime, and alienation. These problems often have shattering effects on the lives of many people, families, and entire communities. Our applications of the most powerful technologies have been irresponsive to issues of general human and ecological well-being. They have had destructive and dehumanizing effects on work, home, and recreational places.

I am being critical not of American culture but of human culture. A visitor from another planet could study my life and get a clear picture of a contemporary, civilized human being. I am a representative of American culture. I am a part of the building and development industry establishment. I know in detail what goes on, where the problems are created, who creates them, and how. My knowledge does not mean much when it comes to finding someone to blame, for there are very few who are not participating in the process of development which alienates man from nature and from other men. It is inherent in how we have been conditioned in our homes, families, schools, work, and our religious, recreational, political, and other pursuits that we operate as we do.

There is a tendency toward arrogance in the psychology of our culture, perhaps resulting from the very esoteric and complex nature of the specialties of most technical knowledge. People who know about new technologies assume without thinking that they are "better" for having such knowledge. They also tend to look at the technological "peasant" as inferior. I know it is arrogance to think that I am better prepared than others to have technological knowledge of my cutlure, to decide who should or should not have such information, or to suggest that I may even be more deserving than others to own the responsibility for this knowledge. However, I have noticed, in my thoughts and attitudes, subtle habits of speech and policy which have been an unconscious part of my communication with others. It is a way of listening that forms what I see and hear. I have sometimes noticed that I have been treated by and have treated others as if we were of no more importance to each other than the machines we use. In researching for this book, I decided to look more deeply into both the philosophic and psychological foundations of my world and to determine for myself the effects that technologies have on people, culture, and nature and what we might have to do to solve these problems.

After reexamining my own position, and exposing my ideas and prejudices, I made a fresh attempt to understand the place of technology in commercial development. This approach rewarded me with a clearer understanding of the effects of technology and development on culture, art, and ecology. When I examined the sociological effects of urban development, i.e., how development affects people and communities, I learned much about things that appear to influence commercial success. I discovered the working of my personal psychology in this process; I discovered the source of personal habits, frustrations, attitudes, and talents and the way I operate in my cultural context—the nature and extent of my own sense of alienation (a sense of not being related to or not being an effective part of my community).

These personal insights helped me to become more productive and satisfied. They also led me to discover an aspect of my personality which I labeled "technological arrogance"—a presumption that the knowledge of fashionable technologies makes one superior. When I was able to identify in myself the source of this attitude, I found it to be just another response to the unconscious process of alienation. I began to notice and better manage the effect that this arrogance has on people in my life as well as on the projects I have undertaken. I began to notice other areas of life that were colored by the same phenomenon. Alienation is clearly a feature of contemporary life. Although it is not the purpose of this book to deal with this subject, it occurred to me that since technological dangers are a constant quality of our culture—and technological arrogance a new kind of bigotry that is infectious because it is regarded as a virtue—I should bring this work about technologies into the domain of greatest value and include issues of psychology and culture which bear on the subject.

Alienation is associated with our use of technologies and with the uncomfortable guilt that we feel in America. We tend to think of ourselves as custodians of the earth, of democracy, of freedom, of God. Given the condition the world is in, we are botching the job and in our technological largess, we amplify rather than avoid the consequences of most damaging activities. In the wisdom of our custodianship, we have unspoken and unclear priorities that determine our decisions about how much oil we spill on coastal beaches, how many forests we turn into paper, and how many Ethiopians need to starve. In very fine detail, we are making decisions every minute of every day, in every purchase, in every job, in every manufacturing process.

I concluded that if I discovered enlightening aspects of my psychology of alienation through my personal relationship with technology, others might perhaps do the same. I decided to make this book an experiment to serve people who aspire to be accountable for the priorities we hold in the arts and sciences of urban and community development, including the administration, design, and other technologies associated with development. Through the discussions about technologies, I have tried to create a clearing in which to view the interrelationship of the individual and technologies in a development project. The possibility exists that readers who become more familiar with technology will develop a new ability to make decisions that take into account complex ecological and sociological as well as technological issues in a development project. At least, the reader will be able to make more money in building development, and at best he or she will find ways to implement technologies that are not only appropriate to personal, professional, and business goals but are also consistent with our national commitment to custodianship of human rights.

HOW TO READ THIS BOOK

Some of the book's content is background information about technologies, which is basic to understanding the design, specification, management, and marketing of intelligent building services. Electronic technologies are constantly evolving, as are the relations among high-tech companies. As a result of this rapid change, minor inaccuracies are difficult to avoid. I have tried to make the descriptions concise, accurate, and readable. Data was included only when I felt it would be needed for the reader to understand the direction and meaning of new developments in technology. There is emphasis placed on building a technical vocabulary to enhance the reader's ability to understand technologies as they relate to his or her own purposes.

Since self-knowledge is the vessel in which all other knowledge is held, it is essential to know technology in the light of personal purposes. Being human, we have a natural commitment to ecological well-being. We want our actions to have a positive effect on the course of land use, urban development, and the care and feeding of the planetary community. The issues with which this book deals are dynamic. The technologies it discusses are subject to rapid and radical change. This book can be useful for readers as a guide to technology, so that in the decisions they are asked to make, as individuals or as members of organizations, they will be better able to make choices consistent with principles and policies that reflect human values as well as concerns for productivity, efficiency, and profit. It is suggested that the reader explore the ideas of this book relative to the particular tasks she or he faces. If questions arise, they can be used as an opportunity for appropriate research and for conversation with engineers and associates who possess detailed knowledge about their specialties. In this way, readers can build practical relationships that include the experience of those in their acquaintance who possess special technical knowledge.

ACKNOWLEDGEMENTS

I acknowledge and express my gratitude to the following individuals for their assistance in making this work possible: Joan Zseleczky, McGraw-Hill Book Company; Liberty Winn, Louise Reding, Dr. Joseph Neustein, Eric Johnson, and Jennifer Smith, Digital Equipment Corporation; Rhonda St. John and Ed Cooper, Sytek Corporation; Michael Bell, Mal Goslee, and Jim Flache, Xerox Corporation; Joseph Baker and Lee Bauman, Northern Telecom International; George Lefcoe, University of Southern California Law Center; John Worthington, Duffy Eley, Giffone Worthington; Bernard Bishop, EOCA, Division of Westinghouse, Inc.; Neil Hadfield, Western Pacific Data Systems; Michael Hoffman, Delphi Information Sciences; John Duhring, Apple Computer; John D. Daly, Planning Research Corporation; Tom Black and Marshall Bennett, The Urban Land Institute; Edward A. Goodman, Tel-Management Corporation; Henry D. Levine, Morrison and Foerster; Werner Erhard and Associates; Mary Hoeve and Stan Gardner, Control Data Corporation; Howard Gordon, Network Research Corporation; James C. Truher, Polaris Network Systems; Miguel de la Peña, Fiber Data Systems; David Abel, Michael Hoberman, Harold Weisbrod, James Rosenfield, Susan Quinn, and Carla Zimbalist, Smart Office Consultants; Piero N. Patri, AIA, Whisler-Patri; Martin Schaefer, Elfi Schaefer, Cynthia Gladstone, Bill Gladstone, Larry Jordan, FileNet, Inc.; Artie Berne, Grass Valley Computers; Dr. Marjorie Hanson, USC Center for Telecommunications Management; James Moran, Bobbi Lona, and Oscar Arnay, Datascope Corporation; Dr. Nicolai Lennox, Maury Cutler, Andrew Zoldan, Gerhard Gessner, Sandee Tiffany, Intergraph Corporation; Susana Lago, ABC Broadcasting Corporation; Mark Nelson, Presto Food Products, Inc.; Dan Kinnamon, Spin Physics, Division of Eastman Kodak Company, Lawrence.

Michael Winn

PART 1

Introduction to the Nature of Technology

The circumstances we face today in our personal quests for achievement require a knowledge base which includes aspects of technology that, until recently, have been the province of high-tech specialists: engineers, mathematicians, and scientists. Perhaps lay persons do not need to understand the chemical or electronic arrangements involved in high-technology processes; yet it is becoming very clear that people who are aware of the opportunities afforded by these processes—and who understand how they apply to their professions, their communities, and the future in general—are doing better and earning more.

Beyond these mundane considerations, the nearly daily deluge of new information about events relating to technology—ranging from the U. S. government's "star wars" strategic defense initiative to local community planning deliberations about new commercial developments—leave uninformed people overwhelmed and underprepared to make intelligent decisions about issues affecting the quality of their lives. Over time, all responsible citizens will eventually be influenced by or will need to make decisions about situations that are vital to their well-being. These decisions may be about ecological issues and development planning, or about personal education, business organization, or the supervision of childhood education. Already, we are regularly called upon to vote on major planning decisions involving technology, telecommunications, and development in work situations and in government policy making. Our choices, unless they are to be inspired by wild guesses, will require some degree of technological mastery. Ultimately, we and our children will bear the costs or share the benefits of these choices in our homes, communities, and jobs.

Architectronics attempts to give readers a knowledge base about technology that enables them to create personal criteria on which to base decisions—criteria consistent with their own vision of personal success and community well-being. Chapter 1 describes the elements common to all technology in order to provide readers with a base from which to understand the complex nature of this subject. Even readers who are already steeped in the highly technical, engineering-related knowledge of some technologies will find in Chapter 1 a refreshing way of looking at the subject, a way which incorporates modern thinking about the philosophy behind our recent technological evolution.

CHAPTER 1

The Mystique of Technology and the Effect of Technology on Building Development

"Man has built his world; he has built factories and houses, he produces cars and clothes, he grows grain and fruit. But he has become estranged from the product of his own hands, he is not really the master any more of the world he has built; on the contrary, this man-made world has become his master, before whom he bows down, whom he tries to placate or to manipulate as best he can. The work of his own hands has become his God. He seems to be driven by self-interest, but in reality his total self with all its concrete potentialities has become an instrument for the purpose of the very machine his hands have built. He keeps up the illusion of being the center of the world, and yet he is pervaded by an intense sense of insignificance and powerlessness which his ancestors once consciously felt toward God."

—ERICH FROMM[1]

WHAT IS TECHNOLOGY?

Technology seems difficult and mysterious to many people. The word is abstract and associated with millions of complex mechanical processes, some of which lurk beneath the surfaces of apparently ingenious machines. The myth is that only engineers can deal with technological matters. The truth is that most engineers don't quite understand the nature of technology, although they are able to master the mechanical processes of a few technologies. Religion is equally mysterious if you don't understand the nature of religion. It is easy to imagine working in a church and not understanding the nature of religion. It is the same with technology. People ascribe unpredictable qualities to things they don't understand, especially if these things are mysterious and even more so if they are phenomenal. Most attitudes and fears about technology are just this illogical.

The starting point is, therefore, to discover the nature of technology and to demystify our concepts about it so that we can observe its characteristics rather than our concepts. The mystique of technology exists in our use of language about it. Since this writing is directed at readers from different fields, and deals with a subject which is cross-disciplinary as well, it is important to define terms. Each object under investigation can then be observed directly rather than through a vision filtered by awe, apprehension, and other more or less rational concepts or emotional perspectives. Many problems created by our use of technologies have their roots in the way we speak about them. Productivity is enhanced when one is able to draw clear distinctions and speak accurately about that which is really before one, rather than dealing with fantasies called upon in the mind by the sound of a word or other symbolic image of that which is being observed.

THE LANGUAGE OF TECHNOLOGY

Technology has been described by the philosopher Martin Heidegger as "that which creates a standing reserve." Heidegger arrived at this unusual distinction through examination of the ways in which human beings do the peculiar things we do. Heidegger felt that people tend to misapprehend a lot of things and that language often obscures rather than assists the ability to see what is actually present. This effect of language to obscure things is easily understood. For instance, for the sake of brevity and utility our language assumes the absolute quality of time. For practical purposes this is fine, but it clouds an understanding of some phenomena associated with processes as diverse as human thought and thermonuclear physics. This kind of unclarity produces in science an effect that is analogous to a sightless person approaching a piano with the unshakable belief that it is a mode of transportation. From the standpoint of modern physical science, there is a degree of probability that the blind person might actually achieve transportation using the piano, based on the proven ability of the individual consciousness to operate on the physical universe.

Heidegger's task as a philosopher was to use language in such a way that his readers rediscovered their ability to make distinctions between things, in order to speak and act as creative beings. In his essay on the nature of technology, he created a distinction for the word "technology" that clearly separates technology from anything that is not technology. This is a valuable distinction.

TECHNOLOGY—CREATING THE STANDING RESERVE

The particular technologies described further on in Part 2 are those which are useful in dealing with the management of information: computer science, artificial intelligence, and telecommunications. There are many kinds of technological operations that have not been included in this work: e.g., genetic engineering, aeronautical engineering, fluid mechanical design, thermonuclear processes, and so on. It is, however, essential to understand a quality common to all technologies in order to see the possibilities for applications or dangers presented by the particular technology one happens to be viewing. Understanding this particular quality provides the context for grasping the relationship in reality between the psychology of man and the physical environment. One sees the possibilities of development only by viewing them from a place

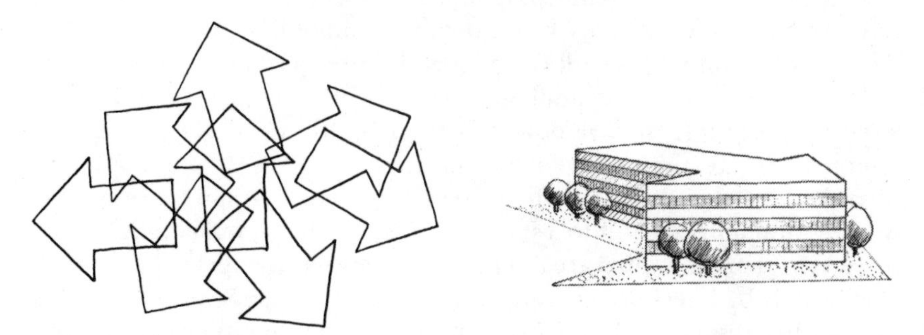

Figure 1.1 Technology transforms things so that they become part of a process to accomplish a useful purpose.

formed by experience and knowledge rather than by opinion, advertising, or the pressure of that which is popular.

When I utter the word "television," I may be talking about a kind of technology, depending on the context in which the word is used. But when I utter the word "technology," I mean something that, in every possible context, consistently implies a very particular kind of thing, common to all technologies. It was Heidegger's thesis that all technologies result in the creation of a "standing reserve." A bridge is an example of a technology. As a technology, the bridge is the sum of its parts and a thing that is distinct from any of its parts. The purpose of the bridge is the creation of a reserved potential for transportation. In this capacity, the bridge does not act on the river which it crosses; it acts on the needs of the human culture on either side of the river. Television, in a similar manner, falls into the category called technology in that it creates the potential for the transmission, reception, and processing of electromagnetic signals resulting in communication. Energies and materials are invested in technologies in such a way that a potential or standing reserve of some kind is created. A very simple example is the lever. The lever, as technology, is distinct from the tree or iron from which it is made; it is distinct from the being, interests, or will of those who fashioned it or will use it. A technological thing (a television set, a bridge, a lever) exists as technology only as long as it is functional, as long as it retains its capacity to work on the standing reserve that its technology is meant to create. A broken hammer literally becomes stick and iron.

THE DANGER OF TECHNOLOGY

In some instances, a technology may create a standing reserve by making a "natural resource" of something in nature such as petroleum, water, or humanity itself. This is the potential in which Heidegger and others have accurately predicted that humanity would face difficulties. The dangers of technology result from several causes: (1) mismanagement of potentially destructive technologies (ecological destructiveness) emphasized by the immensity of power created by the harnessing of atomic energy; (2) creation of management technologies which allow the objective creation of a standing reserve called "human resources"—making humanity itself into a standing reserve (the Orwellian nightmare of 1984). There is a third area of danger, wherein unexpected potentials are created by a technology implementation that results in the creation of standing reserves for ends that are unknown and either counterproductive or pathological, as has been the case with pharmacological technologies.

The first danger appears to be the most frightening. We have already realized dangers in the nuclear power, petroleum, and toxic chemical industries.

The second danger has also been manifested in real problems in our systems of government, commerce, and education; humanity has become a resource to develop. As a culture, we tend to evaluate others based on their value to our own goals. We tend to evaluate their productivity in a material, technological sense. More sophisticated technologies provide greater amplifications of effort (less in, more out), and we are prejudiced in favor of people whom we perceive as being more productive. We are even condescending toward more "primitive" people. Although we value classic art, we give short shrift to the creative genius of our living artists. But art, like technology, is a reality of man—which is to say that art is a quality which defines man, rather than the other way around. Having prejudices which negate contemporary art as less productive, we thus tend to alienate a quality of humanity. In so doing, we incorporate an alienation of many things natural to humans, and eventually humans become secondary to objects. This cycle of evaluation produces continuing effects of alienation that have become pronounced and destructive in highly technological societies. This problem is at the root of the distortion of personal purpose which manifests itself in criminality. It also underlines the willful quality of individualism which seeks personal survival (sometimes explained as "economic independence") at the cost of all else, including personal satisfaction in one's life. As Fromm describes it:

> although man has reached a remarkable degree of mastery of nature, society is not in control of the very forces it has created. The rationality of the system of production, in its technical aspects, is accompanied by the irrationality of the system of production in its social aspects. Economic crises, unemployment, war, govern man's fate.[2]

The third danger, accidental creation of undesirable potentialities for biological destructiveness, has become the nemesis of our age. When Albert Einstein published his first paper on relativity, he may have realized that knowledge about atomic energy gave the human race the potential to release enormous energy, comparable to that being released by the phenomenon we call the "sun." That this technology would be eventually in human hands, whether or not Einstein was to be the medium for the idea's expression, was obvious. He retired to Switzerland for several years before publishing his document defining the mathematics of nuclear reactions. Generations to follow have inherited the legacy of responsibility for the management of this knowledge and the many developments that followed from it. The task before us now is to master technology with an understanding that takes into account the complex variables produced by unpredictable side effects and unexpected interactions. In this monumental task, the related values of individual, cultural, and national self-interest are clearly at issue.

The problems created by technology come in many forms. Because technology can be distinguished as a thing, any solution we invent to manage our relationship with one technology will probably lead to useful understandings about other technologies. In this book, I treat building development as a technology. My assertion is that we can identify the nature of the standing reserves created through the development of buildings and communities. Through this process, we can describe criteria necessary if we are to successfully direct development relative to the social, ecological, and commercial needs of the community. Especially in a free enterprise society, criteria for evaluating development are critical. We must be able to challenge each new project to be developed with a simple request: Identify the intended and potential "standing reserves" created by the project. Just what are we doing, for whom are we doing it, and what is the cost? What do these qualities have to do with what is wanted and needed in terms of both commercial and societal values? Such issues need to be addressed by the inhabitants of communitites where development takes place. More informed choices need to be made by the families and individuals who have the closest relationship to the land, nature, and culture involved. The present process of development permission and review is not sufficient to govern development in the absence of established criteria.

Commercial and other activities in a community utilize a range of technologies for energy, communications, shelter, transportation, administration, and observation. Consequently, the ability of communities to proactively support intelligent building will depend on the degree to which complete ideas can be presented to them. The knowledge base of the community needs to be supported by an approach toward determining the complex intended and unintended results inherent in the design of projects in order to avoid the societal and psychological ills of mismanaged technology.

SOCIAL PSYCHOLOGY AND TECHNOLOGY

In his book *Escape from Freedom,* quoted above, psychologist Erich Fromm wrote about the characteristics of people who are capable of supporting characters like Hitler's. Fromm reached the conclusion that the characteristics of Hitler's supporters were not peculiar to German culture; he found that a tendency toward authoritarianism was prevalent among members of the lower middle class of England and of other societies. He saw this as a response created by the individual's need to feel substantiated by some external cause or reason.

THE CORPORATE PERSON

As a witness to the rise and development of Nazism, Fromm observed that the psychological conditions which promoted Nazism were a reaction on the part of people who were frustrated in their ability to feel secure and satisfied in their opportunity for living. In earlier periods of history, people were used to being guided through life by the precepts of a religious, socioeconomic, or politically feudal order. They could excuse the deprivations of slavery, the brutality, and the degradation of caste through a system of beliefs about life and death which provided a sense of ultimate justice as administered by the divine power through its representative on earth, the church. With the advent of the economic and political systems of capitalism and democracy (associated with the idea of free will), anxieties surfaced due to the awesome responsibility of freedom of choice. The individual needed to understand his or her life as a proactive stand to be taken about things—an assertion of self out of nothing but the ability to assert. In recent years, in addition to this isolating quality of individual responsibility, the self-appointing individual has been given technological skills. Today it is possible to see and even quantify the vastness of the universe and comprehend one's size in the context of infinity. One can either comprehend the personal power

Figure 1.2 In modern industrical societies, man has become a tool for corporate growth.

involved in such an ability or, conversely, experience weakness, isolation, and insignificance.

As if this were not enough, the economic systems of capital accumulation encourage the building of economic megastructures called corporations by relatively small groups of self-appointing entrepreneurial individuals and bureaucrats (empire building). This process has recently reached an apex of frenzied activity in the number of "hostile takeovers" and mergers of big businesses. Megaenterprises operate as a sort of "superpersona" in the society, and the individual tradesperson has become powerless to compete with them. Unlike other forms of social organization (such as family, tribe, club, church, government, and community) the management of megabusiness organizations is indifferent to the individual's complex needs, except insofar as they relate to productivity and the survival of the "self" of the corporation. Fromm, along with Marx, Freud, and others, predicted from these observations that psychological needs have emerged, primarily among the lower middle classes, which produce a social stratum that is willing to submit to and act on behalf of the authority of a totalitarian regime rather than to live with the terror of isolation associated with free will and choice. Fromm's notions about the authoritarian character are relevant to this discussion because the implementation of computer-driven machines is having an effect on people that distances people from their own productivity and aggravates the problem. This is especially a problem in the culture of the United States where, during recent years, the family unit has been weakening while the identification of the individual with a job, profession, or corporation has grown stronger.

Technologies may help provide or reveal solutions. Computer technologies made it possible for megabusinesses to manage enormously large organizations. As computer-driven machines have grown easier to use and understand, they have increasingly extended the power of the individual. One person using an intelligent machine can literally do the work of hundreds. While technologies are taking over the jobs and threatening the livelihood of those who do menial work, the same systems are providing an increased ability for certain individuals to wield enormous influence. Opportunities abound for those with knowledge of how to use high technology and computers.

In many situations, computer-driven technologies have had a dehumanizing effect on the individual's relationship to work. Coupled with such dehumanizing effects, however, opportunities for action and power are available to those who attain technological skills and knowledge. Because the wealthier members of societies have had the greatest opportunity to buy and learn about computers, the lower middle class has been weakened in its economic position while other, wealthier sectors are finding more opportunities. This phenomenon, combined with the continued thrust of entrepreneurial capitalism and the corresponding rise of power as a social and personal goal, is emphasizing economic stratification at a time when material abundance in industrialized societies has reached unparalleled new highs. The potential for individual frustration among those not included in this growing affluence is similar to the working class frustration in Germany during Hitler's rise to power. Because of this, we have as much to fear from a stressful economic catastrophe and the potential consequences of political polarization as we have from a natural disaster or war.

The conditions which Fromm studied are no less prevalent today than they were 50 years ago. There are still totalitarian regimes today. Many conditions have been amplified, not resolved, by the increasing power and use of technologies. Although Hitler and Nazism were deposed by the allied democracies and communist nations, the conditions which provided the ideological fodder for the growth of Nazism are still present today. This is a difficult problem, and it requires a detailed treatment of its own which we cannot attempt here. However, the problem deserves discussion in the context of community development, since the psychological conditions underlying the acceptance of totalitarianism as an escape from the isolation of the individual in modern society are probably the cause of community alienation now being manifested as youth gangs, national defensiveness, and criminal activities (including organized and white collar crime). Fromm discusses the effect of this problem:

> Modern man's feeling of isolation and powerlessness is increased still further by the character which all his human relationships have assumed. The concrete relationship of one individual to another has lost its direct and human character and has assumed a spirit of manipulation and instrumentality. In all social and personal relations the laws of the market are the rule. It is obvious that the relationship between competitors has to be based on mutual human indifference. Otherwise any one of them would be paralyzed in the fulfillment of his economic tasks—to fight each other and not to refrain from the actual economic destruction of each other if necessary.[3]

This issue is relevant to a discussion about technologies of development. Implementations of technology are making possible an international effort to eliminate hunger and starvation, a purpose not dreamed of before the advent of the high-tech age. Efforts such as the commitment to end hunger work directly on the conditions which spawned Nazism by providing the individual with a sense of power, relationship, and responsibility. There are urban areas in the United States which have been afflicted with "urban blight." Huge areas of cities exist in a state of disrepair, giving the appearance of having been bombed-out.

The dollar value of homes in blighted areas in the United States is negligible, though the land value may be great if the area is seen as subject to imminent urban redevelopment to high-density commercial use. The most interesting fact about this "enblightenment" is the consciousness, or psychology, of the residents of these areas who, by tolerating such conditions, permit the blighted state. No change has occurred in the quality of bricks and mortar to transform neighborhoods into ghettos. They are purely a product of consciousness. Blighted communities thus become both a cause and an effect. As a cause, they act as a standing reserve for potential human abuse. As an effect, they become the expression of the powerlessness of people and are evidence that is used by victims to justify (explain as a cause) failure and to validate the fiction that inhabitants of such neighborhoods are victims of capitalism and class discrimination who have been disenfranchised by the political and economic systems of their communities.

It is for these reasons that businesspeople, particularly development firms, have the responsibility of implementing technologies for building and business which enhance an individual's experience of relationship and give him or her the experience of being heard and recognized in the community. In examining development technology as a creation of the standing reserve called "human well-being," social "illnesses" such as juvenile delinquency and criminality become indicators for developing solutions to the major problems of our age. We can measure the success of development by such things as the statistics of juvenile crime.

It is important to recognize that the problem of alienation and isolation of the individual is a real and costly factor. It shows up consistently and colors all areas of human relationship. Fromm pointed out that it shows up even in our closest relationships:

> The relationship between employer and employee is permeated by the same spirit of indifference (as in the case of other competitors). The word, "employer" contains the whole story: the owner of capital employs another human being as he "employs" a machine. They both use each other for the pursuit of their economic interest; their relationship is one in which both are means to an end, both are instrumental to each other. It is not a relationship of two human beings who have any interest in the other outside of this mutual usefulness. The same instrumentality is the rule in the relationship between the businessman and his customer. The customer is an object to be manipulated, not a concrete person whose aims the businessman is interested to satisfy. The attitude toward work has the quality of instrumentality; in contrast to a medieval artisan the modern manufacturer is not primarily interested in what he produces; he produces essentially in order to make a profit from his capital investment, and what he produces depends essentially on the market which promises that the investment of capital in a certain branch will prove to be profitable.[4]

Fromm is describing a condition which we have come to live with without question. We have manifested this problem in modern times by characterizing and labeling people so that, in our language, we appear to perceive them as things rather than beings. This has something to do with the way people think about each other when a problem is perceived, which keeps us from dealing with the problem. We think about and act toward people as if they were equal to the stories we have learned that go with the symbols we have stored. We encounter men, women, children, teachers, employers, politicians, criminals, teenagers, and undocumented aliens instead of beings. We also have attitudes toward criminality, juvenile delinquency, child abuse, and all the problems of confused relationships, from marriage to issues of civil law, which similarly prevent us from discovering and using meaningful solutions to the problems of human relationship represented by these ideas. This manner of thinking is built into our language. In our use of language, the way we speak assumes that we are rational about our problems and problematical people, as though the way people think about things is rational, and as though there is no relationship between the psychology of the individual and the economic and educational conditions which the personality has happened to survive. The only solution to this problem is in our learning to experience our ties and commitment to one another. Relative to this problem, technology is a double-edged sword. Technology reinforces the logic of our language and attitudes. Computers are programmed to make decisions based on very simple criteria. Problems are made worse because of this and yet, computer solutions have come to be regarded as miraculous.

Fromm's conclusion was that the solution is to be found in creating forums in which citizens can discuss and educate each other about economic and social needs in the community, in order to build consensus more constructively and universally and to allow the individual opportunity for more meaningful expression. Our present-day mechanisms for design and control of technologies are oriented toward goals of competitive economic survival. Our public media are mostly given over to competitive commercial purposes. Our educational and news media are dominated by grants from self-interested corporations and other organizations. This results in development and implementation of technologies (including the technology of buildings) without there having been an opportunity to evolve a strategic plan for long-term management of the community resources. There is, therefore, little possibility that many people in our communities will be able to identify themselves with new projects.

This problem has been recognized in many cities in the United States. However, the action taken has been directed toward exploiting the condition. For instance, at the same time as technology manufacturers are marketing technologies that depersonalize transactions between people (such as voice mail and electronic banking), the media advertisements of these same firms depict their businesses as personally interested in the needs of customers and the well-being of employees. Sales representatives have been trained to reflect the personal touch, but relationships usually begin and end with the purchase order. Issues of service and support are stressed in the marketing media of high-tech firms such as banks, telephone and computer companies. They strive in advertising to appear friendly, personal, and interested; but the commitment of these firms is not reflected in their mass media marketing pose. The trade publications and internal communications for these industries correctly reflect the underlying commitment of business—capital investment, capital return, kill the alternative.

Technology planned for business activities needs to address the bottom line and to begin with a definition of business goals which technology is needed to support. Technology implementations in business are costly and rarely designed for results other than a very narrowly defined set of goals. Technology expenditures are meant to support the true interests and direction of a business. This is very promising for business. The unwanted side effects, however, include a further distancing in the experience of individuals from control over the product of their own work and lives, with a consequent suppression of personal experience and expression.

Fromm made an observation which, if true, could be applied with great effect today. He suggested that "the amount of destructiveness to be found in an individual is proportionate to the amount to which the feeling of expansiveness of life is curtailed."

> Destructiveness is the outcome of unlived life. Those individual and social conditions that make for suppression of life produce the passion for destruction that forms the reservoir from which the particular hostile tendencies—either against others or against oneself—are nourished.[5]

Even if Fromm's analysis is only partly correct, it exists as a window through which we can view what we know and do as developers, architects, planners, and managers. With these issues in mind, we can better address our task with regard to the effect our work has on individuals and communities. We may do this by asking these questions: How does a proposed project expand the aliveness of people? What are the potentials created relative to this purpose?

Using as a starting point the proposition that technology works through the creation of standing reserve (some of which may be unintentional), new social, political, and economic criteria emerge for planning, management, prediction, and control. For example, the issues of building and urban development may be understood in terms of longer-term priorities as well as short-term profitability or the exploitation of a tax-sheltering opportunity. With new criteria, architects, engineers, city planners, and entrepreneurs can begin to manage decisions with more emphasis on long-range planning as well as short-term business needs. Since modern buildings may last a century or more, designers, planners, and developers may be able to determine the effects of development in terms of success in the context of human and social well-being rather than just in the hypothesis of a "pro forma" statement. This is an enormous step forward.

BUILDING AS TECHNOLOGY

When building is viewed as a technology which creates the potential for subordinate systems for life and business support, the development of a large commercial office building can be seen as a technology for creating the reserve potential for productivity. The more specifically a builder can examine the kinds of activities to be enhanced by the project, the more perfectly will the building meet its projected purpose. This closer examination of the purpose of a proposed building may also reveal some counterproductive possibilities in terms of its purpose or in view of longer-range policies and community well-being. When one views the development cycle currently in vogue, one sees that the source of many present difficulties in urban development and design (relative to economic and ecological as well as sociological issues) stems from the problem that the present development business cycle allows virtually no possibility to account for any result of development other than return on investment. Given capitalization techniques such as tax-sheltering partnerships, a financial flop can be almost as valuable as a success, so that even in the financial arena there may be no accountability. The development process itself is the weak link in contemporary building technology, and this is the area that requires new thinking.

THE TECHNOLOGY OF THE DEVELOPMENT PROCESS

"We shape our buildings and then our buildings shape us," said Winston Churchill.

Although the financing of development may not seem to be on the same track as a discussion about building technology, an assessment of the development process is necessary—eschewing traditional views of the subject—so as to make clear distinctions about the way things are and find fresh approaches toward urban planning and development that are consistent with the way computers are used and work is done in this age. It is also true that financing itself may be best understood as a kind of technology—one which acts upon the resources of the community to create the potential for development of various kinds.

THE METHOD OF ENTREPRENEURIAL DEVELOPMENT

The entrepreneurial developer's method is to buy a quantity of something and alter it in some fashion so that it can be resold at a profit. In real estate, this usually takes the form of subdivision wherein the development makes one large commodity into a number of smaller units. The sum of the individual values of the smaller units, when resold, is greater than the purchase cost. This logic motivates the development of large parcels of land into tracts of equal-sized lots with nearly identical units. It prompts the wholesale slaughter of forests in order to mechanize development. It finds its apotheosis in the development of high-rise structures, where the construction of multiple levels causes an astronomical increase in the square footage of property for resale. In extremes, a 100,000 square-foot piece of property can produce over 2 million rentable square feet of space.

Based on a business method which emphasizes the benefits of economy of scale in building technologies and begins with the premise of dividing large spaces into more expensive smaller units, the present criteria for building design are dominated by the pro forma for financial investment. The decision makers involved are the financial investment analysts and investors. Developers typically concentrate on market

Figure 1.3 The developer is an entrepreneur. The purpose of development is another matter.

niches in their entrepreneurism. Although directly
proportional to the cost of the construction, since the market for competitive space determines the selling price. Investors, especially corporate holding companies, evaluate a project purely on the financial merits of the deal. They are concerned with information about the market value of the proposed development and the consistency of its design with comparable buildings in the neighborhood (regardless of whether or not the neighboring buildings are well-designed and regardless of the purposes for which the development is to be used). The criteria used by investors relate to theoretical return on investment. These criteria are not associated with the purposes or needs of community development, let alone the productivity potential of a proposed work or living environment.

An important dynamic in the investment part of the commercial building process is the perceived needs of the market, the potential tenant. Corporate organizations, the most likely tenants for speculatively built commercial office buildings, apply technologies with a management view which is necessarily short-sighted. The facilities-planning process views human talent as a technological resource, or standing reserve, called "human resources." Although this view ignores modern thinking about human nature, most businesses do not pay their executive staffs to be social scientists. As long as businesses begin as entrepreneurial quests for personal profit and power, the advantages of a humanistic strategy are generally overlooked. As a result, the creative attention given to building design is concerned exclusively with the development's appearance as a monument to the entrepreneur's ego and personal illusions about lifestyle.

THE FINANCIAL PRO FORMA

Recently, it has become a practice for investors, many of whom are foreign nationals wishing to convert wealth in foreign capital to American dollars, to invest in the development and purchase of commercial structures in the United States without regard for the level of occupancy, condition of the market, appropriateness of design, traffic congestion in the community, or ultimate use of the building. Unlike native investors, the foreign investors benefit just by the exchange of their currency for equity which they can borrow against in American dollars.

They will therefore invest in real estate development even when the economics are absurd. Meanwhile, many American funds such as those of insurance companies and large banks have been motivated by tax-sheltering advantages to invest in building development, again without much regard for the ways in which the building may be used, the soft condition of the market, or the effect of the development on the community or the people who may be employed in it.

FOREIGN OWNERSHIP

Because of the economic forces driving development, many buildings owned by foreign interests are going up in all major urban areas of the world, frequently without the interest of any potential tenants. The building design is based on traditional concepts of what a commercial structure has become as a real estate investment. Site location, building design, shape and size, obtaining of permits, investment pro forma, environmental impact reports, land-use planning, and marketing schemes are all subordinated to theoretical economic issues. Even the physical design of the building and selection of materials are based on criteria irrelevant to the efficient use of the space, the relationship to the surrounding community, or the efficiency of the building as environmental technology. As a result, only by sheer luck does a building development become a contribution to the purposes of a communtiy and even more rarely is the building efficiently conceived relative to the work to be done within its walls. Even in the best cases, local communities have suffered from problems created by projects; these include traffic congestion, destruction of neighborhood relationships, and other problems leading indirectly to crime and pollution.

These factors combine to produce communities which have built into them the capacity to further deepen the alienation of individuals, with a resultant loss of productivity for businesses and the potential for other cultural, and economic problems in the community. We are now in the process of exporting this process to developing nations.

IMPACT ON ARCHITECTURE

Without any reliable or consistent values, the development industry becomes leaderless. Not only has the value of investment in building projects weakened, but also, in the absence of better design criteria, space planning in speculatively built structures is being constrained by building designs that tend to place people in rooms that are like cells. This design limitation results from the absence of any sensitivity to tenant needs. The building developer wants to build economically and take advantage of economies of scale—to increase the profitability of the structure by using a floor plate of a shape and size that provides the most economical building techniques. Especially in speculative projects, the building architects' criteria for efficient space planning are based on concepts of work environments that are derived from history rather than present need. The market survey for most projects, which might shed some light on possible use, is usually a pro forma analysis or statistical data, and there is little or no input from potential tenants. The marketing goals of projects are not well-defined.

EFFECT OF THE FINANCIAL DOMINATION OF DESIGN DECISIONS

Economy of scale in the building process has determined that 25,000 square feet is the optimum floor plate size for a building. This creates a condition in which 59 percent or more of floor space has no windows on the outside world.

To remedy this problem, buildings have been designed with an internal "atrium" in an attempt to give interior space the illusion of an outlook. This use of the atrium idea is not the same as designing a building around an atrium to enhance environmental experience. The motivation influences the design criteria and, consequently, the resultant architecture. As a result, in the reality of the marketplace, atrium window space is not as highly valued, in terms of dollars per square foot, as is exterior view space when the exterior view has any positive aesthetic value.

The issues of productivity are rarely addressed in a speculatively developed building. Beyond the limitations of building codes, conventions, and economics, whimsy and a tendency toward monumentalism determine design decisions about building height, structure, floor plate, and engineering. With regard to usability and marketability, the best guess is the basis for expenditures of hundreds of millions of dollars.

As we continue to build in areas where building vacancy may soon be as high as 60 percent of total space available (Houston, Denver, Los Angeles, San Diego), in an economy which does not signal the growth of business necessary to absorb this space, a kind of mystique has arisen associated with the pretense of need for surplus space. Logic is stood on its head by those who use the statistics of enormous vacancy factors to promote investment in the development of more vacant space. Local industry promoters, chambers of commerce, central city associations, and real estate brokers have used the argument that a community can attract industry by having an abundance of commercial space. The premise seems to be that a community with a vacancy factor of less than 30 percent is stagnant and not prepared for growth. Since a great deal of money is spent in the community when large buildings go up, few civic leaders are willing to argue against the interests of the building trades and others who benefit from the short-term profits of construction. And those who profit are not concerned about the long-term costs of mistakes. The problems of air and water pollution, traffic congestion, and juvenile crime in the community are addressed as if they were separate issues unrelated to the business being done in the community.

THE WINDS OF CHANGE

The converging trends of telecommunications, data processing, and engineering technology are bringing into the cycle of development a new variable which will irreversibly alter the planning process. This convergence has had its greatest effect in the area of communications between machines. Computer technologies are being used to make possible voice, video, and data communications which are changing the way business is being done. This changes the nature of space and location requirements for most businesses, and has a direct effect on the building project pro forma. Very simply, real estate built to accommodate new business technology will destroy the market for space that is not so developed. Also, the need for an urban location for many businesses is changing. The eventual dispersal of large organizations into better-designed buildings in smaller communities is being motivated by factors of transportation, economy, and productivity. This will result in a further increase of commercial vacancy in urban centers which should dim the fervor for urban speculative development by native investors, though foreign investors may not be hampered by this problem for the reasons already discussed.

CHANGING NEEDS IN WORK SPACE DESIGN

New technologies are extending the ability of individuals in all directions. In office situations, people are no longer needed to perform rote or menial tasks. One person with a microprocessor can analyze or monitor a large project in minutes. A lone engineer with a computer-aided design (CAD) system can work out the structural elevations, floorplans, and electromechanical layout for a skyscraper. A single bookkeeper with an accounting program can keep tabs on several large projects with infallible accuracy. Greater individual productivity is having a further effect on the traditional hierarchy of status and control within organizations. The ways in which space is organized and used to facilitate traditional controls and hierarchies is therefore changing; consequently, not only are space needs changing, but the availability of technologies within the space has also become a priority.

The ways in which technologies are integrated within a work environment are becoming more relevant to the work space design. Most significant, the social values of the work environment are also being recognized as a high priority. This represents a major shift or evolution in the idea of the work ethic. Business competition for creative talent is having an increasing influence on site selection and building design as firms seek to enhance their ability to get and keep good personnel.

Since the workspace environment is in such dynamic change and must be designed to respond to the continuing evolution of technology, the change that must occur to accommodate the emerging needs of businesses is not one in traditional building structure (although it may include this). Rather, it is a change in the technology of the building design and development process.

"INTELLIGENT BUILDINGS"

The economic premise with which many developers are now working may soon be upset. This will occur with the development of new kinds of workspace structures which better meet the social and technological needs of the emerging information-technology-oriented work force. Such structures will be more valuable to tenants and may be less wasteful of space and less expensive to build. This will impair the marketability of traditional buildings, which may not be capable of a retrofit sufficient to overcome the limitations of the original design.

There has been movement in this direction. This has shown up in the marketing literature of new projects which are being called "intelligent buildings." However, marketing statements do not provide workspace, and the qualifier "intelligent building" so far refers to tenant-shared private branch exchange (PBX) installations in projects as coventures between developers and telecommunications technology companies (discussed in detail in Chapter 8). The effect of these coventures on the issues of intelligent buildings is slight, because this enhancement is only an attempt to improve the marketability of a traditionally designed structure. There has been little or no investment on the part of developers except in the marketing literature concerning buildings. There has so far been no breakthrough in the design, development, or investment process. The marketing problem, however, indicates the need for a change. This shows a direction for further inquiry about technology that may assist builders to develop more desirable buildings that are easier to rent because of the way they enhance opportunities for productivity and because of their inclusion of designs to facilitate the use of computer-driven technologies by building tenants.

IMPACT OF TECHNOLOGY ON DECISIONS ABOUT BUSINESS LOCATION

Technologies are affecting decisions about location. Many U.S. companies have been using production facilities and people in other lands. Certain parts of complex manufacturing tasks are now being done in the Philippines, India, Taiwan, and elsewhere. Along the Mexican border, a growing number of U.S. firms are building and operating plants in Mexico. In this arrangement, raw materials are shipped under customs bond to Mexico. The labor-intensive part of the process is done in Mexico to take advantage of lower wage scales. The partially completed product is returned to the United States free of import duties. Final assembly is done in the United States. A key feature that makes such international production possible is the corporation's ability to manage and communicate easily with production facilities located abroad.

Foreign coproduction is causing changes in the needs of many firms for commercial production space in the United States. As an example, data for the printing of local and regional telephone directories is currently being entered by workers in the Philippines. The data is then shipped via telephone or on magnetic recording tape to printers located in the United States or elsewhere, depending on the duties, taxes, shipping costs, and other economic factors. One result is that directory distribution companies need less space for production facilities, paper work, and graphics. They also rely more on the ability to transmit large volumes of data at economically rapid speeds over long distances. It is unlikely that these industries will revert back to older technologies, and so the space requirements will continue to become more specialized as management, assisted by computers, becomes leaner and more efficient. Such changes will have a long-lasting effect on the building development industry. Developers and real estate investors should be looking now for new venues of operation and new development stategies. At issue is the question of willingness on the part of the developers and community planners to make the adjustment.

Case Study

THE HEALTHCARE INDUSTRY: THE MEMORIAL HEALTH CARE FACILITY

Hospital buildings provide a good example of a thoughtful integration of building design and computer-driven technologies. Most people have had some experience with modern medical facilities, therefore such facilities provide a familiar example of the problems created by integration of sophisticated technology in a job. This is an interesting example because patient care requires a human element not associated with the technological service implementation. Although the accuracy and availability of information is critical to medical records management and avoidance of malpractice liability, the decisions made by doctors and other health care personnel are based on experience and direct observation of the patient. Patient well-being is undeniably associated with the quality of human relationships rather than with technological systems. The systems are valuable principally because they aid a large staff of people to manage extensive hospital resources and to support each other in the maintenance of responsive patient care.

Medical management has implemented information technology systems more rapidly overall than have other industries. Because of the legal implications of medical situations, information technologies in medical facilities are more exactingly applied than in most other industries. With the recent introduction of regulated pricing of medical services by public and private healthcare insurance providers, there is now an incentive toward greater efficiency in medical information management. Regulated pricing has also given rise to competition between medical facilities for patients who are economically preferable because they are subscribers to health insurance plans with higher pricing standards. Such competition is motivating healthcare professionals toward a new interest in using information and telecommunications technologies in marketing management as well as improved cost management techniques. The negative side of cost management is that cost-saving techniques may be applied by the hospitals serving the "lower end" patients; such hospitals may then carry out procedures only to the letter of the law, regardless of the effect on the patient.

Technology and Personnel Specialization

The traditional role of information management technologies in health care, as elsewhere, has been to make possible the specialization of technical staff. In one day, a bed patient in a typical medical ward may be treated by three medical nurses, three respiratory technicians, a nutritionist, two bedcare assistants, a resident physician, a physical therapist, and assorted laboratory or radiology technicians. This condition alone necessitates an information management system that makes information instantly available to those whose turn it is to deal with the patient. Such a system implies levels of access for doctors, accounting and billing personnel, and food and room preparation staff, as well as persons concerned with matters affecting medical research and public health.

The use of patient management software can lead naturally to the potential for a depersonalization of patient care as staff work more with data about a patient's condition and less with the patient. In patient management software implementations, information about a patient's condition and treatment procedures is held in a database so that medical staff can rotate at will and still deliver consistent procedural care, without having to communicate directly with one another or with the patient. For example, with a portable terminal the physician can monitor the patient's condition and treatment from a telephone booth.

In this situation, the quality of care still depends on the quality of the human interaction between staff and patient. Consequently, even if the quality of care varies, records may show the performance of the hospital's staff to have been correct, providing that procedures as prescribed were justified for the condition and were correctly followed. This reveals the impact that technology has had on the work experience: the effect of these new methods of evaluation on the experience of medical professionals.

Despite such problems, the viability of a medical business in the competitive healthcare market should eventually put technology in the right relationship to the task. Hospitals which are not successful in giving clients the experience of being well taken care of will eventually lose customers.

Hospital administration professionals need support in addressing these problems of appropriate technology management. Information management technology can be implemented in a way that promotes both the quality of care and the quality of the medical professional's work experience. The solution must address the entire venue of medical activity, including building

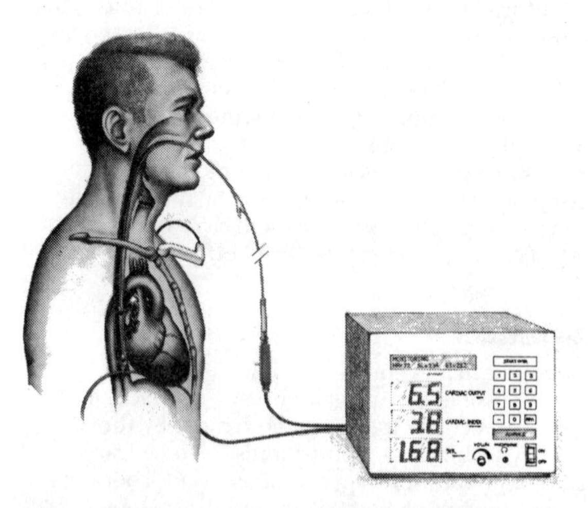

Figure 1.4 Medical science opens the possibility for biological engineering. *(Accucom Cardiac Monitor, courtesy of Datascope Corporation.)*

design, the business philosophy of the facility, and the motivation or psychology of the staff and the patient.

Under discussion here is the way in which technology shapes the human and other resources of the medical facility, and the contribution this makes, if any, to the healing process. The emerging argument is that the design services of an information management technology consultant should be regarded as essential to the task of developing medical service facilities. Consultation should begin with the design process for building development. The issues of depersonalization of care and the quality of employment experience cannot be left to chance in this formula. The community, including hospital staff and patients, needs to participate more in the inquiry leading to facilities design.

Such thinking is considered utopian in today's development climate. Real estate brokers, who must find the tenants for new developments and buildings, are somewhat more sensitive to the needs of the tenant than are developers, whose task is cost-effective construction. But the speculative real estate development entrepreneur is still working with criteria that are unrelated to building user needs. The struggle for economic survival among the medical facilities which serve the prime paying patients may ultimately ensure an improvement in the quality of service for *these* patients. However, these same circumstances are prompting the use of technologies to manage with greater economy and less care. Given the life-or-death importance of quality medical services, this is more obviously a situation in which we need to get out in front of the locomotive of development and lay new track. The direction in which we are now headed costs heavily and is the cause of suffering for a large sector of the population, involving most of the very old and the very young.

In the development of commercial office space, where effects are less apparently critical than in medical development, even less attention is being given to designing buildings for the well-being of those who will use and work in them. Only economic conditions imposed by the use of technology in competitive businesses are considered in retrofitting and redesigning many structures.

Assuming that the choice has been made to incorporate technological design in the design process, what are the changes? The answer to this question emerges from a study of the technologies to be used by prospective tenants. If you are investing in, building, designing, or managing a building, this is the question you need to ask. Information about technologies that will help in asking questions and understanding the answers has been provided in subsequent chapters.

NOTES

[1] Erich Fromm, *Escape from Freedom*, Holt, Rinehart, 1941,

[2] Ibid., p. 138.

[3] Ibid., p. 138.

[4] Ibid., p. 139.

[5] Ibid., p. 207.

CHAPTER 2

The Meaning of Technology to Business

As more businesses automate their office functions, utilizing computer-driven machines, the *trend toward automation accelerates.* The result is that technology prices drop as sales volumes and production levels increase and new tools become readily available to more people.

Major changes occur in the structure of businesses assisted by new technologies. Many of these changes have an impact on workspace requirements, including differences in the kinds and quality of personnel once the new technologies have been implemented. Fewer "menial" employees are needed. More frequent and concise communications pass between employees at different departmental levels. There are changes in people's job activities. In short, it takes a new kind of office environment to support the interaction of personnel with high technology.

THE NATURE OF INFORMATION MANAGEMENT TECHNOLOGIES

"Information management" is a new term. It refers to the procedures necessary when the amount of data about a subject reaches a point requiring—for reliable management—an automated system for storing and accessing reports from the data. This situation occurs when the volume of transactions within any manager's domain grows to exceed an amount that an individual can remember to keep track of. This condition will eventually arise in the growth of any organization.

ORGANIZATIONS AND THEIR INFORMATION NEEDS

For the purposes of this discussion, an "organization" is defined as the network of requests and promises among people involved in a common purpose or enterprise. In a business organization, people are paid for managing their commitments, for meeting the requests they have promised to meet. In practice, in any job situation, there is always a set of requests from the employer, called duties, and a set of promises from the employee with regard to meeting these requests. This same network of requests and promises is paralleled in the relationship between a business and its clients. Information management in an organization thus always relates to the status of requests and promises. The technology for keeping track of requests and promises, for communicating about them, and for ascertaining the nature of promises that can be

Figure 2.1 As an organization grows, the number of management decisions per unit of time increases. Information management is the science of systematizing decision making.

made (and kept) is what information management technology is designed to achieve.

Executives or managers of a business need to know the status of projects, inventories, payments, and production, so that they can make promises with which they are reasonably comfortable. The comfort level is also dependent on an ability to keep track of the process through which their management requests are fulfilled. Along the way breakdowns could prevent the completion of a task, so that a promise would not be kept. In such a case, the managers would have to be immediately informed so as to reevaluate the situation and restate their own commitment appropriate to the new data—make a new promise or request. This orientation of people in an organization around requests and promises is important to understanding the nature of the information revolution and the role which computers play.

THE NEED FOR COMPUTERS

As a business activity grows in size, the need for automated information technology management comes about first at the lowest layers of management. Hourly workers in large organizations do routine, easily learned tasks. Information management systems help to proceduralize

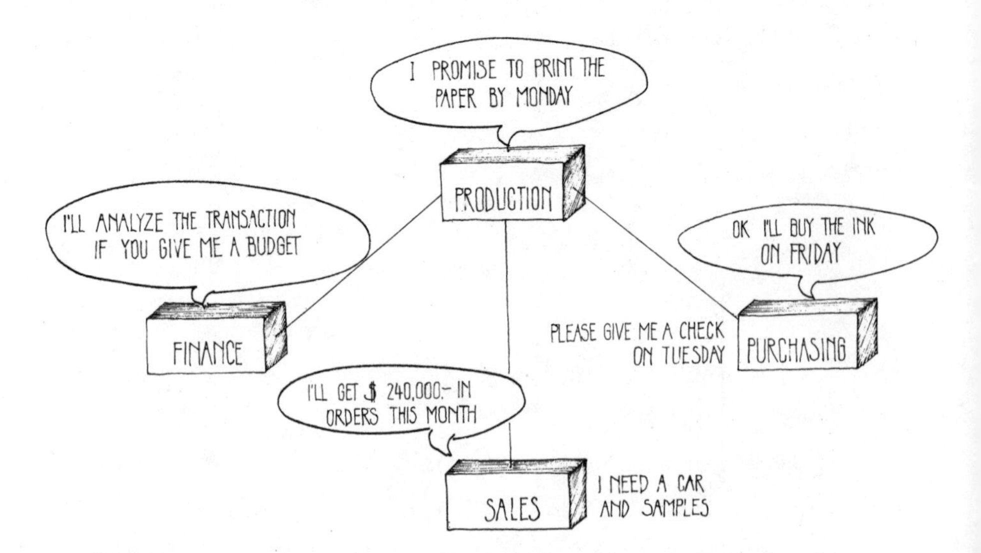

Figure 2.2 A business or other human social organization is a network of requests and promises. A machine, and a chemical or biological organization, are based on similar agreements, except that they exist in nature as physical law.

reporting about job completion so the status of an activity or the quantity of transactions can be reported to managers at upper levels in a timely manner. Such systems extend executives' abilities to comprehend, organize, and manage large groups of people and great volumes of transactions.

The automated proceduralization of business activities into autonomous subgroups has been a major factor in making possible the growth of megaenterprises. With precisely regulated and automated procedures, autonomous groups manage complex administrative tasks in an assembly line process. The Bell System, major defense contractors, large financial and insurance institutions, and government agencies (primarily the Internal Revenue Service, the Social Security Administration, and the Department of Defense) have been some of the forerunners in implementing automated information management procedures.

The first computer systems in private business were installed for accounting functions such as billing, purchasing, and payroll. As computer systems became more sophisticated, cheaper to maintain, and more flexible, a trend developed to increase the usefulness of the installed data systems by expanding access to the systems to other departments within the business and to executive management. This expansion of access not only made the systems more cost-effective but also increased the total overall productivity and manageability of the business. Access to systems has been granted to other departments so that business information organized for one purpose within a business can be used, with a different logical organization, to support other business purposes. For instance, information stored for the purpose of predicting production schedules may also be used by marketing staff to better focus marketing and advertising activities or by financial officers to forecast capital requirements for business expansion.

The design strategy of earlier data management systems followed the design processes of simple business machines that assisted clerks to do specific jobs. There were problems in expanding these existing systems for new purposes. These problems have been addressed by the data-processing industry through the manufacture of data management systems defined by software. Such systems are written in "high-level" business languages, such as COBOL, and are less dependent on hardware manufacture. (Definitions of terms such as COBOL and "high-level language," and other useful distinctions about hardware and software, are given in Chapter 3.) In a modern computer system, the way data is organized by the software determines how the data may later be retrieved and organized in the form of understandable reports.

Recently developed information management systems are programmed so that users themselves can specify the way data is to be used, without the aid of computer specialists.

THE LOGIC OF THE DATABASE

When data is entered into a computer system, with the use of appropriate codes and order, the computer stores data in certain places in its active memory or on electronic storage media to which the machine has access.

When information is managed with a computer "database," logical categories are created for different kinds of data. These categories correspond to the codes used and the order of data entry. A vocabulary is created, forming a database in which certain words are used to define the kinds of reports and other operations for which the data is to be used. In the program, these words are symbols that trigger preset operations. As data is entered, based on the use of code words, the program may attach to it other codes identifying a number of ways the data will be used. There are, therefore, multiple categories into which the same data may be entered, depending on the range of purposes for which the data will be used. In a general sense, the categories used for storing data relate to the result for which each business department is accountable.

Within each department of a business, different kinds of reports need to be generated, often from the same data. For instance, from the orientation of office administration, productivity is measured in terms of the reliability, effectiveness, timeliness, and accuracy with which reports, proposals, invoices, statements, and regulatory and other forms are prepared and delivered. Consequently, the data system for office administration may need to analyze data to record and report statistics about the completion of transactions and preparation of documents. These statistics may be of no interest to other departments.

The financial management department of a business measures productivity in terms of return on investment, earnings reports, or profit margin. This department needs to analyze the content of transactions stored in the same database. The processing of information for each department is set up in advance by a set of word definitions called a "data dictionary." To generate a report from the data, an automatic program for compiling data, called a "query system," is written for each department's particular needs. The language of the data query system is the code by means of which the people and the machine communicate.

SYSTEM INTEGRATION

The purpose of system integration is to create a single information management system which meets the needs of several different departments. The integration of a multitasking computer system must deal with the problems of input of the data from a variety of sources; these include reports made by people using keyboards and other input devices as well as the datastream reports sent to the system by machines. In an integrated system, the following must be considered:

Database management. The job of the database manager is to create a means of compiling sensible reports from all the data for the various management points of view.

Telecommunications management. The telecommunications manager or network communications system administrator of a business has the task of reliably transmitting, storing, publishing, and distributing information and reports. The communications task must frequently include providing for security from espionage and safety from loss of data.

Office hierarchy and semantics. Considerations about information management are secondary to the issue of "office semantics." The term "office semantics" refers to the way the office or production team works within a structure of procedures and a corresponding hierarchy of relationships which often has little to do with the purpose of the business. When a new information access system is implemented, reorganization inevitably takes place. The harmony of a long-standing working environment is shaken. As a result, the only plausible scheme for integrating new technologies in an established business involves the voluntary participation of every level of management, the careful evolution of new procedures, and new systems of checks and balances.

IMPACT OF INFORMATION MANAGEMENT SYSTEMS ON BUILDING DESIGN

When technologies are ubiquitous, concerned with all departments of a business, they may be shared by all. Every worker and manager in a business needs to input, retrieve, and analyze data; to communicate about it; and then to initiate and halt actions of various kinds as a member of a dynamic team. Viewed in this way, information technology management becomes a profession apart from and transparent to all other business activities. Information management professionals and technicians are concerned with the way information is to be used, but they are not accountable for the meaning of the information. Below, some specific information technologies have been explained relative to the ways they affect business goals.

BUSINESS APPLICATIONS OF COMPUTERS

The following list is a summary of some common general business purposes for which computer-driven information management technologies have been implemented. Most software has been written to support one or another of the following tasks:

Word processing & document preparation. Personnel use machines to record and edit thoughts for the purpose of communicating about something to interested or concerned clients, coworkers, or managers. The state of the art of this function, now in development, utilizes voice-activated document writers that can produce printed words from spoken commands. The common form of word processor in present use employs a standard typewriter keyboard to drive a computer program. When an operator pushes a character key on the keyboard, the word-processing program stores a record of the character in its memory and displays it on a screen. The characters and spaces are stored in sequence so they can afterwards be moved around (edited) and printed or transmitted over wires to the machines of other users.

Document storage. Completed documents, messages, and reports prepared by people or machines are stored and indexed in a categorical, alphanumeric, sequential, or other order. Document storage devices record the digital records of data on magnetic tapes and disks or laser-optical disks in the same manner as signals of music and video are recorded for playback later.

Publication & distribution. Documents, reports, or other forms of request, promise, declaration, or invitation are produced in printed or electronic message form and forwarded to other parties. State-of-the-art printing systems utilize lasers to electrostatically charge paper which is then exposed to a toning agent that deposits a color on the paper where it has been charged. The process was pioneered by the Xerox Corporation's Electro-Optical Division. Some laser printers can print at rates in excess of 100 pages per minute.

Accounting, billing, and inventory. Data related to past or future financial transactions is entered by operators or by machine to be later compiled in a form suited to a business purpose. Software for accounting purposes may be highly specialized to the needs of a particular business. Programs which provide a standard set of accounting and bookkeeping tools that can be used by any business are available for running on many kinds of microcomputers and minicomputers.

Financial analysis. Data related to past, present, or future transactions or other events is recorded and analyzed relative to procedures for forecasting business needs. The most commonly used financial analysis programs are called "spread sheets." A spread sheet program presents the user with a grid composed of intersecting rows and columns. Data can be entered into each space in a row and column, called a "cell." The user can then use the program to perform a number of operations with a cell or group of cells. For instance, all the cells in a row or column can be added together. The result of this calculation can then be entered in its own cell or used in another calculation.

Engineering & design. Data related to the physical measurements of a system or product is recorded and subjected to procedural and/or theoretical analysis. Reports in the form of graphic representations or equivalent mathematical statements are generated.

Statistics & research. Data related to the history of an activity, a group of transactions, or other events is recorded by people or by machines for the purpose of determining the effects of actions or controls on a process.

Communications. Information in the form of a bit stream is transmitted between machines in the form of electromagnetic or electro-optical signals. Encoded in the bit stream are cues which activate other machines to process the bit stream; this can result in the delivery of a human-understandable message, report, or statement or the storing of a report in a data storage device. In the case of a telephone type of system which uses digital techniques, circuits are automatically connected in a network to carry a voice, data, or video transmission. Telecommunications technologies are discussed at greater length in Chapter 4.

Procedural management. A machine manages the procedures of a task from start to finish, cuing other machines or prompting personnel to take subsequent actions leading to a finished product.

Facilities & resource management. Data related to the reserves or inventory of a resource or resource system is recorded by people or machines and used in the allocation or control of resources and for predictions by managers about production or other matters.

Data management. Data related to business activities is recorded by people or machines so that reports can later be compiled about the data relative to particular points of view or uses.

Real-time status reports. Data regarding a process in current action is reported by or polled from a machine or from a prompt response by a human operator for the purpose of monitoring and controlling activity, maintaining security, or managing resources.

PROBLEMS OF SYSTEM INTEGRATION

To comprehend system integration, imagine the task of integrating an information management system, containing all of the above elements within one system so that an individual within any department of a business is able to understand the system and order a report on the activities of any other department. The need for this arises frequently in business, for instance, when the accounting department wants to directly check the cost of an item in an engineering department budget, or when a doctor wants to find out about a patient's medication procedures.

Today, system integration problems are compounded by the fact that, in most cases, the machines designed for each of the many tasks of various business departments were developed at different times by different manufacturers all working independently of one another. When these machines were engineered, they were often deliberately designed to be incompatible with the equipment of competing manufacturers. These machines usually cannot easily prepare reports usable by machines in other task areas. For instance, it is unlikely that an elevator control system in a building will have the specific kind of intelligence needed to deliver a record of its energy use requirements per trip to an energy management system, even though it is equipped with technology that is potentially intelligent enough to provide this kind of analysis. Users require that technologies be as simple to use as the standard telephone. But up to this time, the history of technology development has followed the course of proliferation of proprietary systems using noncompatible software. Small systems running incompatible software to work on different tasks within an office have been more affordable than larger integrated systems. This has compounded the problem of system integration. As a result, technology consultants often have difficulty giving their customers easy estimates of the costs of integrating systems or of introducing computer technologies to previously unequipped businesses or departments within a business. This problem has become the basis for the development of the computer time-sharing business, which is discussed in detail in Part 3 of this book, The Intelligent Environment.

THE EFFECT OF SYSTEMS ON BUSINESS POLICY & PROCEDURES

Most people, when confronted with the task of implementing an information management system for the first time, are frightened, halting, suspicious, cautious, reluctant, and timid. They are usually more concerned about not spending their money on the wrong thing, however, than they are about the really problematical issues: the ways in which the system will affect their use of and access to information.

Implementation of a computer system overlays existing business information with forms of indexing, storage, and retrieval which are highly organized and purposeful and peculiar to the way machines operate. When computer systems are implemented, business policies are established which take the place of many of the sensitive decisions made by human managers. Procedures are then automatically administered by machines whenever conditions decree their use. The more sensitive management issues which are too complex for machines may be ignored because of their complexity. Margins for error become smaller, and effects of mistakes are frequently amplified. Communications become faster and easier. More communication is often required, and it is more concise and to the point. As a result, the work habits of personnel are affected. Productivity is measured by more arbitrary standards. Creativity is enhanced for some individuals and restricted for others. In the realm of computer-aided design and manufacturing, for example, the design and finishing of products is governed by tolerances instead of aesthetic decisions. This is why computerization often results in a change in the quality of products and services. This is where issues arise about the weakening of emphasis on quality and the lessening of the human input affecting style and the nature of human employment.

The history of the typical business executive's response to the dilemma of survival in the age of information technology has been marked by veiled hysteria. There has been a panic among management to become educated in order to continue to compete. This panic often expresses itself as a resistance to implementation of state-of-the-art systems, leading to endless conversations and committee meetings. And there has been a correlative panic among businesses to implement productive technologies at the least cost. This "march to the sea" involved endless studies of alternatives punctuated by sporadic purchases of incompatible, interim solutions. The situation created by anxiety over information hidden in electronic storage and the organization's commitment to computerization has often been characterized by decisions which try to involve the least risk. This anxiety led millions to technical seminars, and millions more to try utilization of less expensive microprocessor technology . In larger firms, this same psychology led to overkill involving the selection of elaborate mainframe supersystems which, because of their lengthy software development time, presented other limitations and problems. This subject has been described more fully in Chapter 3.

The one thing that is clear is that implementing office automation precipitates rethinking of business goals in order to determine new productivity levels. The network of requests and promises which make up the organization is likely to change. New procedures and performance expectations are involved that require reeducation of staff and new job specifications.

PERSONNEL REQUIREMENTS IN COMPUTER-ASSISTED BUSINESS

Machines are used to accomplish levels of tasks as part of a total process. Each machine requires a specific set of input tasks usually done in regular order; this has a specializing effect on personnel requirements. As the sophistication of machines improves and people are no longer required to do the menial jobs performed by machines, the question of man or machine tends to be refined to the issue of cost-effective production. Given the ability afforded by modern robotics, voice synthesis, and other machine talents, people need only be called upon for processes for which the programming of machines might be too expensive. These tasks are not necessarily difficult from the human perspective, but they are more difficult for machines. It may never be possible to develop a machine to accomplish an aesthetic judgment. If a task must be done by a worker through making an aesthetic judgment, it is likely to be a difficult job for a machine.

As an example, the accuracy level of optical character reader machines is uncertain because dust, paper flaws, and slight misshaping of characters triggers a best-guess response in the machine, requiring operator attention. Optical character readers (OCR devices) use a video camera to scan lines of type. Each distinct character in a line is compared with a character set in the memory of a computer. When a character in memory is found that exactly matches the one being scanned, the computer enters the matching character in its memory and tells the scanning camera to move on to the next character in line. Because the computer can do its comparison testing in a few milliseconds (millionths of a second), the process can take much less time than it takes to have a typist copy the document. However, a slight flaw in the shape of a character, dirt on the page, or a wrinkle in the paper can throw the machine off, whereas the typist could very easily make the aesthetic judgment needed to identify the character. In an attempt to duplicate this aesthetic judgment, OCR machines have been equipped with electronic dictionaries. If the OCR computer stumbles over a character, it scans the rest of the word in which the character appears. This word is then compared with the words in its dictionary (database) until a match is found for all the characters in the scanned word, and the unreadable character is replaced by the corresponding character in the dictionary word. However, this process takes more time and makes the scanning process slower than human operation. Except when the copy to be scanned is very clean and printed in a standard, simple typeface in which there are no characters that tend to resemble each other, OCR is not effective with other than very common language, is prone to mistakes, and requires the attention of very alert operators who can spot the computer's errors and correct them. This kind of operator attention is impractical when there is a large volume of information to be recorded. As a consequence, rote tasks such as resetting the type of telephone directories [a continual undertaking for publishers of classified advertising (yellow pages)] is now being done by key-stroke workers rather than by OCR. On the other hand, because of computer-driven typesetting machines and presses, the printing industry has been proceduralized to the extent that workers in the Philippines, who are not expert in the English language, are currently preparing telephone directories for the United States. The personnel required for this industry as well as the production facilities required have been changed dramatically by this shift in the work force.

SOCIAL EFFECTS OF COMPUTER IMPLEMENTATIONS

Tasks which are possible but at present difficult for machine programming range from the efficient loading of vehicles to the writing of responses to Department of Defense requests for proposals. A major change in the work force owing to technology implementation is caused by the specialization of people in jobs defined by tasks being done by machines. This specialization has affected the social quality of the work environment. The output of a skilled word processor is much higher than that of a secretary or clerk-typist. People trained to use word processors are highly productive and earn high wages. It is wasteful and counterproductive to ask such persons to make coffee or buy theater tickets for the boss. Traditionally, the job of receptionist in a business has been an entry level task requiring little training. Reception personnel today may be called upon to operate call directors for PBX machines which manage a complex set of software to direct and route calls. In most cases, telephone call management could not be handled as well if the receptionist were sent on an errand. When the call management task is separated from the visitor reception function, the receptionist becomes the host or hostess for the business and must have a presence that commands respect. The menial employee disappears in the automated office.

CHOOSING TECHNOLOGY SYSTEMS

Of all the difficulties involved in implementing information technologies today, the greatest is that in a firm the people in the best position to identify technology needs are the secretaries, clerks, and other workers. Systems purchasing is expensive, and decisions for such expenditures are made by upper-level management. This job frequently falls upon the shoulders of the chief financial officer (CFO) in a company. Although this person may have no background in telecommunications, data management, etc., the CFO has the responsibility of determining budgets and expenses relative to profit. When there is little opportunity for meaningful contribution to the purchasing decision by those who are responsible for getting the job done on a day-to-day basis, management will encounter resistance to automation changes. Under these conditions, the budgetary criteria for technology purchasing are arbitrary and managers of departments within an organization may need to compete with one another for shares in the technology budget.

This problem is compounded because the design and installation of a sophisticated telecommunications and computer system should involve a partnership between the people who are supplying the system and software and the people within the company who will use it. This suggests the need for a data-processing staff within a firm that can operate autonomously to analyze production, implement systems, and train and support other personnel as required. Today, prime characteristics of a succesful firm are the technological education and support offered by its data-processing staff and the presence of policies that include all staff in the decision-making process. A firm with a bright and efficient data management department that is respected by coworkers within the firm should out-perform a firm without this resource.

INTEGRATED SOFTWARE SYSTEMS

Integrated software makes possible the common use of data by various departments of a business. It eliminates the problem created when systems have been independently designed for specific tasks within a business. When, over a period of time, a business has acquired a number of machines from various manufacturers, they will all use proprietary codes and processing methods which are foreign to one another. Data or reports prepared using machines that are running software which is not part of an integrated package will not be alterable by any machine other than the one which was used to generate the report, unless some sort of translation device is available. An accounting system database, for instance, will not closely resemble an engineering or document data storage technique. As a consequence, a manager preparing a report or analysis in a nonintegrated software environment will need the assistance of several people to compile an integrated engineering and accounting report. Reports from different systems will have to be manually reentered as raw data into other systems. In an integrated system, people can access data in usable form without the assistance of others, aside from an occasional telephone conversation. The methodologies of integrated software are discussed more fully in Chapter 3.

The most complete integrated software packages to date were developed by the principal manufacturers of general purpose minicomputers, most notably Digital Equipment Corporation. There are also a number of specialized systems for particular industries such as banking, telephone company management, and real estate property management. These systems provide integration of software for a range of tasks. Instead of a separate system for each task, the integrated system can switch between programs for several tasks. Reports generated by one program in the system can be used as data for other programs. If the databases for each task have been integrated also, managers will be able to access data across and between departments.

Most system companies design software for specialized markets. Each company designs its software programs for multitasking systems in certain industries such as banking, insurance, or the travel industry. By writing their programs in a common business program language like COBOL, the most used business computer language, users can "migrate" their systems onto the hardware of several different manufacturers. In the strictest sense, these kinds of systems are not totally integrated, since relative to the common office functions listed previously, they do not offer utilities for more than one or two functions. However, as the software sold by these firms begins to be delivered on application-specific integrated circuits (chips) with programs "burned in," the indication is that most business systems will be available with totally integrated software packages within 2 to 5 years.

Many of the leading high-technology companies still make and market products which do not integrate. Firms such as IBM, Wang, Xerox, NBI, NCR, Lanier, and other well-known office automation manufacturers have tried to develop integrated product systems by growing outward from an earlier product. They do this by incrementally adding new products compatible with the earlier systems in the product line. A problem with this approach is that the methodology of the earlier products is made obsolete by newer technologies using design techniques that are far superior to and not compatible with the older designs. For example, the earlier systems were deliberately designed to be incompatible with the designs of competitive manufacturers. This strategy is inconsistent with the needs of firms to communicate with one another by utilizing their intelligent machines and is now obsolete.

Information management technologies are developing in predictable directions. We are moving toward more compatibility, better communications between machines, and total system integration. Successful implementation of artificial intelligence is associated with this evolution. This is because the decision-making (intelligent) machines need to control a broad variety of other machines in the application of artificial intelligence. The idea of machines reporting to machines, and machines polling other machines for data required for management decisions, expands the potential of business automation by reducing great tasks to manageable proportions. The technical realities of this have been explained in the next chapter.

SUMMARY AND CONCLUSIONS

The design and development of workspace has been fundamentally altered by new technologies for information management. When one understands the potentials of the new technologies and their methods, it is easier to predict the future of business development and workspace design evolution. This chapter has been about this evolution. It began by posing some questions. By this point the reader should have a better understanding of what these questions mean. A case study has been provided below to illustrate these questions. The next chapter and Part 2 present material that reveals the workings, in specific uses, of various kinds of computers, telecommunications devices, and operations.

Before going on, I want to restate the questions that are providing the context for this inquiry: What takes place in the office? What does information management mean to building development? What are the changes likely in the structure of a business assisted by technology? Consider differences in the activities of workers and the type and quality of personnel involved. Imagine the office environment that is suitable to supporting the activities and interaction of these people. What happens when these technologies are made available to wider bases of the U.S. population and to populations of "developing" nations? Looking at a specific example makes it possible to comprehend the actual changes required—in personnel, environmental support systems, power, space, telecommunications needs, and other needs of businesses that employ state-of-the-art technologies. The effect of technologies on the workplace has been revolutionary, yet what we have witnessed today is just the beginning. In the following example, the growth of a company and its associated technological requirements are graphically illustrated relative to business goals.

Case Study

MIRACLE FOODS

Miracle Foods, Inc., a manufacturer, packager, and distributor of nondairy health food products employed a system integration consultant to assist Miracle in specifying, installing, and implementing technology for a new factory, warehouse, and headquarters offices which were at the time under construction in the City of Industry, California.

Miracle Foods, Inc., began business in 1938 by manufacturing a dairy replacement product to be sold by health food stores. Requests for Miracle's products began to come from other markets—restaurants, caterers, airline food services, etc.—and the company expanded over the years to meet increasing demands. By 1975, after 40 years of operation, the company had sales of approximately $10 million per year of a variety of artificial dairy products and dairy products specially packaged for restaurant use.

Prior to construction of the new facilities in the City of Industry, the expansion of production and administrative facilities at Miracle had progressed by means of piecemeal acquisition of neighboring buildings. The company grew to occupy an entire city block in downtown Los Angeles.

In 1975, a system designer was hired by the company president to write software for and support Miracle's initial implementation of data-processing services, a Data General minicomputer system running COBOL programs. At this time, data-processing tasks were limited to accounting, billing, and aging of accounts along with some purchasing records and payroll management functions. While the automated systems were being installed, Miracle employed a marketing firm to design packaging for a line of new products to be marketed in supermarkets; these were to rapidly accelerate the growth of Miracle's customer base. At this writing, 10 years after the first implementation of computer technologies, Miracle has sales in excess of $30 million per year and shows every indication of accelerating growth.

In the design stages for building its new manufacturing and administrative facility, Miracle requested that consultants conduct a study with regard to any impact which new telecommunications and data-processing system requirements might have on building design elements. After an initial conversation with Miracle management and a meeting with the project architects and engineers, the consultants advised estimating the productivity levels needed to meet future business goals before determining technology requirements for the new building. They also suggested evaluating some new technologies that could improve productivity in sales, marketing, manufacturing, purchasing, and middle management levels. To bring Miracle's staff up to speed on the technologies, the consultants conducted a seminar for Miracle's management team and executives. The seminar was to make management conversant with available new technologies.

As an example of the integration of planning building development with the implementation of state-of-the-art technologies, the minutes of that seminar have been printed below. Any firm can use this material as a guide for similar seminars.

THE HIGH-TECH OVERVIEW SEMINAR
Conducted for

Miracle Food Products, Inc.
924 East 14th Street
Los Angeles, CA 90021

November 9, 1984

Attendance. Present were the system consultants and the following personnel of Miracle Food Products, Inc.:

1. President and general manager
2. Chief financial officer and project coordinator
3. Controller
4. Director of consumer sales
5. Director of administrative services
6. Vice president, sales and marketing

Agenda. Participants were introduced by way of creating a community of interest and focusing the purpose and intended results of the meeting. The session leaders discussed their methods and the agenda of the seminar.

History and background of Miracle. Miracle's history of growth and expansion were reviewed, with a description of the needs which prompted the building of facilities now under construction. Miracle's management each gave a view of her or his job, talked about the technologies employed at present and the problems encountered, and suggested areas which were regarded as bottlenecks. They also mentioned their concerns about planning of the new building with regard to the requirements of their jobs and the tasks of employees in their respective departments.

Description of current technology implementation. Consultants discussed the background and development of Miracle's present use of computer technologies, including a statement about the intention of the initial implementation of the Data General accounting records system and the results of that implementation relative to the company's growth. An analysis was presented of the present limitations on Miracle's growth which have occurred because of this system, as well as unexpected problems and benefits which have resulted.

Definition of "productivity" for Miracle management's use of technology. Participants were asked to examine business and productivity goals for their departments. Consultants began to describe relationships between new technologies and business goals. In each of the following items, some of the individual department managers contributed examples indicating where they would like to see improvement; the technologies which might assist were also discussed.

1. Measuring productivity (less in for more out)
2. Cost reductions through improving efficiency
   a. Saving lineal time through automation
   b. Saving expense by streamlining procedures and communications
   c. Reducing personnel support and maintenance expense by increasing the productivity of personnel and providing procedures that motivate more productive activity.
3. Increasing production
   a. Quantity increase per time—identifying and eliminating bottlenecks
   b. Quality increase per unit—identifying and eliminating errors

Setting production goals. The session leaders summarized the history of Miracle's growth and the ways in which systems were implemented to meet the production required by this growth. It became clear to department managers that the construction of the new facility was not only a real estate and tax-sheltering transaction but also the opportunity for planned-for business growth, which would significantly affect their jobs. Decisions about computer-related technologies, apart from the technologies of building, architecture, interior, and plant design, forced the session participants to focus on two issues: productivity and the well-being and performance of personnel, relative to the following:

1. Miracle's business goals—what they have been, how they have been achieved and measured, what they may become
2. Departmental goals required to meet business productivity goals
3. Plant, personnel, and technology required to meet and adjust to continuing expansion of productivity goals

Describing the total concerns of plant expansion. The task assignment, location, and activity of each Miracle employee and planned-for employee was reviewed, as well as the flow of work and communications, the hierarchy of administrative communication, and the need for security of data and communications. Issues discussed ranged from workstation lighting and other environmental elements to specific technology support requirements for each employee in the following areas:

1. Physical plant (buildings, furniture, factory, etc.)
2. Human resources (personnel, support, etc.)
3. Technology (telephone, data processing, etc.)

Overview of technology to support productivity. An overview of needed technology covered the following topics:

1. *Physical plant. Maintenance and support* of the physical plant relative to technology implementation decision
   a. Heating, ventilation, air-conditioning (HVAC) and power
   b. Security
   c. Administration (facility management system)
2. *Telecommunications.* Detailed description was given of a modern digital PBX—what it does and how it works. This included descriptions of PBX features such as automatic call distribution, voice store and forward features, direct inward line access, and call detail recording plus explanations of how the PBX accomplishes these tasks.
   a. Trunks and traffic management, including a brief history of telephone company management and technology and a discussion of the effects of divestiture and the management of equal access, bypass, and other opportunities
   b. Voice mail and message center techniques relative to specific company communications problems
   c. The integration of voice and data communications, involving a brief discussion about call and traffic management associated with PBX data switching.
3. *Data Processing.* The terminology and techniques of data processing were discussed, with regard to logical and physical data structuring of Miracle's data management system. The distinction was drawn between physical and logical data, and the function of the data dictionary was explained. The requirements for query flexibility to provide newly requested forms of immediate reports was discussed.
4. *Global model.* A global model was illustrated for Miracle's new system, describing electronic office features (word processing, electronic mail, filing, calendar, graphics, etc.). It was shown how such functions may be used in integration with the database and applications programs and how employees will interface with the new communications system.

Roundtable notes. At the conclusion of the session, a roundtable discussion was conducted with open conversation about all of the topics. Several conversations were held and several continued after the session. The conversation was opened with the statement of the question: Where and how can Miracle use technology to achieve a breakthrough in productivity? The following notes summarize the roundtable discussion:

1. *Query capability.* The president and marketing vice president both expressed a desire to have query capability for marketing purposes. They wanted the ability to get immediate answers to questions about customer activity and results of marketing activities and promotions. They wanted to do this without having to talk to or wait for other people to interpret data and prepare reports.
2. *Voice mail.* The purchasing and production managers explained that the existing message-taking and forwarding functions were unreliable and costly in terms of lost sales and improperly completed orders. A voice message system (VMS) was suggested as a possible solution. An argument was raised against automated answering and voice store

and forward; it was asserted that Miracle's customers might not wish to talk to computers and might prefer human interaction. It was suggested that this problem could be managed by implementing the technology so that customers could be appropriately communicated with at all times, while the efficiency and certainty of communications in general would be increased.

The credit and collection manager expressed a need for his phone-answering system to provide a different handling method for incoming credit-related calls than for other kinds of calls. The new PBX software was further specified to ensure that he could program each telephone station independently of all others.

3. *New Automation Software and Methods.* The president, senior vice presidents, and chief financial officer all expressed a long-standing need for integrating the present data processing with financial analysis and modeling software so that financial report preparation would be automated and more timely and usable.

   The production vice president expressed a need for automating the customer order, inventory, and supply report cycle and purchasing system. The cycle had become a bottleneck and frequently threw the company into costly emergency procedures for purchasing, rush deliveries, etc.

   The president wanted to expedite the delivery to headquarters of signed orders, or facsimiles thereof, in order to speed up the turnaround on orders, billing, and payments and avoid sales loss to more responsive suppliers.

Conclusion. Each of the departmental managers was requested to consult with staff and each other to further define where technology could be of value in increasing productivity, so that the priorities of technology design for the new installation could be appropriately planned. A shopping list of tasks was specified.

To-do list. The following list of items needing action was formulated:

1. Miracle management assigned themselves the task of further defining communication needs. They were to discuss, at the departmental level, the possible uses of VMS and direct inward lines. The purpose of this was to see if more direct access could be provided for both managing and marketing tasks. They defined as an objective that customers be provided with more access to and faster response from order fulfillment personnel and that Miracle managers be provided with more direct communication with sales and other staff.

2. Consultants scheduled a meeting with the president and marketing vice president regarding current and near-future database management query requirements and the cost of restructuring the data dictionary, etc.

3. Consultants scheduled a meeting with the financial officer to complete the choice of a new, more powerful computer system (Data General MV8000 versus Data General MV10000) based on a 3- to 5-year business plan. This decision will take into account projected personnel levels in accounting, administration, marketing management, and sales administration.

4. Consultants were assigned the task of developing a detailed implementation plan for Data General's integrated system, the CEO package, accommodating interdepartmental as well as intradepartmental needs, and the integration of this system with the new telecommunications system.
5. A meeting was scheduled to present the relative merits and system costs of the various telecommunications and local area network systems under consideration.
6. A meeting was scheduled with the building architects, engineers, and interior designers to discuss power, cable, and conduit requirements for the new systems, as well as special lighting, furniture, and HVAC requirements associated with the use of the new equipment.

CHAPTER

3

Elements of Computer Technology

TECHNOLOGY EDUCATION— THE NEED TO KNOW

The average adult American owns 39 electric motors, including electric drills, clothes washing and drying machines, vacuum cleaners, automobile starters, electric razors, battery-powered toys, blenders, ice makers, electric typewriters, copy machines, automatic cameras, personal computers, lawn mowers, ventilator fans, and garbage disposals. People in urban communities are involved in daily activities that cause the operation of hundreds of other machines. Although very few people understand the operating principles of a rotating electromagnetic field, this does not prevent their use of the technology of electric motors.

This statement about electric motors has often been used to support the thesis that we should design intelligent machines that do not require people to understand the engineering principles involved in their operation. This is the direction which technology manufacturers have taken in producing machines described as "intelligent" or "user friendly." A recently conducted poll compiled by Media General–Associated Press revealed that people are now comfortable with computers. The MG-AP poll reported that 84 percent of the respondents answered "no" when asked if computers intimidated them. Of those polled, 17 percent owned home computers themselves and 32 percent used computers daily at work. The survey also revealed that computers are generally considered tools for the wealthy and educated—people who are used to having things done for them.

A drastic downturn has been occurring in the sales of personal computers. Computer makers are moving toward a new approach in the manufacture of machines for managing personal, professional, and commercial business—an approach that requires more sophisticated software and more elaborate machines.

Personal computer manufacturers hope that the invention of such gimmicks as voice-activated programs and user-friendly software will encourage larger numbers of people to begin to use the less expensive machines. Their theory is that many people are put off by the typewriter keyboard, which is still the most used input device. Software is being developed which allows people to speak to their computers instead of having to enter numerical values or type in commands using a keyboard.

A potential side effect of voice-controlled machines will be changes in languages that occur as people learn to conform their speech to the

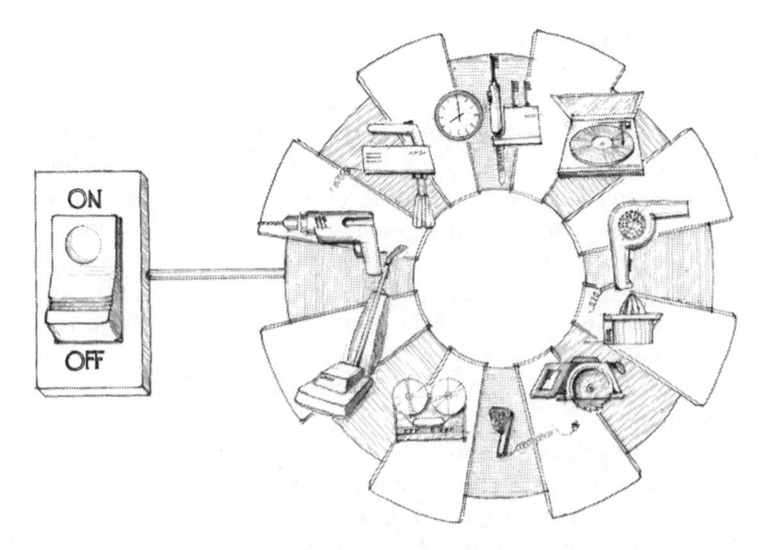

Figure 3.1 Although unable to explain the principles of rotating electromagnetic fields, the typical American householder owns an average of 39 electric motors.

conventions of computer logic. This adaptation is likely to contribute to a change in the way people think as well. It may lead to a more exacting use of spoken language—at least in the workplace.

VERTICAL MARKETING— VALUE-ADDED RESELLERS

Software packaging firms called value-added resellers (VARs), which market packages of software and hardware designed to meet the needs of just one or two kinds of industry, are emerging as the new leaders in computer marketing. Instead of selling a standard set of programs that can be used in any industry (such as word processing, accounting, or database management), VARs (discussed in more detail further on) write a set of programs for a particular industry and build a customer base in this narrowly defined market. This narrow focus is referred to in the computer industry as a "vertical market." A VAR package often includes an integrated set of computer and communications tools sufficient to manage the total operations of a business. This is a change from the computer-store approach which sells special purpose software and machines that can be used by any business.

FRIENDLY COMPUTERS

Computer salespeople like to describe the machines they are selling as being "user-friendly," by which term they imply that one needs little or no knowledge of computer technology to operate them. User-friendliness in computer-driven technology is the result of programming which disguises computer instructions by using a form that can be understood even by a person with subliterate knowledge. One of the best-known examples of a "user-friendly" machine is the Apple Mcintosh. The Mcintosh machine was actually a spin-off of the development efforts of engineers who formerly worked for the Xerox research park in Stanford, California.

Engineers at Xerox PARC developed a splendid technique for combining state-of-the-art video display and computer-programming techniques to display graphic symbols on a computer video monitor. These symbols, which Xerox called "icons," stand for elaborate computer processes. A pointing aparatus is provided, which Xerox calls a "mouse." With the mouse the user can move an arrow around the video screen to point to icons and to initiate the computer processes for which these icons stand. For example, one of the icons looks like a file folder. By placing the pointer on the file folder icon and pressing a button on the mouse, the user can open this folder and see its contents displayed in a "window" of the screen. Alternatively, the file folder icon can be moved and placed on top of an icon which resembles a printer, in which case the file will be printed on paper.

In the Xerox system, the video monitor itself is called a "desktop" and there is a complete range of icons representing virtually every computer process needed to perform office and graphics jobs (see Figure 3.2). The icons are displayed on the screen whenever the user chooses to load the utilities which these symbols represent. Also, the user does not need any computer-related knowledge or language to load the programs. Menus offer a list of utilities including filing and printing. Once the user has selected utilities and set up a desktop, the system remembers. Thus, each time the user logs on, or loads her or his programs to the computer, the screen displays the continuation of the last session.

Xerox is strongly influenced by its roots in graphic processes and has done more than any other company to advance the state of the art of printing, word processing, and other technologies for document prep-

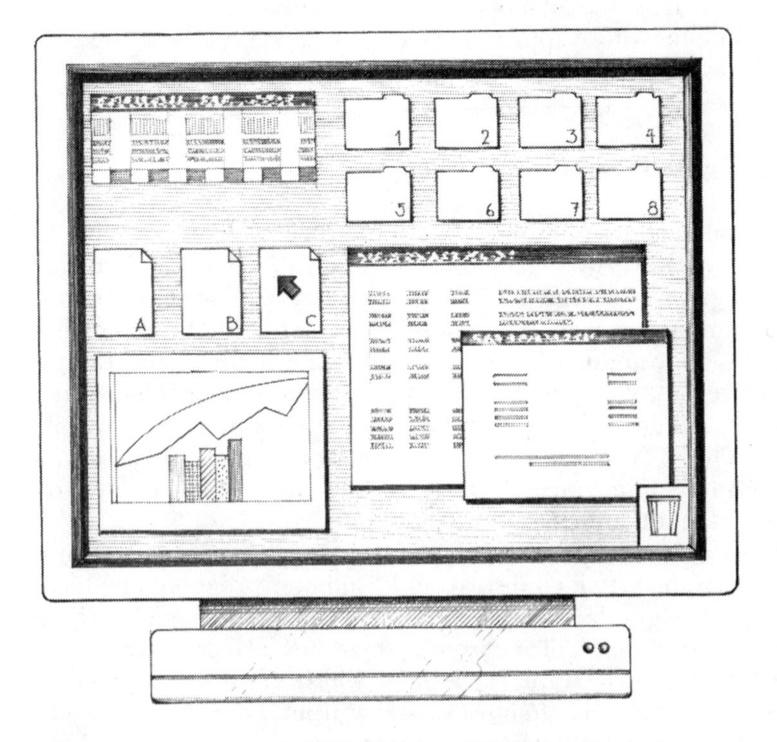

Figure 3.2 The software of the most user-friendly computer systems use commonly understood graphic symbols to represent complex machine processes.

aration and publication. Other manufacturers, such as IBM and the Bell Laboratories (now AT&T Information Technologies), as well as the Xerox Kurzweill Division, have been working on voice-activated systems and systems which make elaborate evaluations using artificial intelligence. They are all aiming at computer systems that will be as simple and natural to use as a common telephone. About development of "user-friendly" technology, we need to bear in mind that the more thinking we allow the machine to do for us, the narrower the range of expression available.

THE NATURE AND RULES OF COMPUTER PROGRAMMING

Although manufacturers of computer hardware pay attention to the appearance and human fit of machines (ergonomic considerations) in the physical design of terminals and workstations, people's working relationship with computer-driven machines is determined by software. Programming provides the language through which people inter-act with machines. Programming is a part of computer design—the "language" in which parts of a machine interact. The way machines and people interact is also determined by software. The analogy to electric motors is less applicable when it comes to software. There are reasons why a person who knows programming, or at least the principles by which computer-driven machines work, has an advantage over one who has less knowledge, irrespective of the "friendliness" of machines. Many practical, routine tasks can be done using user-friendly machines, yet "friendly" products like the Xerox Star or Apple Mcintosh and others have a weakness—the limitation of personal creativity. The machine is always limiting the user to particular ways of doing things. With very powerful systems, such as those used with sophisticated graphics applications for engineering and design, the range of expression available is very wide. However, the way a job is done affects the result. Opportunities for subtle variation are extremely limited using computers as compared to the use of "hand" tools. The advantage of using systems is savings in linear time. The disadvantage is in the limitation on range and quality of expression. More range is available to the computer user who understands more about how systems work.

THE STRUCTURE OF PROGRAMS—MACHINE INTELLIGENCE

In programming, activities are broken up into sequences of tasks or procedures. User-friendly machines accomplish most procedures trans-parently to the user. As mentioned above, they also limit possibilities to those functions for which the computer has been previously programmed. An averaging process is employed in limiting possibilities. Variations slightly outside the parameters of the program are averaged to values which the program has been set to deal with. This produces a result analogous to requiring that a painter must use a certain set of colors as they come from the manufacturer rather than mixing his own palette. Whereas a painter might want to mix a dark umber with cadmium yellow for a new color, the computer provides the painter with a particular color spectrum from which a choice can be made. With powerful graphic systems, the spectrum can be wide; but even so there are limitations. For many routine business-related tasks requiring routine data entry, this kind of limitation is a benefit that helps to avoid mistakes. However, the great future of computer technologies is in creative applications. Knowing how the computer is doing things is crucial to using machines to support the creative process. When people are being creative with computers, they enjoy experimentation and sometimes like to "tweak" programs. Our youthful "computer hackers," far from being criminals, are experimenters with limited outlets for expressing a valuable interest in creative pursuits with computers.

ARTIFICIAL INTELLIGENCE AND NATURAL LANGUAGE PROCESSORS

A sophisticated computer program can translate a machine's language into a user's natural language (English, French, Japanese, etc.) The machine uses processing time and memory to interpret instructions to its own programming and to translate those instructions into human language. The more powerful a computer, in terms of its processing speed and the immediacy of its access to stored vocabulary, the more sophisticated such programming can become.

"Artificial intelligence" is the term used to describe computer systems which attempt to emulate the human decision-making process. By using "natural language processors" (programs which convert human language into machine-processing instructions) software interpreter programs are opening the doors on more creative use of programming by providing better means of interpreting the languages of the user and the machine to one another. The concept of natural language processors goes far beyond what is meant by the term "user-friendly." Artificial intelligence implies that the machine has the potential to become a partner in the creative process and has an active energy which can be an ally or an enemy. The creative manager of a business may become better informed by consulting machines which can rapidly review millions of factors involved in a decision-making process in an instant and summarize conditions in an understandable form. For example, there are systems for determining the best areas in which a business might wish to locate. All of the factors involving the unit cost of making a product or offering a service—tax benefits, availability of resources, materials, and labor—and the costs associated with these factors are evaluated by the system, which ultimately produces a set of recommendations.

PROCESSING SPEED AND INTERACTIVE USE

The design of many modern machines allows them to store and process many separate programs virtually at the same time. They do this by sequentially storing and working with small parts of several different programs in millisecond intervals. Machines can also be equipped with "array processors" which do certain parts of the computing process very rapidly. Speed of processing gives the user the experience of having the total attention of the machine once logged on, even though the machine may intermittently be managing hundred of requests. The machine can handle several or even hundreds of requests from many users, depending on its processing speed and the nature of the programs being used. Faster processing speed therefore equates with more use and usefulness.

MAINFRAMES, MINICOMPUTERS, AND MICROPROCESSORS

The push toward faster processing speeds and bigger, more powerful systems is encouraged by the development of new technology that packs more power into smaller, less expensive machines. Today, a common personal computer, weighing in at 20 pounds or so, is more capable than an entire roomful of equipment, costing millions, was in the 1950s. However, the smaller systems do things differently.

Instead of storing all the data and programs being used in the machine's active memory during processing, small microprocessor systems (such as personal computers) store the programs and data on instantly accessible magnetic recording media. As the machine proceeds through its task, it refers to a magnetic disk or tape to pick up a few instructions, carries them out, goes back to get a few more instructions, and so forth. Micro systems have been excellent single-user systems that need only do one task at a time.

Minicomputer system designers focused on building machines which can load and run several programs intermittently so that a number of users can use the machine at the same time. The processing speed is fast enough so that it appears that the work is being done concurrently. Minicomputers have become the most valuable multiuser, multitasking machines.

Mainframes, which developed more directly out of the roomful era, have reached a point where they can process at the rate of billions of decision events each second. They can process enormous quantities of data through a lengthy analysis and produce in fractions of a second a result that would take a minicomputer a month to complete.

Bigger has traditionally meant costlier—costlier to build, costlier to maintain, costlier to program. Because of the high cost and maintenance complexities of big machines, the smaller machines, both micros and minis, have been employed to assist with a greater variety of jobs. Some of the smaller machines and programs are friendlier in limited applications than are larger mainframe computers. In most situations, once a minisystem is implemented it is not necessary for users to have any understanding of the machine and its programming.

COMPUTER INDUSTRY STANDARDIZATION

With the proliferation of competing computer-manufacturing firms during the first few decades of the information age, the differing approaches of computer manufacturers to the same tasks created totally different codes of instructions for different machines designed for similar purposes. Ideally, this would not be the case. However, the expansion of the industry owes much to the unlimited experimentation in several different directions by competing developers of technology.

By comparison with the telephone industry, which was artificially protected from competition, the computer industry advanced light-years while telephone technology remained a horse-and-buggy operation. This situation persisted until the time of the Justice Department settlement providing for the divestiture of the AT&T monopoly (discussed in greater detail in Chapter 4). Because of the breakthrough in telecommunications made possible through the introduction of competitive services, the computer industry is now quickly moving in the direction of greater standardization, encouraged by continual reductions in the cost of hardware and the expansion of user interest in having machines which communicate with those of others.

Knowledge about the basics of computer design and operation provides confidence and clarity in the confusing environment of humming acronyms such as EPROM (electronic programmable read-only memory), ASPIC (application specific integrated circuits), and ISDN (integrated services digital network), and buzzing words such as plasma screen, local area network, and distributed processing. Even for those who are trying to decide between options for common software products such as word processing and communications, basic knowledge about systems can be helpful.

There are levels of understanding about how computers work. The computer engineer has a level of knowledge which is vastly different from the programmer's. One could not use the engineer's knowledge to do the programmer's job. The knowledge required to write an efficient program to manage accounting tasks may have absolutely nothing to do with the engineering knowledge involved in designing the circuitry on which the program is to run. The knowledge level and understanding that is desirable for the noncomputer professional may be very limited. The desirable lèvel of education is that which is sufficient to allow an intelligent conversation to take place between the computer layperson and the system engineer.

HARDWARE AND SOFTWARE—THE IMPLICATIONS OF CHIP DESIGN

We can think of hardware as the physical machine and software as the set of instructions which tell the machine what to do and how to do it.

Figure 3.3 Different computer manufacturers have followed varying paths in organizing computer operating systems. As a result, there are difficulties in passing information efficiently between systems.

The physical structure of a machine is part of its programming. If a computer were equipped with wings, thrusters, and a few navigating devices, it could be said to have been partially programmed for flight. The differences between that part of a computer's function which is included in its hardware and that part which is contributed by software is of most concern to engineers who must design machines to fit various applications.

CHIPS—INTEGRATED HARDWARE AND SOFTWARE

The engineer might want to design a complex program to be manufactured in the form of a chip. When chips are used, the time it takes for loading and reading program instructions can be reduced immensely. Chips have two important values in computer manufacture: They reduce the cost of hardware literally to pennies and they allow a faster processing of data.

The basis of a chip is a thin slice of crystal. Crystals are the result of very special structural relationships between atoms. Their forms are very logical. Each elemental atom (i.e., oxygen, carbon, iron, etc.) possesses a characteristic number of protons, neutrons, and other subatomic particles, common to all atoms of a particular element. Electrons orbit the atomic nucleus like planets in the solar system. Depending on the energy state of the electrons, they orbit closer to or farther away from the nucleus. The orbits are referred to as "shells" by nuclear physicists and others who study the behavior and composition of atoms. An atom will always (unless found in an "excited" state caused by external influence) have a specific electrical charge associated with the energy level and number of electrons in the outer shell. When atoms possessing complimentary electrical charges associate under the right conditions, they sometimes share the electrons in their outer shells. This sharing of electrons is the basis of the atomic bonding which forms crystals of all kinds. The physical shape and other properties of everything we perceive in the universe are governed by the natural rules of the atomic-bonding processes—the arrangement of atoms to accommodate the sharing of electrons.

The word "crystal" evokes images of diamonds, rubies, and emeralds. The atoms in these crystals are so efficiently bonded that they are very difficult to break loose, and the crystals seem hard. Atoms in a crystal are also very regularly arranged—the pattern of their bonding forms a nearly perfect three-dimensional grid, like a honeycomb. When a crystal is broken, the break produces a sheer face on a plane which is at precise angles to the other planes of the internal crystal lattice structure.

This study of crystal structure is of great interest to science because here the unifying constants of physical science are revealed. More important to the subject of this book, a rudimentary understanding of chemical bonding and crystal structure lies at the heart of contemporary electronic circuit design. They are the elementary basis for the transistor, which is to modern electronic technology as the wheel is to the railroad.

Crystals are used in transistors in the following manner: Silicon crystals about 2 inches in diameter are grown in the laboratory at very high temperatures. The crystal, which may be several feet long, is sliced into wafers about 0.01 inches (0.2 millimeters) in thickness. A wafer is heated to about 1000° C in an oxygenated environment, and a layer of silicon dioxide (a glass) forms on its surface as the silicon atoms at the surface attach themselves to free oxygen in the atmosphere. The silicon is a conductor, while the silicon dioxide is a nonconductive material. By use of a chemical etching process, the glass is removed from certain parts of the wafer. Metals, oxides, and other materials are then deposited on the exposed areas of silicon according to a design determined by the circuit desired.

The material used for the chip wafer is a silicon crystal because of the particular properties of silicon which make it work in this fabrication process and because it is inexpensive. Other crystal materials such as gallium arsenide have been used experimentally because they allow electrons to flow at higher speeds than does silicon. Crystals are used because the electronic bonding of atoms in crystals produces a uniform condition on the surface of the material relative to the free-electron state which determines the specific conductivity required by the technology.

Circuits are printed on the surface of silicon crystal wafers in a kind of photographic process. Such circuits are first designed and drawn in large scale before being photographically reduced and printed on the wafer. In some cases, circuits are printed on a wafer in layers in the form of metallic (conducting) and nonconducting deposits. Sandwiched between these layers, the crystal wafer becomes a part of the completed circuit pattern and its peculiar qualities of electrical conductivity are utilized as required. Once a chip has been designed and tested, chips of that design can be manufactured in mass production. This makes the production of very complex electronic circuitry very inexpensive.

The low cost and high processing speed of chips has been used to develop very inexpensive and, at the same time, very sophisticated computer-controlled devices. An example is the evolution of the microcomputer-controlled digital private automated branch exchange (digital PBX). Digital PBXs are used to manage telephone traffic for large organizations which might have between 400 and 20,000 or more separate telephone lines and extensions. The PBX uses a microcomputer to keep track of incoming and outgoing calls. Because of its speed, the digital PBX computer can translate an incoming call into digital code, shunt the call through its internal circuits, and retranslate it into an analog voice signal for output, all while the callers are carrying on their conversation. The computer also measures and records the time of all calls, makes records of outgoing calls for accounting purposes, and makes decisions about which outgoing lines to use, etc. The computer which manages this task reads and carries out instructions so quickly that even when there are thousands of calls being made each minute, traffic is managed so that telephone calls are not lost, ignored, or blocked. To provide such a utility affordably, the digital PBX computer needs to be small, inexpensive, absolutely reliable, and easy to reprogram whenever telephone extensions are moved, added, or deleted. The system must also be economical to purchase and maintain. By incorporation of the highly specialized programs of telephone call management in chip designs, very efficient, inexpensive machines have been designed to do big jobs. PBX devices are discussed in more detail in Chapter 4.

The chip provides economical and efficient means of employing a program because its circuit logic is prewired. Instead of having the machine go through the process of loading software to arrange circuits in a certain order to set up the processing path for data, the chip embodies these processing pathways in its wiring so that the machine need only shunt data into and away from the chip. The chip itself is in the domain of "hardware," and the structure of the hardware provides the program. The arrangement of circuits on the chip is a program which formerly belonged to the domain called "software."

Today, hardware comes with extensive software functions which are literally built-in. The distinction between the hardware function and the software function is still fundamental to understanding about problems encountered in communications between machines and the difficulty of integrating systems which have been designed to meet differing needs. For instance, hardware designed to run programs for word or records processing will usually present a problem in receiving or sending information to a system designed to run software for a different purpose, such as that used for engineering graphics programs.

HARDWARE

With the qualification introduced by chips in mind, hardware may still be thought of as the physical machine—its electrical circuits, wiring, keyboard, display monitors, data storage drives, cooling devices, power supplies, cabling, and so forth.

The hardware of a machine provides the physical structure through which the electrical signals may be pulsed, stored, accumulated, added together, divided, and subtracted. This physical structure is not random but is peculiar to the purposes for which the machine will be used. The architecture of this structure thus provides the basic order of programming for the machine. When it is "powered up," it will be already programmed so that the first signal received on its input wiring will be managed, read, and interpreted as a particular kind of instruction. It may automatically look into some area of its memory, "load up" an operating system, and run a check on all its components.

PROGRAMMING

Conceptually, it is not difficult to understand how a machine works so that when a person presses the key for the letter "k" on a keyboard, a corresponding letter "k" shows up on a video display screen (VDT). Very simply, the computer is programmed so that an electrical signal of a specific and regular value is initiated by pressing a key. It is also understandable that a sequence of letters such as M-O-V-E can equate to a sequence of electrical signals, the sum of which can be the cue within a program for starting a process. The first step of such a process might be the generation by the machine of a series of electrical signals sent to a video screen to illuminate on a video screen the characters, "MOVE WHAT?" It is conceivable that the next step in this process could be the cuing of a set of circuits so that the value of electrical signals generated by the next input from the keyboard would be automatically compared with values that are stored in a list that identifies the location of blocks of data on a recording device. The next steps in the program could then instruct the recording device to "read" the block of data that is attached to a value that is equal to the value which was inputted on the keyboard. Each step of the process is an electrical signal of a certain value which has an equivalent mathematical value. Mathematical values can thus be used in a sequence to input equivalent electrical signals to cue the flow of other electrical signals. Along the way, these signals can produce the result of turning on switches which activate the display of characters on a video screen, the printing of characters or other marks on paper, or the fluctuation in the control of a manufacturing or other process.

SOFTWARE

In the early years of computer development, an engineer was required to enunciate jobs to the computer by physically rearranging the setting of patterns of switches, wires, and vaccum tubes. Over the years, designers created machines which used electronic switches to change the pathways of electrical circuits. These switches were then designed to be opened and closed by other switches in routine control processes which became the programming for "operating systems." The operating system evolved to become the standard set of protocols for the machines of a given manufacture.

OPERATING SYSTEMS AND PROTOCOL

The first set of instructions to be loaded by a machine each time it is powered up is its operating system. The operating stystem exists as software, yet the computer's wiring is such that the computer hardware and operating system are usually designed and engineered together. The operating system establishes the identity of the computer system's elements: the names, addresses, and physical locations of storage devices, printers, keyboard, video display unit, and so forth. It also establishes the order in which processing will be done. This ordering process is known as the "protocol." The protocol allows the machine to determine the meaning it must assign to data as it is entered. Because of the protocols established by the operating system, the computer will always know, on the basis of the order in which data is received, what to do with data coming from the keyboard, from a storage device, from its own memory, or from a program it happens to be running. The main difficulty in getting computers of different manufacturers to talk to one another centers around differences in operating system protocols. Protocol converters are employed to allow the data of machines running with different operating systems to be inter-exchanged with some limitations. In some cases, manufacturers have licensed the use of their operating systems to other machine manufacturers so that programs can be migrated more easily from machine to machine.

Operating system protocols provide the building blocks for writing applications programs. In the evolution of operating system technology, standard words have evolved which are equivalent to values for complex sets of machine instructions. Usually, these words have natural language meanings to guide the user in understanding the machine's activities. Some of these words have become standard instructions for the functions most computer programs need to apply; these include get, print, find, add, divide, if, but, greater than, less than, subtract, print, go to, display, dump, store, sort, search, start, stop, quit, and log on.

LEVELS OF LANGUAGE—MACHINE LANGUAGE

Between the words used by the application programmer and the computer's functional operation (the physical manipulation of circuits shuttling and regulating a flow of electrons) there are several levels of program language.

A computer is essentially a collection of circuits. These circuits can either be closed (allowing current to flow through them) or opened (preventing the flow of current). The circuits in a computer are arranged so that they can be interconnected with others in functional groups and orders. Depending on the kinds of voltage carried by each circuit in an interconnected group, a certain amount of current will be carried by that group, which triggers switching of circuits in other groups.

Machine language is in the form of numerical code. Each number of the code is analogous to a certain amount of electrical current which the machine can produce through the setting of certain circuits in the closed condition and other circuits in the open condition. Computer engineers can use machine code to create operations in the computer which are accomplished very quickly because there is no need for a lengthy interpretive process or procedure. All the programming of a computer must eventually be translated into machine code before the machine can process it. The relationship between machine code and higher-level programming language can be explained in a few simple steps.

NUMERICAL CODE—BINARY, DECIMAL, AND HEXIDECIMAL NUMBERS

Because we constantly use the decimal number system, it seems second nature to quantify things in multiples of ten. The number system natural to the computer is based on a choice between two states: 0 and 1—the essence of a binary number. This is natural because computers operate on the basis of two possible states: the presence or absence of voltage in a wire. Zero can be equivalent to an open circuit (no voltage), and One then is equivalent to a closed circuit (some voltage). Binary number systems are based on two possible states, expressed as 0 and 1. The binary number system is not limited: It can be used to represent any possible number, however large, just by increasing the number of places, or digits. Larger numbers are, however, cumbersome and may be hard to remember. A bank account number like 1001111 100100001011 would be impractical. Because of these inconvenient qualities of binary numbers, programmers found it infinitely easier to write machine language code using a third number system, called the "hexidecimal system." Hexidecimal has characteristics which allow it to be easily translated to decimal numbers for human consumption and binary numbers for the machine to use.

UNDERSTANDING VARIABLE-BASED SYSTEMS

The hexidecimal system uses 16 unit states. Hex numbers are more compact than decimal numbers and are easily translated by machine into binary equivalents. To understand hexidecimal numbers, take a closer look at how number systems work by examining the elements of the decimal system. When 123 (one hundred and twenty- three) is written in decimal code, the code 123 means

3 ones	3
2 tens	20
1 hundred	100
Total	123

In writing notation for all of the above-mentioned number systems, units (ones) are in the first place (on the right). The value given to each other place in the numbering system, counting from the right, depends on the base of the system being used. (The base of the decimal system is 10, that of the binary system is 1, and that of the hexadecimal system is 16). In the second place, counting from the right, there are multiples of the base. In the third place, there are multiples of the second place, etc. Thus, in the decimal system, we have units (0 through 9) in the first place and tens in the second place (10 through 90); tens of tens (or hundreds) are in the third place (100 through 900), and tens of hundreds (or thousands) are in the fourth place (1000 through 9000); and so forth.

HEXIDECIMAL BASED NUMBERS

In the hexidecimal system, the base is 16. The first place is ones (0 through 16). Since the hexidecimal system contains 16 unit states as compared to 10 units in the decimal system (0 through 9), computer scientists have used alphabet letters to represent the units above 9. When you want to count to 10 in "hex," the sequence is 0, 1, 2, 3, 4, 5, 6, 7, 8, 9, A, B, C, D, E, F, 10. Thus the expression "10 hex" represents the same number of units as "16" does in the decimal system, and the second place is sixteens (10 hex = 16 dec, 20 hex = 32 dec, 30 hex = 48 dec, etc.). The third place in hexidecimal is 16s of 16s (256s). Thus 100 hex = 256 dec; 200 hex = 512 dec; 300 hex = 768; etc. The fourth place in the hexidecimal system is 16s of 256s (2096s). So 1000 hex is 4096 dec, 2000 hex is 8192 dec, and so forth.

The value 123 in the decimal system is therefore written 7B in hexidecimal.

B ones	11
7 tens (16s)	112
Total	123

Hexidecimal numbers are usually written with the suffix h or the prefix $. The expression $36 or 36h should be interpreted as 54 decimal (three 16s + six 1s). Hex numbers are of more manageable length than are decimal numbers. They are easier to remember, and they convert easily to binary numbers with fewer chances for mistakes because base 16 has a geometric relationship to base 2.

ASSEMBLY LANGUAGE

Once the computer engineers have assigned mathematical values to a machine process, it is possible to write a translation program that replaces machine code with natural language words, called "pneumonic symbols," that are interpreted by the machine as specific hexadecimal numbers that are used to represent the mathematical values of the processes. Pneumonic code is not quite natural language; it is a rudimentary and abbreviated approximation of human language, and it must be ordered and presented to the machine in a rigid format.

PROGRAM LANGUAGE

Program languages are computer applications languages that have been designed to work with specific computer operating systems, often for certain kinds of purposes. They consist of human language words and symbols for more complicated machine operations. Common programming languages include COBOL, used for many business management programs, and PASCAL, extensively used in scientific applications.

All programming languages have a few things in common because the essential elements of all computers are ultimately based on the principles of binary logic. Typically, each line in a programming language expression is a separate instruction. The entire set of instructions is called a "program." The program (which consists of this sequence of instructions) can be stored in the computer's memory circuits or in an external medium. When the computer is given a starting instruction (usually the name of the program), it proceeds to read the instructions, one line after another. This is known as running a program.

APPLICATIONS SOFTWARE

Applications software consists of sets of programs for accomplishing specific tasks. Word processing is an example of an application program. The application is writing, editing, and formatting human language text. The word-processing program exists as a list of program language instructions which, when loaded into the machine, causes the computer to respond to input at the keyboard in a prescribed manner so that characters are displayed on the video monitor and recorded in memory as required.

EXPERT SYSTEMS AND ARTIFICIAL INTELLIGENCE

Computer scientists have been working with psychologists to figure out how people think and to duplicate the process with machines. Because computers are able to analyze a tremendous volume of rapidly changing data very quickly, they may theoretically be able to assist us in making decisions about complex issues. Computer systems that work this way are called "expert systems." They have been successfully implemented to assist with such tasks as oil exploration, navigational guidance, and air traffic control. Computer systems are excellent expert consultants when the task requires decisions to be unaffected by criteria other than those for which the program has been designed. However, to get a computer to tell you when you should take a raincoat when leaving the house has proved unreliable.

Expert systems are the practical applications of what is known as "artificial intelligence." The essence of artificial intelligence is an ability of the program to learn by experience. This means that the results of each program decision must be fed back and included in a database for future reference. This capability, most notably demonstrated by the grandmaster status awarded to several computer chess-playing programs, is significant because it involves the ability of a machine to write its own programs and to analyze and evaluate the results in accordance with specified criteria. The distinction between artificial and authentic human intelligence must therefore exist in the ability to create relevant criteria.

Very simply stated, artificial intelligence programs analyze data and write instructions for processing until a result is produced that satisfies some preset condition. The conditions for satisfaction may be continuously modified by the results so that the machine continues to learn through the feedback of experimental data.

SOFTWARE—FUNCTION AND DOCUMENTATION

Computers are very simple machines, yet much of the jargon about computers and applications software is not very understandable for those who use them. As mentioned above, the step-by-step process by means of which computers do complex tasks always is preprogrammed. This way of approaching tasks is foreign to a human approach, which is a mixture of intuition and logical deduction. Consequently, there is a difference between the way a computer does its job and the way in which people use the computer program. The manual that helps the user escape from the madness of the program's inescapably plodding logic is called "documentation." The choice of words is unusually succinct. Documentation simply documents the way the program will unfailingly respond to user input. For instance, a user manual for life on the planet Earth might contain instructions such as, "every action has an equal and opposite reaction" and "what goes up comes down."

The language of documentation, which is initially prepared by programmers, is sometimes more arcane than the expressions of physical law. Computer engineers and marketers often give a name, such as "word processor," to a program. It is important to learn not to be intimidated by arcane language and to be willing to investigate the real possibilities of technologies that are sometimes misleadingly named.

WHAT'S IN A PROGRAM— THE "WORD PROCESSOR"

Actually, a word processor provides the utilities of a kind of automated typewriter. A computer running a word processor program is crunching numbers and does nothing with words. A writer uses language and is primarily concerned with editing ideas expressed as written words consisting of regular alphanumeric characters that are formatted in sentences and paragraphs. The word-processing program causes the computer to cumulatively store, retrieve, and transmit electrical equivalents of alphanumeric characters in the order arranged by the writer. From the writer's orientation, the word processor is a tool for creating, storing, formatting, and printing documents and images. "Word processor," in contemporay usage, is a term which should be understood to mean the following: A typewriter keyboard is used to enter text into a computer's memory; the text also appears on a video monitor screen. The writer is allowed to move, delete, or add words or phrases at will. Access is provided to large volumes of previously stored words in the computer's active memory and/or on peripheral data storage devices. The word processor is capable of driving a printing device that can be connected to the computer, and it allows the writer to print any part of the material that is in or available to computer memory. It should also allow the writer to send or receive data over the telephone to other computer users where the material can be read, edited, or printed by others.

PROGRAMMING SKILLS

The skills required to operate a program are not the same as those required to write software. Skill with one program does not necessarily equate to skill with another. A data entry program utilizes words to identify, store, sort, and report about data, while a "text editor" functions to arrange and edit reports. The skills necessary to run a data processor or data management program are unlike the instructions for a word processor program. There are also extensive differences in the way files are kept by different programs. A database file may consist of fields of data which are organized only when reports are generated, whereas each word-processing file is a complete sequence requiring no reassembly before displaying or printing. Nevertheless, since the methodologies of computers are inherently based on electronic functions and the binary system, knowledge of one program and, better still, knowledge of one operating system will open vistas of understanding about all programming. Similarly, an understanding of how one computer printer is driven by a computer provides a relatively thorough education in the basic principles of computer communications.

DIVISION OF LABOR— THE COMPUTER ENGINEER

There seems to be a natural division of labor between those who are responsible for the result of the computer's task and those who maintain and support the use of the system. One reason it is valuable for computer laypersons to develop a basic understanding of program development is that eventually this will provide the means whereby both teams will be educated to have common understanding and knowledge of each other's tasks. A more important reason is that the effect computerized procedures have on most jobs is such that a little knowledge about how systems behave will provide one with great economic power. On the other hand, total ignorance of systems destroys the creative potential of new technologies. It is a little like putting a surgical laboratory in the hands of a bushman.

OPERATING SYSTEMS AND THE CENTRAL PROCESSING UNIT

In contemporary machines, the operating system determines the order in which tasks are done by the central processing unit (CPU) of a machine. If the computer had an identifiable thinking unit, it would be the CPU. As a thinking unit, the CPU has almost as much intelligence as a traffic signal. When a computer receives an instruction from the operator or another machine, the CPU is so structured as to always process the information it receives in a certain order. In this way, the machine "knows," by the order in which it was received, what to "do" with the data as it arrives. Operating systems determine the order in which the data is delivered to and managed by the CPU. The operating systems of machines of different manufacture differ in the order in which they do things based on the functions for which the machine was designed and the design preference of the system designer. The efficiency with which the hardware moves data within a system to accomplish a task depends on the operating system design. For this reason, some operating systems are better suited to certain kinds of applications than are others. As many different operating systems have been devised as engineers have developed machines for special tasks.

TWO APPROACHES TO MACHINE DEVELOPMENT

Since the operating system is the first level of programming in a machine, in many state-of-the-art systems designed for specific applications, the operating system software and the hardware for each processing function are designed together in order to optimize the efficiency with which each function is done. Each function of the system can then be worked on by a separate engineering group. Each group is charged with the development of the interfaces between adjacent or interacting functions.

Machines have also been designed to support popularly adopted operating systems. The manufacture of machines for standard operating systems for which numerous useful programs have already been written has been the key to the successful expansion of the personal computer market.

Early computer manufacturers purposefully designed operating systems to be incompatible with those of other manufacturers. This was seen as a beneficial competitive strategy during the early epochs of computer science, since the market for computer systems was concentrated among a relatively small number of high-volume purchasers such as the federal government, major banks, and larger industrial accounts. As usable systems became smaller and more affordable, and the markets for systems grew larger in number and volume, the proliferation of proprietary exclusive systems began to create a virtual Tower of Babel, with vendors clamoring for the validity of their own particular systems approach to programming. To the purchaser, the vendors all seemed to be making the same claims, in slightly different ways.

One result of the competitive proliferation of incompatible systems was that, with few exceptions, one can transfer information between machines made by different manufacturers only through a complex translating technology, if at all. Also, machines made by the same manufacturer for different markets will usually not communicate with one another. The competitive motivation for incompatibility is now being superseded by a motivation to promote communication and connectibility. Because of expansion of the marketplace, it is becoming easier to transfer files and data between machines. This eventually equates to being able to create reports and documents and send them over a telephone system to clients, coworkers and others for reading on their machines.

STANDARD OPERATING SYSTEMS

Independent software development requires that manufacturers of computers adopt standards for both operating systems and communications so that their software can run on the machines of any manufacturer. The manufacturers have responded to this need because the availability of a library of individually tailored or special-task software extended the value of their systems and encouraged sales. The operating systems for microprocessors which have become most popular are CP/M and MS/DOS. They are very similar but different. One cannot run a CP/M program on a machine which uses the MS/DOS operating system or the other way around without the intercession of a translating program. CP/M was designed by the Digital Research Corporation for the original Intel chip which first commercially incorporated microprocessor technology as a computer CPU. Because so many practical programs were developed by independent software programmers for CP/M machines, CP/M became a standard through popular acceptance. MS/DOS was created by MicroSoft, Inc. It is nearly identical to CP/M. It was developed at the request of IBM for IBM's entrance into the microprocessor market to help IBM's PC machines dominate this market by excluding CP/M programs. IBM wished to establish an operating system which was not compatible with the products of its competitors. MS/DOS would not exist as a standard were it not for the fact that IBM had a powerful position in the marketplace and wished to create product differentiation for its PC product.

SINGLE-USER AND MULTIUSER SYSTEMS

Neither CP/M nor MS/DOS, nor any other early microprocessor operating system, was designed to support a multiple-user environment. (A multiuser environment is a situation in which two or more people are using computer terminals to access a common computer memory or data-processing facility). As a result, much of the valuable software written for use on these early microprocessor operating systems is not efficiently usable when an organization wishes to network individual microprocessors together. Multiuser, multifunction software is very different from the single-user, single-tasking products which were written for CP/M and MS/DOS. More recently developed microprocessor chips are capable of supporting more sophisticated operating systems. But a standard comparable to MS/DOS or CP/M for multiple-user software has not been forthcoming. There is a trend today to migrate the multiple-user software developed for minicomputers onto "supermicroprocessors." Supermicros use chips capable of reading the 32-bit word structure used by minicomputers. Some of them can support minicomputer operating systems. This approach is proving to be more successful than the approach which favors the redevelopment of entirely new software for a new operating system as, for instance, is being attempted with the Western Electric (AT&T) Unix system. Although the Unix operating system supports multiple users, it has qualities which are problematical for much application programming. For these reasons, AT&T is releasing Unix operating system personal computers which include MS/DOS and CP/M operating systems as standard software as well.

MICROPROCESSORS

A microprocessor is a central processing unit (CPU) on a chip. As previously mentioned, the CPU chip is manufactured using a type of photographic reproduction process. The logic and wiring circuit is designed in large scale, photographed, photoreduced in size, and then deposited as a metallic image on wafers in making an integrated circuit chip. In a personal computer or other micro system, there are other chips in addition to the CPU chip; these provide the logic and circuitry for memory, timing, power supply, input/output, and other system components. In a typical personal computer, all of these parts are assembled by plugging them into larger printed circuit boards. The board containing the CPU chip is called the "mother board." Other boards typically included are main memory, memory expansion, printer, bus, graphics, disk drive controller, and communications. All of the other boards are plugged into the bus board, which provides standard interconnection wiring. The bus is a circuit-wiring facility. Originally, the bus was a bundle of wires with multiple pin connectors that attached onto the various components of a computer system. In large modern mainframe computer systems, the bus may be a single coaxial or fiber optic cable into which all of the components are connected. The bus acts as the communications medium between parts of the system. This subject is covered in detail in Chapter 6, Data Communications and Local Area Networks. In state-of-the-art microcomputer systems, the bus is a circuit board into which the user can plug other circuit boards which carry the logic for the jobs the computer does as well as its internal utilities and system components (keyboard, disk drives, video monitor, etc.). In microprocessor computers, the entire works is packaged in a box suitable for placing on a desk.

DISK OPERATING SYSTEMS (DOS)

In most micros, the box contains one or more disk drives. The disk drive was a key feature of early microprocessor technology. All computers need to store data. Some of the data consists of the step-by-step instructions, called the program. Other data to be stored is the information which the program is used to process, analyze, or manipulate. All of this data needs to be stored in randomly accessible storage—random-access memory (RAM). Because the earliest micros had very small active memory storage (8K to 16K bytes of RAM) disk-operating systems were designed so that program and other data could be stored on a disk and only the parts of it necessary for use at any given moment would be loaded when the program required it. Systems which store operating system instructions on a disk to be loaded in parts during the running of the program are known as "disk operating systems" (DOS, as in the IBM PC operating system MS/DOS—for MicroSoft/DOS). Using DOS, the microcomputer is able to carry out extensive programs by loading up from and dumping data to a disk drive, so that a lengthy program is done in piecemeal fashion. Modern micros have extensive internal memory, measured in millions of bytes. The DOS operating systems and associated applications software are still used. It is simply unnecessary for the machine to consult the disk storage as often as it used to, which tends to speed up apparent processing speed.

MICROPROCESSOR SYSTEM DISK DRIVES AND OTHER COMPONENTS

The most modern disk drives are optical signal recorders which use miniature lasers to imprint billions of signal modulations on a plastic plate as a means of storing data which can later be read. Older disk technology collects electromagnetic signals on a rigid plate (rigid disk) or a flexible plate (floppy disk) which has been coated with a material similar to that used on audio recording tapes.

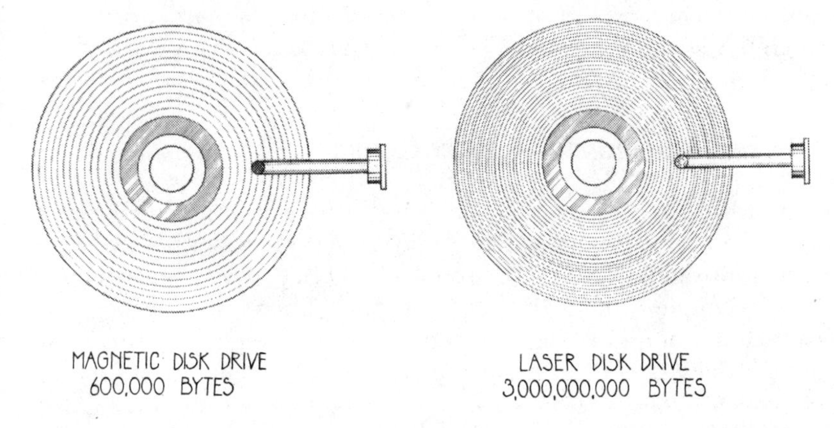

Figure 3.4 For each succeeding generation of computers, the cost per productive unit has been lowered by more than 50 percent.

INTERFACES

The connection between a computer and other devices; such as external data storage devices (disk drives, tape drives, etc.), printers, and telephone modems is called an interface. Interface connectors, in the form of multipin plugs and sockets of a few standard types, are mounted on the back of most computers. Connectors are usually provided for a keyboard, video display monitor, printer, telephone connection (modem), and external memory storage device (tape or disk recorder). This assemblage of parts makes up a computer system that can then be given a name and marketed.

CHARACTERISTICS OF CPU CHIPS

Because the manufacturing costs of CPU chips, also called "very large-scale integration (VLSI) devices" are so low, microprocessor systems found a huge market and a wide variety of applications. The term "microprocessor" commonly refers to these small systems. Strictly speaking, the microprocessor is the CPU-emulating chip. This chip is referred to by a code name or number such as "Intel 8080," "Intel Z80A," or the "Motorola 68000." Later-designed chips do their job faster. What makes them faster is their design. Different generations of microprocessors differ in the logic of their operation and the size of the bit word readable in each register of the processor. (The logic of a microprocessor places data being processed, in the form of data words, into one of a series of locations, called "registers.") An 8-bit word is only capable of describing one or two characteristics of an idea, whereas a 32-bit word can be used to make very specific distinctions. A chip with registers that can only contain 8-bit words would have to read four times as many words as a 32-bit chip in order to arrive at the same descriptive idea.

BITS, BYTES, AND WORDS—BINARY LOGIC

A word or byte, in computer jargon, is a sequence of bits. A bit is either a one or a zero. A word, or byte, in an early microprocessor is a sequence of 8 bits, for example, 00111001. In the 68000 chip, a word or byte is 16 bits, for example, 0001100011001010. In a binary number system, which includes only two digits (1 and 0), every possible number, from negative infinity (2−00) to positive infinity (2+00) can be represented by a sequence of ones and zeros. Clearly, a chip that can read, recognize, and store a binary number with 16 elements can operate faster than one which recognizes information at only 8 bits at a time. The current state of the art of microprocessors is a 32-bit machine. Chips that are capable of storing 1 million bytes are now in production. This means that very extensive programs can be incorporated on thumbnail-size wafers of silicon compounds.

MICROPROCESSOR SOFTWARE AND COMMUNICATIONS

With the advent of microprocessor hardware technology and the growth of data communications capability, which together enable the connection of computers to valuable data resources through the public telephone network and local data communications networks, today's computer market has been driving manufacturers toward implementing standard communications protocols and more compatibility. The trend toward standardization of protocols for computer communication was partly motivated by the needs of specialized software programming, which requires some compatibility so that the same software need not be reinvented for various kinds of machines or each time a new and better machine is developed. The previously phenomenal growth of the personal computer market was the result of this kind of software development. Standard disk operating systems (DOS) have emerged, for which many programs have now been written for such common purposes as word processing, financial spread sheet analysis, database management, and accounting.

Most software for microprocessors now consists of programs sold to users as off-the-shelf, ready-for-use packages. The programs have been written by individuals and software development firms and are sold in the form of prerecorded flexible magnetic disks (floppy disks) on which are recorded the coded set of computer instructions for a task. A documentation manual, included with the software, provides the user with simple, step-by-step instructions on how to use the program.

MINICOMPUTER SYSTEMS

Minicomputer systems were developed to provide medium-sized businesses and engineering, scientific, or manufacturing projects with the capability of managing large volumes of data economically. When the microprocessor was invented, the workhorse minicomputer system had an average working memory capacity (RAM) of 256,000 bytes (256 k bytes) of information. (The microprocessor started with less than 16,000 bytes—(16 k bytes). Today a microprocessor may have an active working memory in excess of 3 million bytes (3 megabytes or 3 M bytes), and the minicomputer a virtual memory of more than 70 million bytes (70 megabytes—or 70 M bytes). Given the development of the million byte chip, one can no longer distinguish between micro and mini systems by means of hardware capacity. One important aspect that differentiates minis from micros is that the minicomputer has defined hardware circuits for its central processor functions whereas the microprocessor uses a computation technique to emulate these functions. It therefore takes microprocessors much longer to do everything. The large capacity of the micro's random accessible memory is of no consequence to this issue. The micro can only process at speeds allowable by the process of the machine's logic. Consequently, mini programmers have always taken a different approach in the development of operating systems, applications programs, and network architecture for minicomputers because of their greater speed as well as their capacity.

DISTRIBUTED PROCESSING

A distinguishing quality of minis is that the way in which they execute instructions makes them very suitable for distributed processing applications. In distributed processing, several machines are each assigned specific ranges of tasks. These machines are interconnected in a local area network (LAN—see Chapter 6) or by means of a common bus. They may be connected over common telephone lines, subject to limitations in the speed of transmission. When a user accesses (logs on) a distributed processing system, part of a job may run on one machine and part on another. The user, at his or her terminal, need not be aware of which machine is doing what. Minicomputer machines can run several programs simultaneously. Various users, doing different tasks, may be in virtual interactive conversation with several different programs. Although these programs are actually running intermittently, the computer is keeping track of all the conversations and the user experiences instantaneous response. Because of the throughput speed of minicomputer systems, the user experiences no delay in a well-designed system. Minicomputer software has been developed to handle large numbers of interactive transactions. A relatively inexpensive cluster of minicomputers can provide total system services for a Fortune 1000 firm.

MINICOMPUTERS VERSUS MAINFRAMES

Although mainframe systems make better news copy because of their occasional great size and expense, most of them aren't very large nor are they necessarily very expensive. For most business applications, they are far less versatile than minicomputers. More minicomputer systems are in operation than mainframe systems. IBM is a leader in mainframe system development and has a better-known name in high technology, yet more Digital Equipment Corporation (DEC) minicomputers and software are used in business than any other make. Minis have been much more successful in providing for the needs of most vertical market applications—situations where the size of the individual business enterprise could not support the expenditure of millions of dollars on a system.

The most interesting software for scientific, engineering, and graphics modeling has been written for minicomputer systems. One example is the Intergraph Corporation's three-dimensional multicolored graphic imaging programs used in the design and engineering of space vehicles. Engineers working with this software are able to enter the mathematics of structural systems, and the machine will display a three-dimensional representation of the designed object and even rotate the object in a field with other objects in the background or foreground. Using such software, it is possible for architects to create video models of buildings and virtually look inside doors and windows, examine interior space, and observe the effects created by light entering the windows at different times of the day. Aside from its entertaining aspects, such a program facilitates the design and selection of window cornice treatments, reflective glass, and furnishings.

THE SYSTEMS HOUSE

In the earlier days of the commercial computer industry, a type of business called a "systems house" was prevalent. A client of a systems house can give up the entire problem of purchasing and maintaining computers and automation services to a systems house consultant. The systems house provides a one-stop answer for all computer-related questions. This is an effective but costly alternative for most companies. Only the more expensive systems houses can afford to keep the kind of high-quality personnel needed to deliver solutions responsively for the complex problems involved in implementing new systems into the established hierarchy of a business.

THE VALUE-ADDED RESELLER

The value-added reseller (VAR) is a recent outgrowth of the systems house concept. The VAR usually carries a particular line of computers, peripherals, and software packages written for a specialized industry. The VAR puts together packages with add-on products that turn general purpose computers into systems that do a specific set of tasks for an industry. An example might be a computer system for dental offices. The system can record patient appointments, print payroll checks and bills, do tax accounting and reporting, and assist with laboratory analysis; it may even produce quarterly and year-end financial reports to forecast business cycles. The success of the VAR concept is that VAR systems more specifically serve the dentist's needs than a general purpose system might. The VAR system will be much easier to implement into an established business than a collection of off-the-shelf unrelated programs for word processing, accounting, etc., as is typical of solutions using a personal microprocessor.

Unlike the retail computer shop, a VAR business does not sell a group of generic products for a client. The VAR dealer markets a total system implementation for businesses within a narrow range of industries and specializes in very intensive and knowledgeable support of just those industries. This is known as "vertical marketing." The VAR goes after every business of a certain kind, rather than business in general. There are VARs specializing in property management, law, food processing, and defense contract auditing (see the case study at the end of this chapter).

VARs traditionally utilize relatively inexpensive minicomputer products. They hire independant software writers to create programs for specialized purposes; these are usually written in a standard business program language (COBOL). They have the software written so that it can be quickly and inexpensively modified to suit a client's special needs. They also design it so it can be migrated to newer, faster, or less expensive hardware that may become available. Because of the way the VAR focuses on specific industries, the service available is similar to that offered by a systems house, but often at a much lower cost. This has made it possible for the VAR to support businesses that range in size from those that employ a few persons to several hundred. Since more than 85 percent of the approximately 7 million businesses in the United States employ fewer than 20 persons, it is probable that VARs, working with increasingly affordable minicomputer technology, will eventually dominate the high-volume business systems market. In the long run, they will ultimately be replaced by more affordable service available when integrated services digital networks (ISDN) become a reality. This topic is discussed in Chapters 4 and 5.

MINICOMPUTER HARDWARE MANUFACTURERS

Principal manufacturers of minicomputers include Digital (DEC), Hewlett Packard (HP), Texas Instruments (TI), Nippon Electronic (NEC) and Data General (DG). HP systems are known for their workhorse reliability in engineering, business, and scientific applications. HP3000 systems have been used to run the networks and accounting functions for telecommunication companies such as MCI. TI minicomputers, such as the Business Pro systems, are some of the most attractively priced systems and have been successfully coupled with the components of other manufacturers to run specialized applications software for business and engineering applications. DG is known as a source of relatively inexpensive systems for running COBOL programs. DEC is the most highly regarded minisystem manufacturer. DEC systems are extensively used for scientific, engineering, and business purposes.

MINICOMPUTER SOFTWARE

Software written for DEC, DG, and HP systems has assisted virtually every kind of profession and industry in which management can utilize a data-processing or computer-controlled function. Over all, there has been an accelerating trend toward integration of departmental elements of systems, in order to allow people within different departments of a business to access common information and to enhance interdepartmental communications. In 1984, DEC and DG both began to release multitasking programs that promise to provide integrated office automation and to interface with database management and other applications programs. Thus, every employee and manager in a business will be able to access information, generate reports, and communicate with everyone else using an inexpensive desktop workstation. This kind of software is not available with microprocessor systems or with mainframes.

MAINFRAME SYSTEMS

Mainframes have enormous computing capacity. They were developed to manage large scientific, archival, statistical, and financial computations. The software that has been developed for these machines is appropriate to situations which involve the processing of a huge volume of information at the time of each transaction. Newer supercomputers can do in seconds a number of computations which it would take a microprocessor 1000 years to complete.

In mainframe software, there is no real interactive conversation between user and machine. The user requests information or sets up a scientific experiment; the machine processes the request and a screenful or more of data is dumped to the user's terminal. The user can then make adjustments to the information and send it all back for processing or for updating of a file. This process is distinct from the minicomputer approach wherein once the user establishes a session, the user converses with the program interactively until the task is completed. In the mini approach, communications may be in quantities of just a single character or a "yes" or "no" response to a prompt within a field. In the mainframe approach, the user adjusts a screen and the contents of the entire screen is then sent to the host for processing.

Several qualities of mainframe systems make them unwieldy and uneconomical as compared with minis or micros for many business tasks. Such a use would be analogous to using an atom bomb to swat a fly. Mainframes are usually large installations, costing tens of millions of dollars and requiring a large staff to maintain. They are sequestered in high-security buildings that need to be equipped with special environmental systems. Their programs are also cumbersome and difficult to modify. Most attempts to implement mainframes for business purposes have failed. They fail for two reasons: because they take so long to implement that the nature of the job has changed by the time they are operational and because they are revolutionary in their effect on traditional office activities. They are not able to grow into a situation and adapt to changing demands.

The technology for business application machines is becoming more and more compatible with traditional environments and activities. Most machines used in businesses run on standard 20-ampere, 110-volt ac circuits. However, mainframes, especially those called "supercomputers," have been growing more exotic in demands for special environments, sources of power, and communications methods. Understanding the nature of supercomputers—and why they have special needs—reveals interesting information that helps one also understand the directions of emerging technology.

SUPERCOMPUTERS

The growth of scientific and engineering mainframe computer systems has taken an entirely separate direction from that of micros and minis. State-of-the-art systems, primarily used in the simulations of scientific and practical models, are being called supercomputers. Supercomputers are providing cost-effective means for doing complicated modeling as compared with traditional, mechanical means of analysis. Examples of current applications range from the computer-assisted analysis of underground oil reserves to simulation of wind tunnel experiments for aircraft and automobile design.

Undoubtedly, scores of applications for supercomputers remain as yet not thought about, largely because we have not addressed many problems for which these systems could provide simple solutions. There are many areas of human and resource management for which systems could be designed if the professionals in the field had sufficient background to request the application. Manufacturers tend to find new applications for existing products wherever there seems to be a possible market with the budget to support the purchase. The price of a supercomputer at this time is $10 to $20 million. The economical practice of timesharing supercomputers will probably become more available as the telecommunications feature of the public telephone network becomes more capable of supporting high-speed data transmission through the use of fiber optic cables and satellite transmission. This in turn will spur the construction and use of supercomputers and increase the range of available new applications.

EFFECTS OF EMERGING COMPUTER TECHNOLOGY ON BUILDINGS

We are designing and erecting buildings today to house businesses that may be using technologies for which we cannot predict exact power, space, and cooling requirements. Although many computer products are being designed to fit comfortably in a standard office environment, the most advanced technologies are creating new kinds of demands for power, space, and cooling. Future requirements are unknown because, when dealing with current technologies, we cannot foresee many of the possible applications. Nor can we predict where a breakthrough may result in entirely new methods for solving problems related to circuit design, power sources, cooling, and telecommunications. Understanding the mechanical problems of computer technology relative to the creation of heat and use of power will allow one to understand the impact of emerging technologies over the next 5 years.

HEAT, POWER, AND COMPUTATION

To put it very simply, computers work by using a flow of electricity from one switch to signal the operation of other switches. Based on the numbers and locations of switches that are opened and closed, computational results are produced which can be interpreted. The interpretation is a matter of equating voltages at certain levels and in certain locations as having certain mathematical values. The mathematical values may be assigned logical equivalents with nonmathematical meanings. These ideas have been more completely explained in the earlier section of this chapter concerning programming and languages. The crux of the matter is that the moving parts of the computer system are electrons, and they are flowing through narrow paths called circuits.

A by-product of electron motion is the dissipation of heat. Heat results from the displacement of atoms in the medium in which the electrons are moving. What we experience as heat is actually a vibration. As the electrons move through the medium of the circuit, the atomic particles of the medium through which they are flowing are vibrated in sympathy with the vibrating movement of the moving electrons. This movement or vibration in the circuit medium is a by-product of the electron flow through the circuit. Unless this vibration or heat is efficiently dissipated into a cooling medium, it builds until the circuit gets too hot to function and it fails, burns, or melts. Designing methods for dissipating heat has

Figure 3.5 We are erecting buildings today which will someday need to house machines the purpose and requirements of which we can only guess.

become a crucial objective in the design of new computers. The cooler you can keep the machine, the faster you can maintain the flow of electrons. One cooling method being employed by the latest supercomputer designs surrounds circuits in liquid helium. This technology is similar in principle to the cooling jacket on a common automobile engine, except that instead of surrounding the heat-producing elements (the combustion cylinders in an automotive engine) with water, liquid helium is used. Helium liquefies at a very low temperature and is chemically inert.

SUPERCOMPUTER DEMANDS FOR POWER AND COOLING

Computers work because of the flow of electrons (electricity) through circuits. One way to make a computer that computes faster is to speed up the flow of electrons through the circuits. Shortening the distance the electrons have to flow is one way of accomplishing this. The closeness of circuits packed together in chips is thus a key value of microminiaturization and chip manufacture to computer design. Shortening the distance between circuits produces a very compact arrangement of circuits. Using chips makes it possible to pack millions of circuits into small packages weighing only 2 or 3 pounds. A relatively modern supercomputer such as the Cray II uses approximately 170,000 watts of power. This amount of power flowing through circuits generates a lot of heat, which must be dissipated or the circuits will be destroyed.

VECTOR OR ARRAY PROCESSING

There are differences between the kind of software being run on supercomputers and software for micros or minis. This is due to the extreme speed of these machines. Because they can process so much data so quickly, new techniques for processing have been developed; these include vector or array processing. Vector processor packages have also been designed as accessories to enhance the performance of minicomputers and microcomputers. However, this has nothing to do with the processing speed of the CPUs of these machines. An array processor used with a micro or mini usually handles a part of a program which would otherwise require a long, time-consuming computation of a large amount of data.

SERIAL (SCALER) PROCESSING VERSUS VECTOR (ARRAY)— PROCESSING

"Vector" and "array" processing are synonymous terms. Vector processing differs from the kind of processing done by older techniques, called serial or scaler processing, in this way: Microprocessor or scaler processing does things in a sequence using locations in the computer's memory, called registers, to store the data while it is being used in a process. If you wanted to add $A + B$ to find the sum C, the microcomputer must put the value of A in one register and the value of B in another register and the operand, "find the sum," in yet another register. The processing results in the placement of the sum in a register given the value C. In an array processor, the logic for the entire operation is set up like a matrix and the values of A, B, and the operand can be changed independently of one another; the value of C will automatically vary based on these changes. In the Cray-II all this happens at speeds in excess of a 1.2 billion computations per second.

MEGAFLOPS

The common convention for measuring the speed of computers is based on the length of time it takes for a computer to calculate a floating point operation. Supercomputers average no more than 4 to 6 nanoseconds per calculation. In 1970, the first large computer, called Illiac-IV, ran at a clock speed of 50 million floating point operations (50 megaFLOPS or MFLOPS) per second. By 1976, the Cray-I was running at 180 MFLOPS per second. In 1980, Control Data Corporation's Cyber-205 was running at 400 MFLOPS per second. The 1985 Cray-II model is calculating at speeds of around 1200 MFLOPS per second. Engineers are now thinking in terms of having 10,000- to 20,000-MFLOP per second machines in production within the next 5 years.

APPLICATIONS OF SUPERCOMPUTERS

It is difficult to specify all the potential applications for these machines. They have already revolutionized many design processes and are making possible many achievements in space travel, ballistics, fluid mechanics, nuclear physics, biological science, and mechanical engineering which have produced phenomenal practical results. It is unlikely that there is an engineering problem that could not be simulated and solved through the use of these machines. An architect or civil engineer might look, for instance, at the possibility of using a supercomputer to simulate the bending algorithm of a high-rise structure under various stresses, using various materials.

TELECOMMUNICATIONS AND SUPERCOMPUTERS

The speeds of data transmission available on the existing public telephone network are impossibly inadequate for networking supercomputers. Networking supercomputers could provide a new means for informing and educating people working in common fields all over the world and could provide a substantial support for international commerce. Given the potential of the supercomputer, there is a possibility of a breakthrough in technology applications associated with development of a state-of-the-art universal telecommunications technology. Both AT&T and IBM are in hot pursuit of these developments. Fiber optic communications offer the most potential for providing a usable link between machines. Fiber optics and other methods of data communications are discussed in the chapters to follow about telecommunications and networking.

FRONT END DEVICES

Because of the incongruous differences between the velocities at which data flows in supercomputers and the millions of times slower speeds of user terminals and communications channels, minicomputer systems are frequently used as "front end" machines by supercomputers. The front end machine collects the data coming in from a communications source or a user terminal so that it can pass the information on to the supercomputer at speeds which are appropriate to the supercomputer's internal clock (which is running at 4 to 6 nanoseconds, several million times faster than the terminal speed). Likewise, when the supercomputer produces the results of the calculation, the front end device catches the output data in a buffer and then relays it to the user's terminal at speeds appropriate to the receiving capability of the terminal.

MAINFRAME VERSUS DISTRIBUTED PROCESSING

In a mainframe implementation, the user is usually remote from the data processing center. Tens of millions of dollars' worth of equipment and personnel are locked away in a high-security environment. The user communicates with the processor over phone lines through formalized, cumbersome, and slow communication channels, rarely exceeding a transmission rate of 1200 bits per second (1.2 kbs or 1200 baud). The total information of an entire screen is sent to the data-processing (DP) center for processing and then returned to the user's terminal.

In a distributed processing situation, the DP equipment is local to the user. User terminals are either hard-wired or connected via a high-speed networking medium capable of transmitting data at speeds in excess of 10 million bits per second (10Mbs). Information within a field (part of a screen) may be transmitted, processed, and returned. The result is more user-friendliness, faster response time, and true interactive participation.

Because the data-processing user's needs are not static but instead are changing all the time, with few exceptions, most mainframe implementations for business purposes have failed. Because of their size and highly cumbersome structures and procedures, they tend to have a revolutionary effect on the way jobs are done. They are so difficult to cut-over (implement on the job site) that by the time they are installed, the job they were designed for has often changed. The mainframe programs are then difficult to modify and adjust to changing circumstances.

Distributed processing, on the other hand, is an evolutionary approach to DP solutions. Equipment is comparatively inexpensive and easy to install. The user can be provided with a few programs at the outset and then gradually implement more software, meeting each priority as it emerges as the next logical step. A complete system for a company may take 3 to 5 years to evolve, but in the meantime people will have access to workable, flexible modules of a system all along the way. The finished system will have evolved harmoniously with the business which it supports. Unlike mainframe software, as changes are required, only the program module affected needs to be adjusted causing no disruption for other modules.

HYBRIDS

The memory capacity and processing speed of microprocessors has been growing as chip manufacture has gradually improved. Recent developments include 32-bit-word CPU chips which provide micros with the ability to support the running of minicomputer software. The speed of the processor still does not compare with operations of a state-of-the-art mini, but new integrated software packages enhance the possibility of networking together stand-alone personal systems to provide utilities such as word processing, accounting, financial analysis, and graphic analysis, all utilizing a common data resource. With such an integrated system, users in various locations can do projects independently of the rest of the system and other users; they can also connect to a shared network of resources, access a remote data base, communicate with others, or order work done on a special purpose machine such as a laser document publishing machine or a supercomputer.

DATABASE MANAGEMENT

Most of the work that computers are doing involves managing a collection of information. The root form in which the data is stored is always binary code: a series of 1s and 0s. Sometimes the information is statistical, sometimes records of transactions, sometimes engineering data for design of a project or product. Sometimes the data is an on-line resource management file such as airline travel reservation information, and sometimes the data is the compiled documents of a business, hospital, or public agency. Depending on the purpose for which the data is stored, it is accessible in various forms. For instance, an accounting database will usually be accessed by requests for standard forms for tax filings, financial statements, payroll checks, client billings, etc. An engineering database may be accessed by a request for a video display or printed plot diagram of a stored design or calculation. A travel or theatrical booking database may be accessed by inquiries regarding dates and destinations.

DEFINITION OF A DATABASE

A database can be defined as a collection of data designed to be used for a number of purposes, sometimes by a number of different programmers. It is a collection of interrelated information that has been stored so it can be used for several purposes. To accomplish this, the program automatically stores each input of information in several different locations according to a prearranged format relative to an intended purpose. The data is stored so that it is independent of programs which use the data. Standard forms are used in adding new data and when modifying and retrieving existing data within the database. The form is either a data entry or query system. The query or manual data entry system usually consists of a sequence of questions, called prompts, which require a user to respond by typing in data.

Data may also enter the system automatically. Other machines may feed the computer a stream of data regarding current transactions or other events. An example of this is the automated bank teller. When a user puts a bank card into the machine's card reader, the machine reads the card and then requests that the appropriate file be brought up into active memory. Each transaction regarding that file, whether caused by the card holder or the bank, automatically updates the file. The computer system may contain a collection of databases, with each database existing as an entirely separate structure. For instance, the database for each branch of a bank may be kept as a separate unit. Data regarding checking accounts, savings accounts, and credit cards may also be kept as separate databases within a bank branch system.

QUILL PENS AND LEDGER BOOKS

To understand database management, it is helpful to take a close look at the job actually being done. Big business is a major part of our culture and a very recent phenomenon. Less than 100 years ago, the size of a typical business was such that record keeping—including accounting, correspondence, inventory control, and other records-keeping functions—was managed by clerks who kept the data current in ledger books. Data processing was done by a clerk equipped with a quill pen and an ink jar. On the table in front of the clerk was a set of ledger books. If a customer ordered a certain quantity of goods, a clerk would deal with this transaction in its entirety. He or she might look at the stock sheets to see whether the order could be filled from stock or whether some of it had to be manufactured or purchased from a supplier. The clerk would update the order book, and if any goods were sent, he or she would

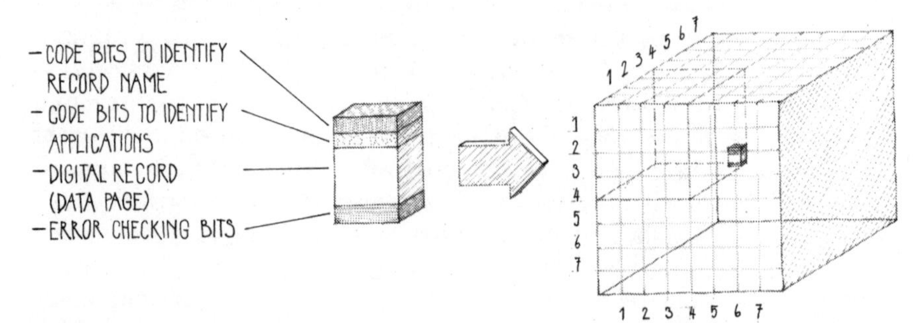

Figure 3.6 Database software uses numbers as coordinates to locate and assign importance to blocks and collections of information.

modify the stock sheets, make out a bill for the customer, and make an entry on the appropriate pages of the ledgers. The clerk could immediately produce the answer to any query. As the business grew, the size of the ledgers increased until several clerks were needed. At a certain point, the labor was divided to make the job easier and one clerk would maintain stock sheets while another did the billing.

BATCH PROCESSING AND PUNCHED CARDS

Around the turn of the century, various means for mechanization were introduced. The work was split up into batches. An accounting function would be carried out on all the transactions within one file by one clerk or machine, then the next function would be performed by another clerk or machine. Punched-card accounting introduced the possibility of having large batches. In the punched-card process, data is entered by punching holes in cards (which should not be folded, spindled, or mutilated). The punched holes corresponded with numerical places in fields representing account identification, quantities, dollar values, or other data. Each transaction in a business using punched-card processing creates a card. Many trays of cards have to be fed through a machine while it runs a particular program before the setup of the machine can be changed for the next function it might need to perform with the same set of cards, or another set.

In the use of older automated methods requiring batch processing, some flexibility of the old clerical method was lost. A transaction could not be given individual treatment. It was no longer possible to give instant answers to inquiries about the status of an account, the creditworthiness of a customer, or the amount of an item in stock. The answer to an inquiry might be a week or two out of date by the time a report could be generated. When items were posted, it was necessary for the computer to read every item in the file as it scanned its way to the ones to be updated; often every item had to be written out in sequence whether it was to be updated or not.

Batch processing with the data divided into separate files for each use, as it evolved from ledger book procedures, is not the best way to operate with computers. As businesses grow and cash flow fluctuations become larger and small adjustments by management become more critical, it is much more convenient for management if all the information about the organization is timely and immediately available. The use of a modern database is like having one super ledger clerk keeping the data for the entire company. This superclerk organizes books so that he or she can search them with x-ray vision and immediately answer every query that comes along, providing only relevant information in the report. Unlike the clerk's forerunners, who only managed one task, this superclerk does them all. When a report of information is received in one task, the superclerk automatically updates all the other application references, as required.

Relational database management software developed for modern minicomputers is of the superclerk type. It was developed to run on moderate-sized (it all fits in one room), efficient, reasonably priced (at $100,000 to $500,000), fast (instantaneous response) minicomputer systems.

MAGNETIC TAPE AND OTHER MEDIA

An invention following the punched card approach utilizes magnetic recording material similar to that used to manufacture common audio tape. Data entries are entered by machine reports or by data entry clerks as consecutive electromagnetic signal recordings on a "streamer" tape or disk. During processing, the data is read off the tape or disk to be processed in a batch, using one program at a time. This form of processing is still in use for many banking, large-scale billing, and other record-keeping tasks. Newer media for recording the data include laser-optic recording devices that can concentrate the records of billions of transactions onto very small surfaces which are read using laser-optic techniques.

SUMMARY AND CONCLUSIONS

Microprocessors popularized the computer-driven technologies because of their affordability and the availability of programs for applications which range from controlling traffic signals to cooking a roast. Minicomputers have made it possible for very humble companies to grow into multibillion-dollar corporate giants. Aside from the scientific and engineering applications of these machines, their use in relational database programming has enabled expanding businesses to manage literally millions of transactions every hour.

The famous McDonald's Hamburger chain utilizes microprocessor-controlled point-of-sale machines (cash registers) which are polled automatically by a remote central computer system. At every moment, the production, costs, profits, supply needs, and activity level of every franchise can be queried. The production and transportation needs for the supply of buns, meat, pickles, and Coca Cola are processed daily to determine purchasing, manufacturing, and shipping requirements. Product managers can instantly review the effects of a marketing program as it is implemented in a city or region. Cash analysis can respond to corporate cash needs with up-to-date predictions about cash flow requirements. This is possible because of the use of relational database software.

With more business functions being managed by machines and the growing availability of intersystem communications, there has been a growing need for network support and communications ability. With the availability of communications standards and protocol translaters (which translate data to a common form that can be reinterpreted to and from different operating systems with comparative ease), and the establishment of standards for international data communication, the opportunity for sharing the resources of larger systems has prompted the development of software for new services based on the possibility of connecting computers through the public telephone network. These issues are dealt with in greater detail in Chapter 6, Data Communications and Local Area Networks.

The evolution of intelligent machines is creating something like a knowledge-base among machines. Evolving standards foretell a future of greater compatibility among most machines. At present, nearly every machine can load communications software that allows the machine to emulate the terminal of a host computer. Also, a host machine can be loaded with operating-system programming of foreign machines. It can then run software designed for other machines.

Case Study

WESTERN PACIFIC DATA SYSTEM—
SOLVING THE AUDIT PROBLEMS
OF GENERAL DYNAMICS/CONVAIR

Western Pacific Data Systems (WPDS) is an entrepreneurial, small firm operating in a narrowly defined vertical market and dedicated to a specific, well-defined task. The company entered its field because automatic systems were needed for control of government assets, ranging from fine details (nuts and bolts) to telescopes.

Faced with the problems of managing an elephantine internal accounting procedure—in order to satisfy government auditors that it was professionally competent to manage large contracts— General Dynamics/Convair (GD/C) was directed by the Defense Contract Administration Service to employ WPDS. WPDS has set up simple methods requiring little maintenance or attention.

WPDS is typical of many small firms that use relatively inexpensive but high-powered distributed processing systems to provide methods of managing specialized business operations. The trend away from mainframes and toward distributed processing technologies is at the heart of this kind of business and points to the eventual evolutionary direction of the DP, networking, and telecommunications industries. (Implementation of distributed processing is a major factor driving the telecommunications and local area networking technology markets.) Although many large companies have realized that distributed processing is a better way to do things, they have difficulty in adapting to a modular approach to data processing. Their organizations have been based on the concept of centralized data processing, and their personnel have little experience with the kind of proactive and autonomous direction which distributed processing techniques require. This creates an opportunity for small firms like WPDS to be hired by giant firms like Boeing and GD/C to implement systems which are cost-effective, manageable, and easily integrated with the already established hierarchy of the organization.

WPDS was formed out of an initial contract to provide software for inventory control for a fastener manufacturer (Kyocera). WPDS began operations by developing programs to keep track of supplies, materials, and products (commercial asset management and inventory control). Certain aspects of these programs lent themselves to the government asset control requirements. They were also easily adaptable to the varying audit requirements of the Department of Defense Contract Administration agencies. The adaptability results in part from the use of high-level COBOL language for minicomputers, rather than mainframes. In 1981, WPDS, working with GD/C, began to develop software to control inventory for spare parts. Another division of GD/C later requested a modification to suit its needs. In the meantime, Boeing managers heard about the system and asked to buy a turnkey installation from WPDS. Boeing implemented the first WPDS Government On Line Data (GOLD) system. The system ran on inexpensive Texas Instruments Business System 990/12 minicomputers, beefed-up with array processors, 2 Mb of RAM, high-speed disk drives (Fujitsu 474 Mb and TI 425 WD 800 series), and a COBOL accelerator which increased processing speed by a factor of 4 to 10 times normal speed.

The Plight of the Defense Contractor

Many billions of dollars' worth of government property is placed in the hands of civilian repair and maintenance contractors by the Department of Defense each year. An aircraft or a ship may be in the hands of a private company for weeks or months. In the interim, hundreds of thousands of items need to be accounted for. Because of a history of enormous losses due to mishandling, loss, and theft of public property, contractors are audited as to their management and control procedures. In the case of GD/C, two full-time government auditors perform audits daily on the premises in San Diego. The WPDS software provides a method for automatically meeting the government audit requirements and keeps track of every inventory item. If government audit procedures did not require signature documents (which are necessary until electronic signatures are legitimized) to establish the acknowledgment of accountability, government asset management could become a virtually paperless enterprise. This prospect entails substantial cost savings for contractors. Not only has the system made an impossible task manageable, but the savings in administrative costs should become a factor in the process of competitive bidding and will ultimately produce savings passed on to the taxpayer.

Much paperwork is being eliminated by the WPDS system. Every transaction regarding the movement of any government property prompts an audit trail report and triggers the next required action. The system also automatically forwards statistical reports to the corporation's mainframe information management computers, including audit prompts required by anyone within the system.

A good picture of the task being managed by the WPDS system may be seen by reviewing the manual operation which the system replaced at Boeing Military Aircraft Corporation (BMAC). Traditionally, parts records were being kept on ledger cards. There was a card for every part, and whenever a part was moved an entry had to be made on a card. As contracts became larger and more complex, the number of cards multiplied geometrically. Keeping track of parts and cards became a problem. The manual process of entering data on cards and culling reports caused a bottleneck. The difficulties entailed in keeping track of parts made the government demand new audit procedures. New audit controls made manual systems and procedures even more difficult, seriously impairing people's ability to keep up with the volume of data transactions each day. By the time an inquiry regarding a part could be answered, it would be inaccurate. Moreover, the physical task kept getting bigger, the tubs of cards for the parts in complex modern aircraft got bigger, and the staff required to manage the task grew and required further management.

Technology, a Morale Booster

The first WPDS contract with Boeing involved asset tracking for a relatively small modification project for the F4 aircraft for the U.S. Air Force and Navy. There were 20 people working on the task of accounting for F4 project parts on the first shift at BMAC, another 10 working second shift, 7 days a week. The job was still not getting done. The supervisor for the task was in ill health. She had not had a day off in months and was having family problems as a result of her long hours at work. Following implementation of the WPDS program, the job required only 12 people on first shift and 1 person on second shift, 5 days a week. As a result, the supervisor found time for a 2-week vacation with her family. The system cost was justified in 6 months' time, according to Boeing Computer Services (BCS), the purchaser and operator of the system for BMAC. BCS was able to purchase the WPDS system and take over the reins completely in 3 months. WPDS attributed this quick turnover to the professional quality of BCS personnel. The cost of implementing a system is governed by the quality of personnel who will use the software. When firms like WPDS can work with professional, competent DP management, an excellent professional relationship is developed allowing shorter cut-over times.

Sink or Swim

The Department of Defense Contract Administration Services recommended that GD/C consult WPDS and advised GD/C that recertification depended on implementation of an automated asset management program before the year ended. The GD/C contract is the largest installation of the WPDS GOLD system to date. Unlike the case of Boeing, the DG/C Data System Division is only providing data and is not supporting the installation. WPDS is therefore much more involved with GD/C staff, providing more support. Although tiny by comparison to the GD/C mainframe systems, this installation is the second largest installation of TI minicomputer equipment in the world.

Daily Random Audits

To comprehend the size, importance, and value of the task done by WPDS, it helps to understand the government audit procedure. When an audit is conducted (which may be a weekly, monthly, or quarterly occurrence), the government auditors conduct a physical trace on a random sample of parts. To give an idea of the size of the job, a staff of 50 people works in the government's auditing offices located within the Westinghouse Electric Newport News shipbuilding facility, which is just one division of the company. In the auditing process, auditors may request the records for 10 or 15 parts at random. (There may be 10,000 parts involved in the inventory of the entire project). The auditors check the records of these parts and ultimately physically count them to determine the accuracy of the accounting procedures. Results of the audit are statistical. Certification depends on the accuracy of the records. The WPDS system provides for automatic updating and checking of these records. When a part is moved, the data regarding the move is inputted at a data terminal. The move is visible on the system immediately and, since the system is a network with a gateway allowing reports to be made out of information in the system (it is unidirectional for security puposes), reports of value to corporate level management are also instantly updated. It is possible to trace the path of every single part from the moment of its entry on the system to its eventual installation or disposal. All checks and balances required by the government-approved procedures are provided for in the software. When changes are made or requested in procedures, or when parts move between departments which use different procedures, the program is adjustable to be consistent with the new procedures. Either WPDS or the client is able to alter the program to adjust for new procedural requests by the government.

Technical Information

The WPDS GOLD system is an excellent example of distributed processing. The hardware for the Convair installation consists of five TI 990/12 minicomputer systems equipped with Fujitsu high-speed disk drives, printers, plotters, and several PCs, all communicating via an ethernet LAN provided by 3-COM.

The WPDS system utilizes industry-stranded protocols (IBM SNA 3780) to provide direct transactions with the GD/C mainframe installation, providing instant uploading of transaction results and also providing capability for IBM 3278 terminal emulation for TI and other workstations. These standards are used to provide the greatest compatibility with other systems and terminals in the GD/C mainframe environment. This allows data inputs regarding transactions, or moves of parts, to trigger direct reports to management, keeping corporate visibility as high as possible. Because there is no two-way gateway into the system—no one can peek at or subvert the process—this automatic updating of pertinent balances allows the corporation to see current end-balances on parts supply inventory.

The use of minicomputers and a distributed processing network is one key to the WPDS system's easy and relatively inexpensive implementation. Data relevant to each task is processed instantaneously by the appropriate program, generating reports and triggering the processes of other discrete and separately acting units. The end result is real-time audit tracking capability.

Retraining and Support

For the GD/C contract, WPDS provided 6 hours of training per person for each level of personnel. When one considers the enormity of the task and its impact on administrative effectiveness, contract negotiation, and corporate integrity, this is a very small amount of time, given the results obtained. Classes of six persons each were taught about the software to a level of detail appropriate to the particular task which the student needed to do. Key personnel, for instance, required an overview, managerial, *conceptual* understanding of the system operation (who does what, when, and how, system checks, etc.). Operations personnel were trained only with regard to the particular routines of data entry and report making for which they were responsible; they learned a *repetitive procedure*. In all, 105 GD/C personnel have been trained by WPDS. The educational process began with the 12 highest level management personnel. Following their training and feedback, the next level was introduced to the automated techniques, and so on. The result on morale has been almost as valuable as that on operations. People were relieved that the problem which had for so long overwhelmed them was at last contained.

WPDS Corporate Direction

WPDS sees a bright future in the sale of asset management packages for two markets. One involves an expansion of sales of its present system, which includes over 400 separate programs for large corporations. (The GD/C system utilizes 237 WPDS GOLD system programs, as compared with 150 programs used by Boeing. The difference in the number of programs results from the different methods of the two companies. GD/C's system hardware for the dual installation cost around $600,000. The entire contract involved an expenditure of $2 million and required the work of three full-time programmers for 6 months. WPDS estimates that the more typical high-end user will spend only $250,000 to $500,000, with support included.

After placing advertisements in the trade journals of the National Property Manager's Association and the National Contract Manager's Association (the users and buyers, respectively, responsible for asset management and accountability in defense contracting corporations), WPDS found that 75 percent of inquiries were from PC product users, indicating a demand for a product in the $50,000 price range, with a moderate monthly maintenance charge for update and modification of software.

WPDS staff believes it would be very feasible to provide the low-end customer with a product which could track the receipt, storage, issue, and consumption of materials for structured parts of an overall system—which describes the needs for the great number of small defense industry subcontractors. Such a system would run on one of the new supermicros, such as the PCAT, DX10, or TI Business Pro. It would not contain as many of the programs as the larger system operates and would entail more modification of customer procedures to fit the program design, rather than vice versa, but would produce identical results and lend itself to timely reports to major contractors for their audit requirements.

Conclusion

WPDS indicates a trend in the direction of the high-technology industry, utilizing the design economics of distributed processing. The implications are more important than the achievement. WPDS reflects an important source of the American technological success—small groups of entrepreneurial men and women providing the solutions which enable enormous corporations to operate with efficiency and integrity.

PART 2

Telecommunications Technologies

The future use of computer technologies is tied to the role of telecommunications and common access to shared resources. In other words, there will be little or no growth in state-of-the-art technologies that is not associated in some way with telecommunications. The potential for economic growth of most businesses is similarly tied to the use of telecommunications. For this reason, technology firms such as IBM, which recently purchased major interests in Satellite Business Systems, Rolm, and MCI, are constantly maneuvering to control a share of the telecommunications market. It would be unfortunate if the Bell operating companies, AT&T, IBM, and the independent telephone companies eliminated competitive enterprise through monopolistic control of telecommunications services. This would stifle creativity in the development of new technologies business in general by inhibiting competitive pricing for crucial technology services.

The most serious problem of monopoly results from control of economic development that is influenced by technology designs. Much of Part 2 speaks about the motivations, strategies, and business techniques of the telephone companies. Because of the controls that are vested in public agencies, the public needs to become better informed about the meaning of tariff requests and other issues and more knowledgeable about protecting their own interests from the self-interested pursuits of AT&T and local telephone companies. For the sake of corporate profitability, these firms would prefer it if people would have to pay a fee to the phone company each time they wished to use a computer resource, which for certain purposes may someday be possible only by way of remote access to a computer system. Although this idea seems an extension of the imagination, the AT&T monopoly pursued exactly such a course for nearly a century. *And although we are beginning to regain public access to telecommunications technologies in this nation, our gains have been slow and they are bitterly opposed by the established telephone companies.*

Divestiture and The Responsibility of Choice

It is popular today to blame the AT&T antitrust settlement and divestiture for the complexities involved in deciding about telecommunications services. Would that it were so! Prior to the freeing of competitive participation in telecommunications services, the complexities surrounding communications technology could not be considered. Since divestiture, we have begun to deal with the possibilities offered by telecommunications technologies which were not being made available to telephone subscribers by the Bell System monopoly.

The corporate policy of AT&T subordinated implementation of new technology to the issue of maintaining the monopoly. Since there was no competition to deal with, there was no need to go to the expense of improving service offerings. Prior to the antitrust settlement, firms that wished to improve their communications systems were forced to deal with the problem in a roundabout fashion. If those responsible for market development in AT&T decided that it was not in the corporation's interest to implement new technology then it wasn't done. Many of these new technologies had to be developed for private in-house use by individual businesses, and prior to 1968, they could not be connected with telephone company lines without confronting the legal rights claimed by the monopoly. This situation led to the artificial separation, in the telecommunications industry, between telephone-related technologies and local area networks for data communications.

As for the small firms or individual subscribers, although they have been offered sweeping promises of future technologies there has been very little technological improvement forthcoming from the Bell System. At a time when the cost of manufacturing and supporting high-technology services has been moving dramatically downward, telephone usage costs have consistently increased and service has not improved commensurate with the increase in cost.

It did not make good business sense for the monopoly to make a product available which was more difficult or less profitable to manage than existing service. Since there has been no competition and the setting of rate structures with state public utility commissions has been based solely on industry-generated data, there has never been much reason to implement new technologies other than to meet expanding demands due to population and economic growth.

The Politics of Regulation

It has been argued that the long years of monopolistic operation, which allowed AT&T and the Bell System to grow into the largest and richest private business in the world, should be considered a form of public subsidization for the creation of universal telephone service at "affordable" rates.

What is Affordable?

What is affordable has become open to question. In today's economy and culture, it is necessary to have telephone service. A business cannot survive without it. The nature of much business is becoming more geographically widespread, requiring extension of telecommunications access. In California, people now speak about doing business in the Pacific rim (meaning the nations bordering the Pacific Ocean) as a business venue in the same way as they used to speak about doing business in a city. The costs of using telephone company services, for both local and long-distance calls, is a major expense of business. Compared with other means of communication, the costs are immense. Telephone service has become essential to business enterprises and public agencies. It can also be considered necessary to the safe and efficient management of homes, farms, schools, and so forth.

Monopoly as a Form of Subsidization

All of us, over several generations, have paid a portion of the subsidy of the AT&T and Bell System development costs each month over several decades. In many cases, we have overpaid. An audit conducted by the auditor general of California in 1985 determined that subscribers to the services of General Telephone, Pacific Bell, and Continental Telephone in California were overcharged in excess of $103 million during 1 year (1983–1984). The auditors ascribed this to a failure, on the part of the state's Public Utility Commission (PUC), to appropriately analyze the rate increase requests made by the telephone companies. Such mistakes have probably been made in other years and places when and where audits have not been conducted. (The PUC commissioner's reply to the charge of the state auditor is evidence for the likelihood of there having been previous abuses. He said that the problem arose because his staff was too small and underpaid. He expressed the opinion that the public would be better served if they focused on the money they will save in long-distance costs due to equal access, rather than worrying about the dollars they have lost due to inappropriately regulated local rates).

Since divestiture, the role of the state PUCs in administering rate structures and regulating telecommunications has been subject to scrutiny and criticism. The PUC involvement in telecommunications has been recognized as being not necessarily beneficial to the public interest and as being protective of the telephone company monopoly. The PUC now seems to be struggling to keep telecommunications within its regulatory domain as state-of-the-art technologies tend to extend into activities beyond the domain of state regulatory powers. The purpose of the PUC is to oversee a public utility which owns a sole right to operate in return for delivering a universal and affordable service (traditionally called a "natural monopoly"). Using fiber optic cable, cellular radio transmission, coaxial CATV cable, microwave relay antenna, and other transmission technologies, universal telecommunications services can now be provided to telephone subscribers in much better ways in a competitive environment than has been possible with the Bell monopoly which consists of a twisted wire network. The new technologies have created the potential for providing universal service, the price for which can be driven down by competition among several vendors, making regulation, other than to protect small new telecommunications firms from monopolies, obstructive to the interests of the public.

Bypass and the Strategy of Telephone Company Rate Increases

Large business customers have long since learned to bypass the telephone company network by using alternative communications methods. These methods are described in the following two chapters. The strategy of the Bell operating companies has been to argue that without the income from the businesses that are bypassing their exorbitantly overpriced services, they will have to raise rates to residential users. They are clamoring at the same time for deregulation which would allow them to use their wire network to provide "enhanced" services in competition with smaller telecommunications firms, whom they could easily destroy through cross-subsidization of services.

Advertising and Rate Increases

In its current advertising, AT&T is appealing to customers with a suggestion that the firm is more reliable than its competitors because of its size and history rather than its pricing, technology, or responsive service. Although the company still accounted for more than 90 percent of all long-distance traffic carried during 1984, a look at competitive pricing structures shows that prices for products and services continue to rise. While its competitors consistently lower their rates, the AT&T network and the Bell operating companies adjust shorter-distance rates up and longer-distance rates down, in a ratio of about 3 to 1. For example, short-haul rates go up 10 percent and long-haul rates go down 3 percent.

Many people believe that AT&T, the Bell operating companies, and the other independent telephone companies may well have an obligation to the public not only to provide inexpensive service but also to share both technological knowledge and the network that has been developed with money earned during the long period of monopolistic control. However, the present policy of AT&T is to lend engineering support only to firms and individuals that are not operating as competitors.

The Science of Telecommunications

Telecommunications is a young science, born around the same time as talking pictures. Because of the confinement of telephone industry activities within the Bell System, the language surrounding the art and science of telecommunications has become specialized and esoteric. The principles of operation are relatively simple. One vibrates a medium at one end and then interprets the vibrations at the other end. One can connect different pieces of wire together so that a vibration started in one wire can be carried through another. Subscribers to traditional telephone services are supplied with instruments which can vibrate and listen to vibrations on a copper wire. In today's technology, these vibrations may either be analogous to the inflections of voice or other sounds (analog transmission) or consist of pulses of only two possible electrical signal levels—equivalent to a 1 or a 0—representing digital bits of information (digital transmission).

Traditional Analog Telephony

Analog signals are the proportional electrical equivalent of the original form of the communication. When we speak into a telephone, the telephone generates and transmits an electrical signal that represents our voice. The signal is proportional to the intensity of the soundwaves striking the mouthpiece as we talk. One way this signal varies to represent different voice sounds is by frequency. High tones, for instance, occur at higher frequencies than do low tones. Traditional telephone, stereo, and public address sound systems are all based on analog communications.

The way telephone subscribers are connected to one another is also easy to comprehend. Let us imagine that subscriber A has an instrument connected to wire number 259 0819 in area section 619. Subscriber B has an instrument connected to wire number 277 5308 in area section 602. In between section 602 (Phoenix, Arizona) and section 619 (San Diego, California) are other wires called trunks. In the old days, calls were connected by manually connecting the incoming call wires from subscribers' telephones with the appropriate outgoing trunk wires.

Operators set up a call by physically plugging the jacks of wires into sockets. The wire patch device was later replaced by a switchboard. Instead of plugging jacks into sockets, the exchange operators closed rudimentary knife switches. The trunk wires connected the switchboard in the local exchange where the call originated with the exchange switchboard local to the wire of the intended receiver of the call. An operator at the receiving exchange would manually connect the incoming trunk call to the receiver's wire. She (for some time, operators were always women) would then generate, using a handcrank, a surge of voltage on the wire which would ring a signal bell in the terminal set of subscriber B. Sometimes a call would be routed through several exchanges until, having connected a series of trunks, the end-to-end circuit would eventually be completed along a path of wires linked together by switches. All of this connecting and disconnecting of wires and switches was initially performed by operators who instructed each other along the route as the pathway circuit to the recipient was incrementally created. Later, the manual switchboard was replaced by electromechanical switches. A dial was placed on the subscriber's telephone which set up a series of pulse interruptions on the wire's carrier frequency, or dial tone. Depending on the number of pulse interrupts in a sequence, certain switches would automatically close and a pathway to the recipient's phone would be created accordingly. In more recent years, the electromechanical switch has been replaced by the electronic computer-controlled switch. The call set-up follows the same procedures; however, microelectronic circuits manage the call set-up more quickly and efficiently and in a way which permits the use of advanced processes for multiplexing calls.

The Bell system telephone network remains essentially unchanged at this time. All the functions of a modern digital-controlled network—telephone company wire center, central office, etc.—are simply automated forms of the original manual switchboard operations. Instead of trunk wires, transmission media such as terrestrial and satellite microwave and fiber optics are doing the job that copper wire did in earlier times. The switching of calls (connecting the originator's wire with trunks, etc.) is being managed by automatic machines which interpret the caller's dialing as a series of instructions to connect a pathway to the recipient's wire address. When the connection is established, a voltage is automatically pulsed along the wire circuit to "ring" the phone.

The importance of most new telecommunications technologies is not that they have changed the methods of organizing the telephone network business but that they have reduced circuit costs and switching time. They have also provided the capacity for higher-speed transmissions, allowing more people to use the network at lower costs. This lowers the overall cost per call and per circuit. Since divesture, the advantage of the lowered cost per circuit has appeared in the form of discounted long-distance services and less expensive terminal equipment. However, except in the case of larger users of transmission services who can afford to install their own microwave, cable, and other technologies, local phone service remains a de facto monopoly operation in most parts of the world and the economic benefit of improving communications technology has not been shared with ordinary telephone subscribers.

In the next three chapters of this book, sufficient data has been presented to provide the reader with an understanding about the emerging technologies used for telecommunications services, including fiber optic and cellular grid transmission, and digital PBX call management. The services of different kinds of telecommunications companies are identified, and industry trends have been pointed out. The methodologies of technologies have been described along with historical and analytical data about the telecommunications industry so that the reader can develop a working knowledge of the language of telecommunications and the interests of key industrial elements. A strong argument has been advanced which asserts that the future of the telecommunications industry resides in the creation of supportive and flexible small, alternative local communication service networks, which can integrate with one another as independent units, in order to best utilize the forthcoming merger of data, video, and voice services in integrated digital networks.

CHAPTER

4

AT&T and Telecommunications Standards

Any serious interest in telecommunications technologies must include an understanding of the strategy of AT&T and the Bell operating companies. For many years, implementation of technology innovations in telecommunications was hampered by the perceived need of the AT&T Company, holder of the Bell and other patents, to maintain a monopoly on the sale of telephone services and equipment which could be connected to the telephone network. With this business strategy as a priority, technology decisions were made and standards adopted which were limiting and often not in the public interest.

In 1968, the U.S. Supreme Court decided that people could connect to the AT&T network any equipment that was privately beneficial and would cause no public harm. The 1968 Carterfone decision reopened the opportunity for three new industries: long-distance resale, interconnect technologies, and bypass technologies.

Long-distance resale involves the purchase of long-distance services at high-volume rates and the resale of those services to aggregate groups of service users who share some of the benefit of the discounted rates with the service provider.

Interconnect companies manufacture and sell equipment that interconnects with the telephone network. The most simple kind of connection is a standard telephone set, and the most elaborate equipment is a digital PBX ranging in size from a few hundred lines to the capacity of a small telephone company central office. The PBX provides in-house communication switching as well as the capability of dialing outside the premises into the local and long-distance networks.

Bypass technologies provide means of transmission between points as an alternative to using the local or long-distance telephone networks. They are typically microwave, fiber optic cable, or coaxial cable circuits which connect two points together for high-volume, high-speed transmission capability. Satellite transmission is also being used for bypass by some of the larger firms such as RCA and Hughes and by the Department of Defense.

DIVESTITURE—THE ANTITRUST AGREEMENT

Following the settlement of the antitrust law suit brought against AT&T by the Justice Department of the U.S. government, many new developments in telecommunications technology began to appear. AT&T's ability to control the telecommunications market has been challenged by a requirement that AT&T divest itself of the regional Bell operating companies and accept restrictions of business intended to allow the

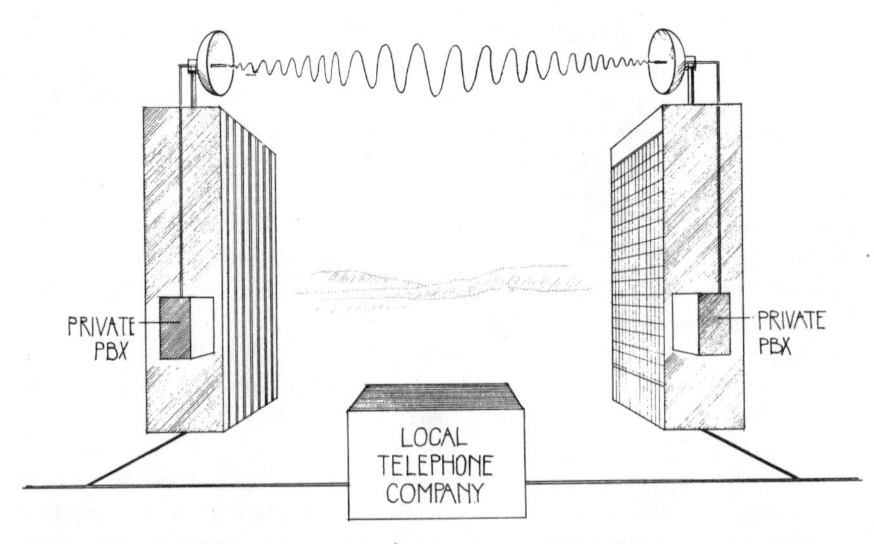

Figure 4.1 "Bypass" is the term used to describe situations where people are telecommunicating without using the facilities of the established local telephone operating company.

growth of competitors and to prevent cross-subsidization which would unfairly discourage competition. (*Cross subsidization* is the practice of using revenues from one part of a business (long distance charges) to pay for the cost of another business area (local call service) so that prices on one part are artificially high and on the other artificially low.) The business strategy of AT&T has not been altered by the stipulations of the legal settlement; it is only being expressed a little differently. Obviously, there would have been no need for an antitrust suit and settlement were the firm friendly and encouraging toward competition.

Whereas the traditional posture of AT&T has been preservation of monopolistic control of the industry, the new objective is preservation of control of the market. There is no difference in AT&T's approach, which is to make the most aggressive stand possible against competition; however, there are now at least legal opportunities for competition. Tactics aimed at preservation of market control are no less aggressive. It is important to recognize that despite the prominence of firms such as MCI-SBS, GTE-Sprint, ITT, Western Union, and others, AT&T still carries in excess of 90 percent of the long-distance traffic in the United States, which is an enormous share of the market to preserve. Company marketing executives are measured by their success in conserving this share.

This condition has an effect on technology development which is similar to the earlier condition of monopolistic control. The firm has a huge influence on the implementation of technology in the world. There will presumably be a need for government-imposed restrictions on AT&T as long as the company continues to make technology implementation and other decisions which are oriented toward keeping others out of the business rather than toward the creation of opportunities for expansion and improvement of service.

TELECOMMUNICATIONS STANDARDS

The AT&T–Bell System monopoly often established arbitrary standards which were not responsive to the needs of subscribers or of the computer equipment manufacturers. Management saw this as consistent with the intention to support the AT&T dominance in the telecommunications field. The use of proprietary communications standards used to be the norm among computer manufacturers, to the extent that even the different product lines of the same manufacturer could not be depended on to integrate. In recent years this strategy has given way among most computer-related manufacturers to the need to integrate office and business equipment into compatible systems. The voice transmission standards defined by the AT&T network of telecommunications services have produced a technology bottleneck for digital communications which the aggressive development of competitive smaller-scale services is now being asked to relieve. AT&T and the Bell operating companies are offering strong resistance to this, both in the marketplace and in the form of strong lobbying activities before state and federal legislative and regulatory bodies.

Until very recently, the Bell System telephone companies were exclusively responsible for "public switched" telecommunications services. The words "public switched services" refer to a service through which a subscriber can communicate with all other subscribers to the service. In the United States, as elsewhere, standard wiring schemes have been used by the Bell System to permit the greatest possibility for the interconnection of all system subscribers. As a result, the world is mostly wired with universally standardized but outmoded and inefficient wiring. The costs of replacing this wiring and the equipment and personnel to manage it are large. In 1983, before divestiture, AT&T estimated that plant costs for approximately 100 million existing access lines were $150 billion, or $1,500 per line. The costs associated with installing the approximately 1 million new lines added during 1983 was $17 billion, or $17,000 per line. Presumably, the costs for replacement of old plant with state-of-the-art technology could be as much as $17,000 per line.

This has been cited by experts as an important factor in the willingness of AT&T to undergo divestiture as part of its negotiated settlement with the Justice Department. Consistent with the terms of this settlement, AT&T was able to divest itself of a tremendous problem—the retrofit of the entire physical plant of telephone communications—while at the same time it maintained access to the entire body of telephone customers' long-distance needs, which was construed as the superior source of revenues. The terms of the settlement also opened for AT&T the opportunity to enter other fields, such as the computer industry, which it had been prevented from exploiting as the result of its conditional status as a natural monopoly.

THE BELL OPERATING COMPANIES

The local Bell operating companies (BOCs) have also enjoyed a monopoly as a public utility in the business of providing local telephone connections. They still enjoy a protected status because of the fears among politicians about the cost of supporting the "residential network." The traditional hold of these firms on the telecommunications industry has been shaken loose by the development of technological alternatives that are both superior to and less expensive than Bell services. Because of the availability of inexpensive equipment and the pronounced need for better high-capacity digital technologies for communication, many companies have installed various means of bypassing the local telephone company's local network except for calls which need to be made within the local dialing area.

LOCAL TELECOMMUNICATIONS FRANCHISING

The local franchises for telephone operations were granted by communities during a time when the Bell System maintained a monopolistic industry and long before the industry was known to be the immense profit center which it has become. Because of state PUC regulation, communities cannot now benefit from franchise fees attached to the rights of established local telephone companies to use streets and other common areas for transmission between users. Since the introduction of cable television and the competition among cable television companies for the right to plant cables, franchises are now being granted by municipalities for the purpose of transmitting signals of various kinds, for various unregulated special purposes. These franchises are accompanied by royalty fees paid to the city. Most localities are encouraging competition with the established telephone companies and seek to benefit wherever possible through granting franchises with associated fees and royalties.

Many cities are granting new franchises to firms wishing to operate competitive communications services. The franchises allow a nonexclusive right to place conduit under and above city streets, extending through major commercial areas. Governments all over the world are licensing franchisees to deliver communications signals of various types.

The first of these franchises to be developed was for coaxial cables to carry television signals. Referred to as community antenna television (CATV), these franchises use coaxial cable, which has a higher bandwidth potential than twisted-wire pairs. Coaxial cable has an inner wire core that is shielded from both electromagnetic and radio signal interference by an outer layer of conductive metal. It is therefore able to carry higher-frequency signals, capable of providing the bandwidth required for television signal transmission. This has resulted in the creation of a coaxial cable communications infrastructure which is already capable of providing a range of services beyond that available on the telephone company's twisted copper wire lines.

Most cable TV franchises were granted prior to the divestiture of the AT&T and Bell System monopoly; consequently, they expressly prohibit the use of the cable for exchange of information between subscribers. In the current climate, there is no reason why such exchange services may not be successfully applied for by cable companies. In many instances, such services are already being provided by cable companies. Many firms have purchased the right to use certain frequencies on CATV coaxial cables in order to carry communications between their own locations, bypassing the telephone network. For instance, point-to-point connection services are now being provided by many CATV companies between terrestial microwave relay towers and satellite uplinks owned by long-distance carriers and corporations.

Because of the confusion in regulation procedures and the overlapping responsibilities of the Federal Communications Commission, state public utility commissions, and local government agencies regarding common-carrier franchise agreements, new franchises are being limited to particular telecommunications services. This situation is analogous to allowing one person to use a car only to go to the dairy and another only to the bakery. Conversely, franchises sometimes require that a firm which seeks to provide CATV service to one profitable area must also provide service to less profitable areas. As a result, some CATV companies have not been able to meet their service initiation schedules, and many have failed as businesses. These failures would not be so frequent were the new franchisees allowed to provide other communications alternatives which the technology could support. For example, coaxial cable which is being utilized for broadcast of television signals has sufficient bandwidth to provide other services. Local franchising has begun to include licensing of new firms to provide business communication services on fiber optic cable networks and private exchange service using cellular grid systems for mobile telephone services. Meanwhile, the emerging technologies are integrating all telecommunication services on compatible networks using a range of different transmission media and techniques.

Confusion exists in local franchising today because the transmission medium is associated with the service or application. For the information management professional, the transmission medium has nothing to do with the way the medium will be used. The selection of a transmission medium is a matter of simple economics. The problem is stated as a need to provide information resources and communications ability at the desks of a staff. The business manager asks, What is the most cost-effective means of getting the job (of communicating) done? The answer to this question entails a review of the communications traffic habits of the organization. When these habits are understood, the technology of a network can be decided upon by a comparison of costs and benefits. This same kind of analysis could also be used for community planning and by municipalities of new franchises for telecommunication services. For instance, cellular telephone technology is at present being licensed exclusively for mobile phone service, though it has much broader application. An alternative is to allow a cellular franchisee to provide whatever services are consistent with federal regulations. Telocator Network of America (TNA), the trade association of cellular service companies, regards wire line services as competitors and does not grant TNA membership to wire line company subsidiaries which operate cellular franchises. The industry, at least, is clear about the matter.

TELECOMMUNICATIONS—STATE OF THE ART

Telecommunications is not a technology but an industry. This industry is not committed to a specific set of technologies but uses whatever becomes available. Somewhat like the theories surrounding light wave technology, the modern medium for signal transmission, telecommunication is difficult to pin down scientifically. The word "telecommunication" is used to describe phenomena which are rapidly changing. If you combined into one category all the telephone companies with those companies which provide products for all services related to the transmission and receipt of communications signals of all types, telecommunications could include all of this. Under subheadings, you would list concepts such as telecommunications media, telephone companies, telephone classified advertising, data communications switching, digital transmission technologies, TV and radio broadcasters, analog signal switching, integrated services digital networks, private terrestrial networks, wide-area networks, long-haul and local networks, CATV companies, local area networks, cellular transmission services, packet-switching networks, signal multiplexing, and PBX systems.

Knowing the meaning of these categories can be valuable relative to business planning and development, commercial facilities management, commercial real estate development, and community planning. However, if the average citizen had a better grasp of the opportunities possible within the field of telecommunications, this would become a different world, if only because the franchises granted by communities and the decisions of public utility commissions might become more appropriate to the potential of the technologies.

TRANSMISSION MEDIA

Transmission media provide the physical channels which carry the signals to connect users on a network. Media are generally classified as bounded—as in wires, cables, and optical fibers—or unbounded—as in radio, microwave, infrared, and other broadcast signals.

The capacity of a transmission medium is measured in bandwidth.

Bandwidth determines the possible applications of a medium. Transmission of digital code, at speeds approaching the working speeds of very smart computers, and the multiplexing of calls so that thousands of calls can be transmitted on the same cable at the same time are only possible if the bandwidth on the medium is great enough to accommodate the traffic.

For any given application, there needs to be sufficient bandwidth available relative to the volume of traffic at peak periods. The criteria for evaluating any transmission medium are economic. The economy is determined by the amount of available bandwidth possible relative to the cost of the medium. As a comparison, all of the traffic between a large office building (1 million ft^2) and another remote place can be carried through one fiber optic cable or microwave signal. An equivalent amount of bandwidth on copper wires would require hundreds of wires. There is sufficient bandwidth in a fiber optic cable that television signals can be transmitted in digital code, allowing video signals to be sent simultaneously with voice and data signals. This is why fiber provides the capability for two-way picture telephone services. State-of-the-art telecommunications transmission requires much higher frequencies than are practical with the antiquated standard of telephone technology utilizing twisted pairs of copper wires.

BANDWIDTH

Bandwidth refers to the range of discrete frequencies, measured in cycles per second, which can be carried by a given medium. This provides a numerical index for the capacity of a communications channel. Each kind of transmission medium has a different amount of capacity, and the technology needed to encode, transmit, switch, and receive signals has been developed to accommodate that capacity. For example, the circuit-switching methods of the public telephone network and the use of twisted-wire pairs has been optimized for transmitting 4000 Hz voice (analog) signals. This is a major reason why much of the existing public telephone technology is inadequate to the needs of modern data communications, despite the attempts of AT&T and the Bell operating companies to adjust the system.

ANALOG VERSUS DIGITAL SIGNALS

Analog signals are exactly what the name implies, signals that are proportional representations of other wave forms. The fluctuations in frequency and amplitude of an electromagnetic telephone analog signal exactly duplicate, in a different scale, the fluctuations of a human voice. As a voice lowers in pitch, the electromagnetic wave form generated by the telephone mouthpiece becomes lower in frequency. Louder sounds produce wave forms of greater amplitude.

Digital signals are actually signal pulses of constant frequency, amplitude, and duration. As described in more detail in the foregoing chapter, computer messages consist of 0s and 1s. Since there are only two possible signal elements, the digital code signal requires only two electrical states, one representing 0 and one representing 1.

CYCLES PER SECOND—HERTZ

In an electromagnetic or other waveform signal transmission, each complete oscillation of the signal waveform is called a "cycle."

The number of cycles occurring each second is referred to as number of hertz (abbreviated Hz). The word "bandwidth" is used to describe the difference between the highest and lowest frequencies used in a signal. The transmission of analog voice signals requires a bandwidth of about 3100 Hz and is commonly transmitted over public telephone wires in the bandwidth range of between 300 and 3400 Hz. In discussing purely digital communications, bandwidth is often expressed in terms of the amount of data (number of bits) that can be transmitted on a channel in each second. Voice-grade telephone lines, used in conjunction with modems, can provide bandwidths capable of carrying 300 to 9600 bits per second (b/s). For comparison, dedicated point-to-point public telephone data communications lines (not switched) may provide a bandwidth range of around 1.54 million b/s. Certain varieties of CATV cables offer bandwidths of 300 megahertz (300 million Hz = 3 MHz) with a digital capacity of over 10 million bits per second. Optical fibers have bandwidths of several billion hertz, called gigahertz (GHz), with potential digital capacity of billions of bits per second.

UNBOUNDED MEDIA

The most typical form of unbounded transmission medium is the common home radio receiver. It is designed to "tune in" frequencies

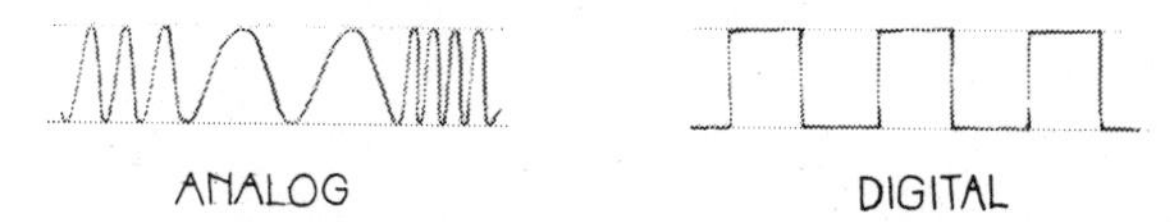

Figure 4.2 Analog signals are proportional representations of sound or video waveforms. Digital signals are composed of only two distinct energy levels, equivalent to one or zero.

within a narrow range of radio frequency (RF) transmission. There is a limit to the total number of frequencies possible in RF transmission. RF waveforms of various lengths have some limiting characteristics which make certain frequencies usable for certain uses. In addition, by both international treaty and national regulation (as administered by the Federal Communications Commission), RF ranges in specific bandwidths have been assigned for special purposes such as commercial broadcast, citizens band, national defense, aeronautical and marine navigation, and various industrial and private purposes.

Because the quality of RF tuners and transmitters varies over time and with atmospheric conditions, to prevent transmissions from spilling over into neighboring frequencies each frequency band has been separated from others by separation bands, which reduce the total bandwidth available for transmission. Unbounded media for telecommunications purposes include microwave, satellite relay, infrared, laser, and semidirectional radio diffusion.

MICROWAVE

Microwave transmission requires line-of-sight capability, where the sending unit can "see" the receiving unit. Under conditions where that can be accomplished, a microwave communications system can become a cost-effective alternative to a wire or cable system. Microwave has been

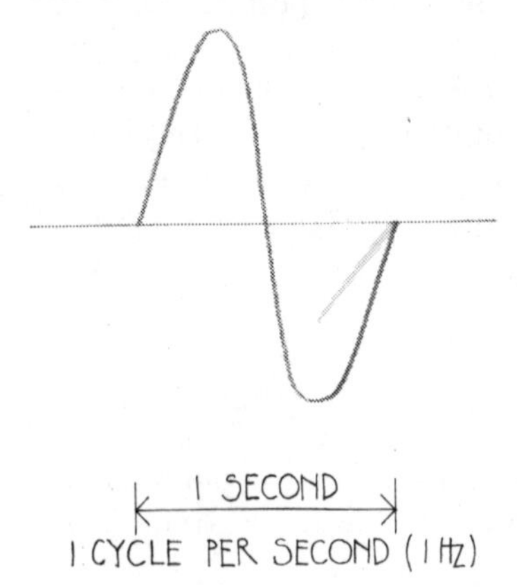

Figure 4.3 Hertz (Hz) is the unit used by engineers to show that a number is a representation of the frequency of a waveform. 1 Hz is one complete cycle of a wave; 1 kHz (1 kilohertz) means 1000 cycles per second.

in commercial use for telecommunications since the Carterfone decision in 1968. The best-known new telephone long-distance carrier, MCI, takes its name from the initials for Microwave Communications Incorporated.

Microwave transmission offers greater bandwidth and higher transmission speeds than are possible with wire cables. Microwave is an effective short-haul carrier and works well between buildings within a city, or across rivers and other natural divides. The radio transmitters and receivers for microwave are relatively inexpensive to build and maintain and are far less troublesome than the installation of underground or overhead wire or cable. Microwave radiation is distorted by atmospheric interference (fog, dust, etc.); thus, it is limited in the distance it can span and it is affected by weather conditions. There is an appreciable loss of signal strength over distance.

A microwave circuit consists of two antennas located within a few miles of each other, transmitting and receiving signals in the low-gigahertz bandwidth (6 GHz to 17 GHz). To employ microwave technology, the analog (voice) or digital signal is multiplexed and the multiplexed signal is converted to the gigahertz range to which a microwave radio transmitter is tuned. Incoming signals are reconverted to the multiplexed wire signal. Microwave towers have been erected at intervals in remote areas to provide a chain of linked transmitters that relay signals over long distances. They require less maintenance than copper wire cables, and in fair weather, provide excellent signal quality.

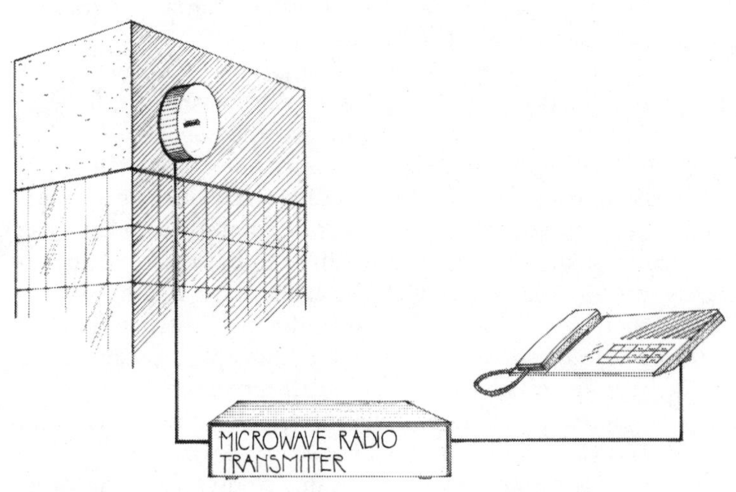

Figure 4.4 Microwave radio transmission is efficient and cost-effective for high-volume telecommunications traffic where line-of-sight transmission is possible.

WAVEGUIDE

As described above, microwave is highly directional and affected by interference from particulate matter in the atmosphere. Waveguide technology uses a tube to confine and protect microwave transmission and direct it around corners. It has been employed by AT&T over long distances to avoid atmospheric interference. But the expense of waveguide tubing has not proved cost-effective as compared with fiber optic cable, a more recent invention. It has been used to relay microwaves in order to complete a microwave circuit in areas where line-of-sight transmission is impossible and to carry signals to and from microwave radios and antennas within buildings. Signal loss is negligible in waveguide tubes because the signal is not affected by atmospheric conditions or electromagnetic interference. The technology is expensive to construct and appears to have been made obsolete for long-distance use by more economical developments in optical fiber that offer greater bandwidth at a lower cost.

CELLULAR RADIO TRANSMISSION

Cellular transmission uses a radio frequency diffusion technique. It was initially employed as a mobile phone service technology. The technology places transmitting/receiving stations at regular intervals throughout a geographical area. The term "cellular" refers to the assignment of a narrow band of frequencies to small geographical areas, forming a cellular grid pattern (see Figure 4.5).

In cellular systems, the transmitters of adjacent cells operate on different frequency bandwidths. Low-power transmitters are used so that cells not adjacent to one another can use the same frequencies without interfering with one another. The subscriber has a telephone equipped with a radio transceiver. When a subscriber places a call (using a handset similar to a standard push-button telephone), the transceiver of the caller's instrument is automatically tuned to the radio frequency of the transceiver in the cell from which the call is being made. The call station which receives the call reads the dialing instructions and retransmits the call directly to another user's radiotelephone transceiver, utilizing a frequency for transmission that is different from that used for receiving. Alternatively, a call may be switched into the local phone company's wire network and then sent by wire to the recipient, or the cell transmitter may transmit the signal by microwave or some other means to a distant cell for retransmission or connection to the wires of the public telephone network.

Based on the volume of calls and the bandwidth made available by the further sophistication of telephone transceivers, there is no reason why cellular technology may not completely replace the need for the residential wire network in some instances. When a radio incorporates a microprocessor computer, time-differentiated digital transmission as well as frequency separations can be used to increase the total number of calls carried on the same bandwidth simultaneously. Given that the intervals of time-based differentiation of signals operate at the level of nanoseconds and that the intervals of human speech are millions of times slower, cellular technology is a possible future candidate for replacement of the local wire network.

SATELLITE TRANSMISSION

Communications satellites in geophysical (stationary) orbits are equipped with antennas and transponders. A dish antenna on the ground focuses a signal onto the dish antenna attached to the satellite. The satellite may be equipped with intelligent signal-managing equip-

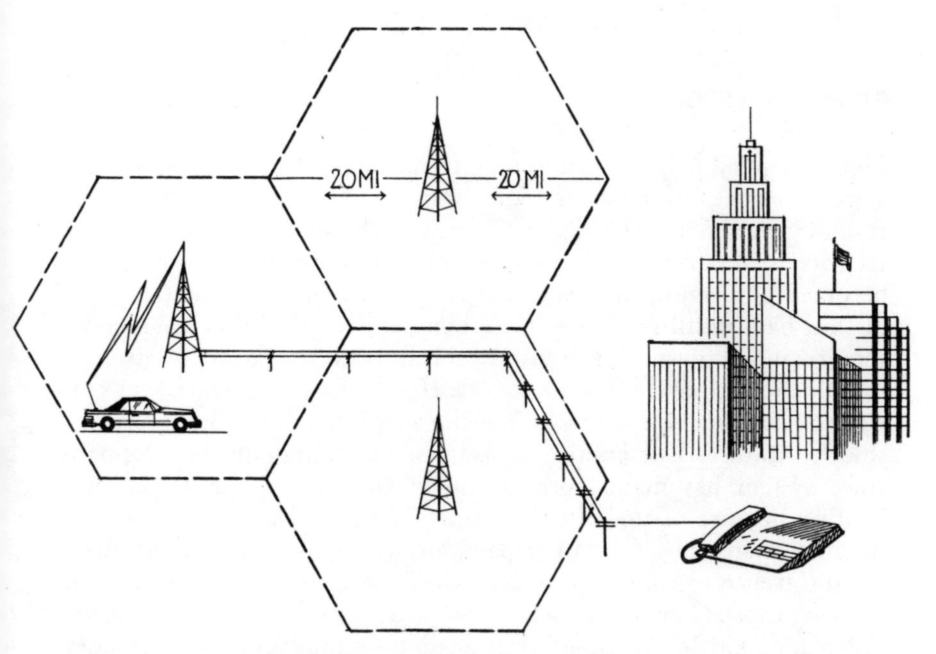

Figure 4.5 Cellular radio telephone uses limited-distance transmitters that are networked together by a computer. The technology makes it possible for more users to occupy a relatively narrow bandwidth, since several users can use the same frequency at the same time if they are far enough apart not to interfere with one another.

ment, called "transponders," which can receive a signal from an earth station, amplify it, and redirect the signal through a transmitting antenna that is focused on another earth station's dish antenna or to another satellite. The two earth station dishes for the call may be located hundreds or thousands of miles from each other.

Before a signal is transmitted to a satellite, it is encoded in a digital format by a device called a coder/decoder (CODEC). Digitizing the signal allows for the use of a greater number of multiplexing techniques. Digitized voice, video, and data signals may be ubiquitously mixed together and streamed onto the same frequencies. This process can also set time delays in order to avoid signal echoes and other problems caused by the distances the signals travel to and from the orbiting transponders. Satellite relay service is limited by bandwidth, expense of transponder installation, and difficulties which result from the extended distances over which the signal must travel. It is successful as a commercial long-distance medium because it has a fixed cost irrespective of the distance, terrain, or geopolitical factors. However, only a small percentage of satellite capacity is currently being used commercially.

BOUNDED MEDIA

Radio frequency signals can also be transmitted through copper wires. Wire absorbs and emits a high amount of electrical interference, resulting in a relatively high error rate and posing a problem where security is important. The problem of signal loss and distortion also becomes more aggravated as higher frequencies are attempted. Because of this, bandwidth on twisted-wire pairs is limited. Lower frequencies require more power for transmission and tend to drop in strength rapidly over relatively short distances. Higher frequencies are subject to electromagnetic noise which, unless the wire is protected by a grounded shield, can distort or entirely cancel a signal. Although the telephone voice system has made optimal use of twisted-wire pairs, they are limiting because of their narrow bandwidth and high signal loss over distance. When twisted copper pairs are compared with optical fibers, the difference in bandwidth capacity is analogous to the difference in carrying capacity between a school bus and a spaceship about the size of the planet Earth. All other transmission technologies (wave guides; satellite retransmission; dispersed, quadrant, unidirectional, and cellular radiofrequency transmission; infrared light; and coaxial cable) fall between optical fiber transmission and the common twisted-wire pair.

TWISTED-WIRE PAIRS

Twisted copper wire pairs are still the standard used by the descendants of the Bell System companies for telephone transmission. Homes and commercial buildings have all been strung with these wires. In an attempt to market AT&T and Bell services, AT&T has developed a new computer-networking system that uses twisted-wire pairs as the network medium. (The intention of this system is to support the embedded plant of Bell System wiring rather than to provide an optimal networking method, and it requires the installation of additional twisted-pair wiring.)

COAXIAL CABLE

In coaxial technology, radiofrequency signals are transmitted along a copper wire. Unlike twisted pairs, the wire is surrounded by a shield of fine copper wire mesh or an extruded aluminum sleeve to prevent electromagnetic interference (EMI) or RF interference which can distort or change the signal. Shielded cable has a central metal conductor surrounded by and insulated from an outer concentric layer of conductive material which is grounded at either end to carry interfering signals to ground (see Figure 4.7).

This concentric shielded cable is called "coaxial cable" and, depending on the diameter of the internal conductor, it has a bandwidth proportionately wider than that of twisted pairs and lends itself well to the

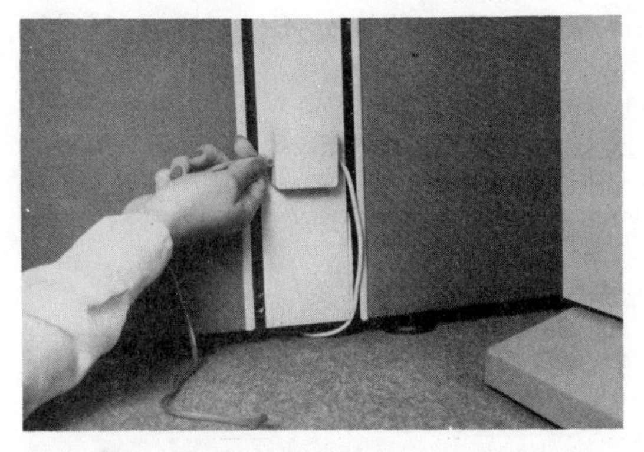

Figure 4.6 The modular telephone jack is a de facto standard for voice telecommunications. It is optimized for voice and not engineered to accommodate high-volume data traffic, which requires more protection from electromagnetic interference than a jack of this technology allows.

support of wideband signals such as are required for the transmission of television signals—typically 6 MHz for a color TV signal. The gradual drop in the strength of a signal as it proceeds along copper wire is managed by the placement, at periodic intervals along the length of the cable, of signal-amplifying equipment. This is an expensive process and one of the more limiting factors associated with all copper wire technology. In the school bus analogy, coaxial cable is equivalent in carrying capacity to a commuter train about 5 miles long. One coaxial cable has the capacity to simultaneously carry 50 standard 6-MHz color TV channels or thousands of voice-grade lines and low-speed data signals (9.6, 19.2, or 56 kb/s).

TRANSMISSION OF SIGNALS USING LIGHT IN THE VISUAL SPECTRUM

Using visible light to transmit signals provides a greater number of discrete transmitting frequencies than does microwave. The bandwidth of the visual spectrum of light is enormous as compared with radio frequency signals. Light is channeled down long continuous filaments called "optical fibers" so that readable light signals can be carried in cables within buildings or above or below the surface of streets.

LOWER COSTS, GREATER CAPACITY OF FIBER OPTIC CABLE

A light signal traveling along a fiber cable will not suffer appreciable loss in signal quality for 9 or 10 miles. This compares very favorably with electromagnetic wave signals in copper wire, which require much more energy and suffer appreciable losses over several hundred meters. A great expense associated with the copper wire present in the public telephone system infrastructure is the need for amplification and

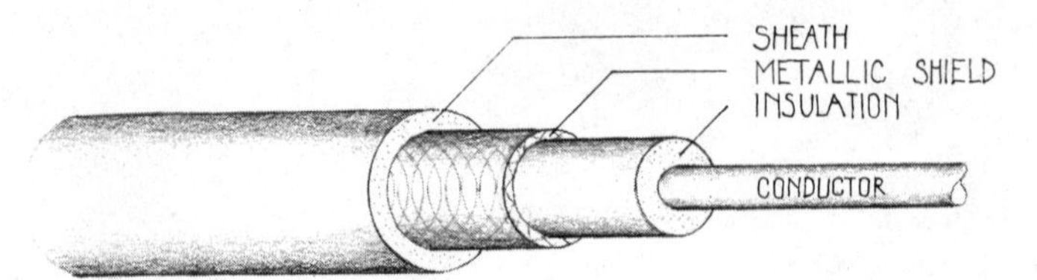

Figure 4.7 Coaxial cable is a de facto standard for television signal broadcast transmission. It is shielded and provides higher bandwidth than do twisted-wire pairs, but it is subject to balance problems and cannot be easily optimized for high-volume two-way transmission.

signal-balancing equipment. These costs are significantly reduced in optical fiber transmissions. And, while costs of the technology are reduced, the greater bandwidth available in visible light signals allows much more signal-carrying capacity and much faster rates of signal transmission. This leads to the possibility that a broader range of computer-related and video communications services could be offered to businesses and individuals on a fiber optic cable network. Such services may include direct connections between state-of-the-art computers, switched call service at transmission rates fast enough to support picture phone service, and the extension of local area networks for high-speed digital communications (see Chapter 6).

OPTICAL FIBER CABLE

Fiber optic cable design utilizes the differences in the ways different kinds of materials refract and reflect light. Refraction refers to the bending of light as it passes from one medium to another. We notice this as distorted vision when we look through water or thick glass. It is the principle upon which optical lenses are constructed. Light from one medium meeting the new medium at certain angles will be redirected (refracted) through the new medium.

Fiber optic cables are designed in two parts: An inner core material carries the motion of the signal along the length of the fiber. An outer shell material, which is also translucent, helps to contain the signal and maintain its velocity down the channel by concentrating escaping elements of the signal back into the center of the channel (see Figure 4.8). There is a difference in the refractive indexes of the inner core and the outer shell materials. As a result, light is propagated down the inner core. Parts of the light signal that bend or bounce in directions other than the direction of travel down the central core are forced by the outer shell medium back toward the central core medium, so that the light is continually propagated along the length of the cable and there is little signal loss. The fiber is sheathed with an opaque cladding to prevent the light signal from escaping and outside light from entering.

The fiber strands are made of glass or plastic. Glass fibers provide the highest performance. Plastic cables are serviceable and less expensive for many applications. Currently available fibers have usable bandwidths of over 3.3 billion Hz (3.3 GHz), as compared with the upper-limit capacity of 500 million Hz (500 MHz) for coaxial (copper wire) cable. Data communication rates of over a billion bits (1 gigabit) per second have been supported, with error rates of only 1 in 1 billion, with the result that most error detection and retransmission costs have been eliminated with fiber cable. Fiber optic transmissions are not affected by electrical or electromagnetic interference nor do they emit noise; this makes them inherently secure. Fiber cables are very small and light, allowing space savings.

OPTICAL SIGNAL CONVERSION

In fiber optic communications, electrical signals are translated into light pulses by a modulator which controls a light source. Light can be transmitted as analog or digital signals. Analog signals vary by light intensity, while on/off light pulses create the equivalent of 0/1 bits in digital signaling. The light pulses are transmitted over the fiber and are detected and converted back into electrical signals by photoelectric diodes. There are different varieties of each component of a fiber optic system, including the following:

Light signal sources. There are two types, light-emitting diodes (LED) and laser diodes. These elements use an electromagnetic signal to drive a light-generation device.

Transmission fibers. There are at present three types in general use. *Single mode* fiber uses a very narrow inner channel surrounded by an outer shell. *Stepped index* fiber uses multiple concentric layers of fiber so that there is a graduation of the refractive indexes of the medium progressing outward from the center of the fiber. *Graded index* fiber is similar to stepped index fiber except that the refractive index changes within a single medium material in an almost imperceptible shading from the center outwards.

Signal detectors. Either P-insulated N-channels (PINs) or avalanche photo diodes (APDs) convert the light signal into an analogous electromagnetic signal.

FACTORS AFFECTING THE PERFORMANCE OF FIBER OPTIC SYSTEMS

The performance of an optical fiber system in terms of transmission speed, bandwidth, and distance is a function of the amount of signal dispersion which occurs. There are two types of signal-degrading dispersion—chromatic and modal. Chromatic dispersion is governed by the bandwidth of light produced by the light source. The wider the range is at the source, the sooner the signal degrades. LEDs are less expensive light sources than are laser diodes. They emit a broader range of light frequencies and thus allow systems to achieve speeds of only 150 Mb/s over 1 kilometer as compared with the 2500 Mb/s achieved by laser diodes.

Modal dispersion is an effect caused by the tendency of light to travel in a wavelike motion rather than in a straight line. The larger the wave fluctuations, the greater the dispersion of the signal and consequent degradation of the signal.

Optical fibers are produced in varying thicknesses and densities. Each type is a trade-off between ease of use and performance.

Single mode fibers. These produce the highest performance. They are extremely thin and force light pulses to travel in a very straight path, with very low modal dispersion. The thin fibers make connections to light sources, detectors, and other cable segments very difficult. There must be precise alignment in order for a signal to continue its path.

Stepped index fibers. These are thicker than the single mode variety and are more amenable to connection and splicing. Since the signals are not forced into a straight path, the fibers allow greater modal dispersion. They carry signals at a rate of 20 Mb/s as compared with the 2500 Mb/s of single mode fibers.

Graded index fibers. These are the most common commercial fibers available. The density of the fiber varies from the inside out, which has a modulating effect on the light pulses as they disperse and forces them

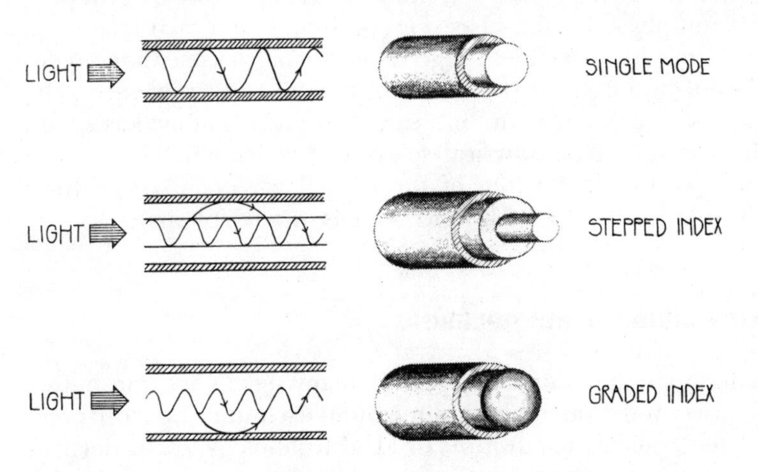

Figure 4.8 Fiber optic cables are manufactured in several designs which vary according to cost, ease of use, and performance. The single mode fiber is the best performing, most expensive, and most difficult to splice.

to travel toward the center of the fiber and to arrive in synchronization with signals that have not dispersed. These fibers achieve transmission rates of 1 Gb/s.

Detectors on the receiving end of a transmission detect the light signals and convert them back into electrical signals through the use of photoelectric diodes—either a PIN diode (which is less costly) or an APD (which is more sensitive and effective).

MULTIPLEXED SIGNAL TRANSMISSION

In long-distance telecommunications the analog or digital signal is invariably multiplexed. Multiplexing is a technology for adding signals together at a transmitting point, sending them over long distances at high speeds, and then unmixing them at the receiving point. This permits a greater economy in the use of the bandwidth of a medium. Instead of the cable carrying only one call at a time, it might carry hundreds or thousands, depending on its size and type. There are three types of multiplexing: space division, frequency division, and time division.

SPACE DIVISION MULTIPLEXING

Space division multiplexing is the creation of a single cable by grouping together many physical cables (see Figure 4.9). Traditional telephone wiring works on this principle. Large cables strung on telephone poles are bundles of hundreds or thousands of individual twisted-wire pairs that connect with pairs that run into each home. Each home has a wire dedicated to it—an actual physical space in the channel. This is very inefficient since only a fraction of the twisted wire pair's bandwidth capacity is used for the 4000-Hz voice signals of a telephone.

FREQUENCY DIVISION MULTIPLEXING

In frequency division multiplexing (FDM), many signals are transmitted simultaneously on the same physical medium, each utilizing a different portion of the available bandwidth. In FDM technology, each subchannel may be assigned a frequency range which is tailored to the bandwidth requirement of the signal it will carry. Channel capacity is well-utilized, which makes FDM a very efficient method of channel allocation. In the example of standard telephone technology, the signals from our telephone sets are carried to a central switching office on physically separated channels. At certain points, where large volumes of calls are to be transmitted between two points, it becomes inefficient to run a single wire for each call. Many calls are then frequency multiplexed onto a single, high-bandwidth cable (see Figure 4.10).

For example, if a particular cable provided a bandwidth of 48,000 Hz spanning the 60,000 to 108,000 Hz range, the first call would be transmitted in the 60,000 to 64,000 Hz range, the second in the 64,000 to 68,000 Hz range, and so forth. In this way, thousands of calls could be transmitted simultaneously on cables of great bandwidth. Conceptually, FDM is similar to space division multiplexing—one physical channel is divided into a number of smaller channels by frequencies instead of by separate physical wires.

FDM is accomplished by Modems (from modulator/demodulator) which shift the 4000 Hz signals up to successive frequencies and modulate them onto carrier signals. At the receiving end of the multiplexed transmission, a modem is again employed to demodulate the signals back into their original frequencies.

Analog-to-digital (A/D) and digital-to-analog (D/A) converters are often integrated into multiplexer modems when there is a need to convert digital signals to analog in order to transmit data communications over the analog (voice) type of FDM channels of the existing AT&T long-haul telephone network.

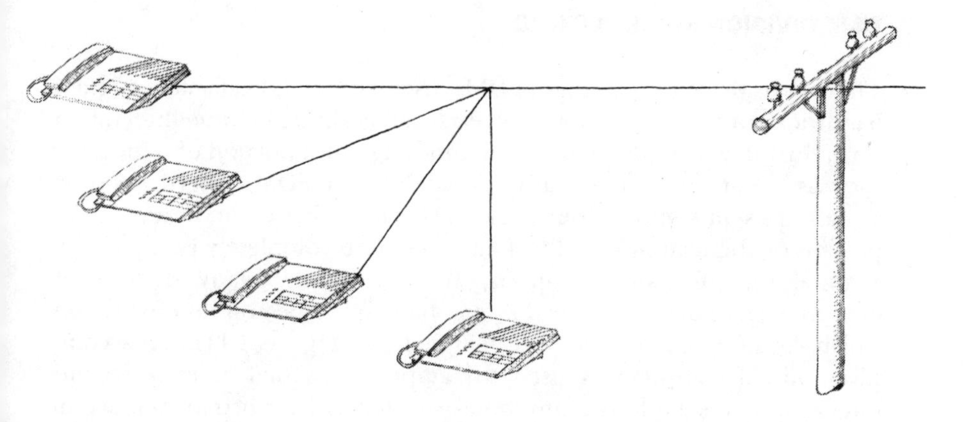

Figure 4.9 Space division multiplexing combines many separate wires into one cable bundle.

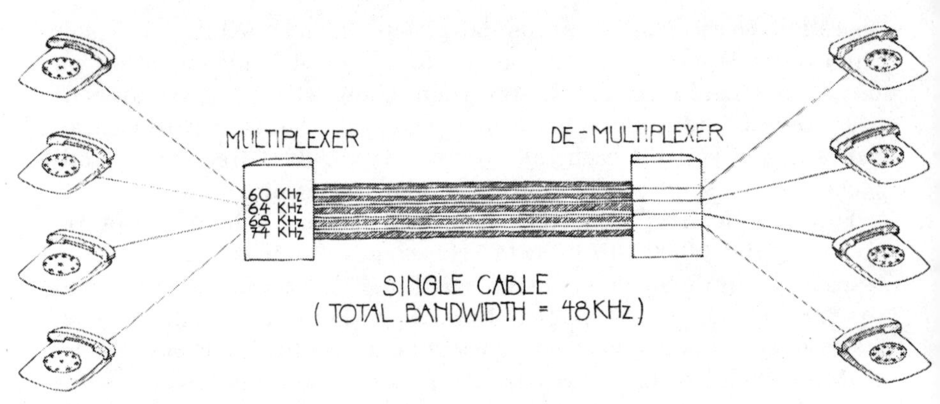

Figure 4.10 Frequency division multiplexing assigns each call to a narrow-bandwidth channel so that many calls may be transmitted over a single cable simultaneously.

The FDM technique of positioning each signal in a unique frequency range creates the possibility of establishing dedicated channels. This provides the potential for further subdivision of the frequency subchannels by other multiplexing techniques (such as time division multiplexing) for even more efficient use of available bandwidth. Also, more levels, qualities, and types of service within one network channel are made possible. For instance, bandwidth may be allocated for specific groups of users or for special tariff services.

TIME DIVISION MULTIPLEXING

Time division multiplexing (TDM) uses the full available assigned bandwidth of a channel; however, each call is allotted a time interval, in turn, during which it may transmit a message or a portion of a message such as a data packet. As differentiated from FDM, where multiple signals are sent simultaneously and each call is allotted an independent portion of the channel, in TDM each message completely occupies the channel (or subchannel) capacity for an instant. Many streams of discrete signals are interleaved sequentially into one continuous stream which consists of portions of each signal (see Figure 4.11). To accomplish this, a computer is used to sample the signal at microsecond intervals. The sample is many times shorter in length than the actual signal. It is the sample which is transmitted, not the original signal. On the receiving end, another set of logic circuitry uses the samples to reconstruct the original signal. This process is done exactly enough so that human voice quality and music can be encoded and reproduced

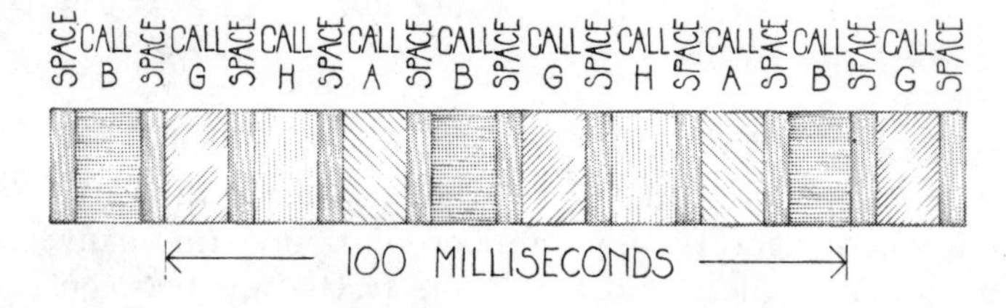

Figure 4.11 Time division multiplexing is a digital technology. Signals are compressed and encapsulated so that a number of different calls can be interleaved and transmitted on a single cable at very high speeds.

satisfactorily. Digital signals are very easy to code and decode in this fashion.

TDM produces a greater utilization of a channel. Either analog or digital signals can be multiplexed with TDM, and modems for data communications are not needed, as they are with FDM. In TDM, voice (analog) signals are converted to digital code. Instead of the entire analog signal being converted, samples of the analog signal are taken at millisecond intervals and these much shorter samples are coded in digital form. This has the effect of compressing the signal length and increasing the signal velocity. The samples of different signals are intermixed at the sending station and sent at high speeds to a receiving station where they are sorted out and reconstructed. In reconstruction of the signal, the sample is followed as though it were a statistical model for an ideal signal and the blank places are filled in according to rules of probability.

TDM is also used for techniques of call management by digital PBXs. The technique of multiplexing samples at millisecond intervals of a signal compresses the signal to a fraction of its length and permits a digital PBX to float calls around from circuit to circuit and make more efficient use of hardware which would otherwise be tied up with one call at a time.

MULTIPLEXED DATA COMMUNICATIONS

Computer to computer communications also multiplex signals. Bandwidth on a cable can be divided into separate frequencies for different functions or different users. A computer can be receiving information from several sources at the same time that it is sending responses. In optical fiber systems, the multiplexed signal is converted to a frequency in a visual spectrum bandwidth and then propagated along the cable either by lasers or light-emitting diodes.

THE PRIVATE BRANCH EXCHANGE

A private branch exchange (PBX) is a telephone exchange switching unit that serves a private company or other organization. During the early decades of the twentieth century, the number of phones in many businesses had grown dramatically. Much of the traffic was between on-premises extensions, and it was technologically awkward and expensive to connect these calls through the telephone company central office. This prompted the installation of private switchboards and call-managing operators in large organizations, hotels, government offices, and so forth.

The modern PBX, now often referred to as a "switch" in the professional vernacular, developed out of the specifications for these early private switchboards. PBXs followed design criteria that differed from the telephone company's central office equipment. They evolved from private company switchboards and were designed to connect calls between parties on the same premises and to switch calls between the premises and the outside telephone network. The PBX eliminated the necessity for every phone in the building to have its own line to the telephone company and provided the facility for a number of extensions to share lines to the outside on an as-needed basis. Since most calling is intraorganizational, the number of lines connected to the telephone company central office is dramatically reduced.

Like other forms of telephone-switching equipment, the PBX began life as a manual plug and wire switchboard. Electromechanical switches replaced the manual plugboards. For a time, on-site operators received a call from the outside and then switched the call manually into the called party's wire extension. Later, crossbar switches were employed to store the incoming dialed number in electrical circuits and make the internal connection automatically. This technology was later superseded by electronic switching of circuits.

As the need for data communications emerged, lines of the public telephone network and the PBX were employed for user to computer and computer to computer communications. At first, the computer signals needed to be converted to voice (analog) telephone signals. Modems were engineered to provide digital-to-analog and analog-to-digital conversion. This method for data communications was awkward, slow, and cumbersome and subject to intrusion by computer "hackers." However, the telephone network was extensive and available and provided a cheap, if slow and sloppy, means for networking computer devices.

PBX equipment supplied by AT&T made little progress until 1968 when, as a result of the Carterfone decision, other companies were permitted to make and sell equipment that could connect to the lines of the common carriers. The Bell Canada company had been experimenting with customer premises equipment for the purpose of providing groups of customers in large office buildings with PBX-supported services, as a means of more efficiently delivering service. A division of Bell Canada now known as Northern Telecom International (NTI) purchased a Texas firm called Danray, which had developed a digital-controlled PBX. The Northern Telecom digital switch has since led the market through several generations of successfully implemented products. Since the inclusion of microprocessor intelligence and VLSI (chip) circuitry, the modern digital PBX performs far more sophisticated functions than the electromechanical equipment allowed.

Signals coming into a digital PBX from the outside network may be either digital or analog and may be received as time division or frequency division multiplexed signals. This means that data equipment can send signals directly into the switch (PBX) over private lines, and long-haul digital carriers, such as microwave, fiber optic cables, and other trunks, can route data streams from remote data devices through the switch to on-premises data-processing resources.

Telephones within a digital PBX line system may be equipped with codec chips which convert voice signals so they can be sent to the switch in digital form. Digital PBXs can be equipped so that older-style telephones can still send analog signals (which are converted to digital signals by a codec at the switch, as are incoming analog calls from the local telephone network). The fully digital switch multiplexes all call signals internally in order to allocate available channels more efficiently and avoid blocking. (Blocking occurs when the PBX cannot accept a transmission because its circuits are completely occupied.)

The hardware and software for a PBX are configured by the manufacturer to meet the customer's specifications. Modular parts are assembled to provide the desired number of lines for telephone extensions and trunks for connection to the public switched network, private dedicated lines, and other service connections (see Figure 4.13). Small PBX installations average 200 to 400 lines. Larger units range from 2000 to 25,000 lines. The entire PBX system is assembled in a modular fashion. There are cabinets, shelves, and cards. The cabinet contains some cable and connector provisions. The shelves carry connectors to receive the cards. The cards are microcircuit boards which serve various purposes. For instance, each card in a current Northern Telecom (NTI) PBX system currently manages 16 separate telephone line extensions. Each NTI trunk card can carry 8 ports to outside network trunks. NTI data line terminal cards support 8 lines each and incorporate modems.

Figure 4.12 Since the Carterfone decision, the telephone terminals available for private or business use have increased in complexity and decreased in cost. Clockwise from the upper left: The Meridian M4020 integrated terminal; the Meridian 2112 digital telephone; the Meridian M3000 Touchphone; the Meridian M2018 digital telephone. (Courtesy of Northern Telecom International, Inc.)

The CPU which controls the operations of the PBX and runs the programs that determine call features consists of several cards on one or two shelves. Another shelf is equipped with a power supply. Commonly, there are optional battery back-up power supplies and even redundant CPUs and power supplies. Down time for a communication system is to be avoided at all costs.

A wiring panel, called a "punchboard," is attached to a wall or rack beside the PBX. All wires coming out of the PBX lead to stations on the punchboard. To connect a line into the PBX with an extension, a technician simply pushes the wire leading to the telephone extension into a slot opposite the desired line to the PBX. To complete the installation, the PBX computer is then programmed with the extension number of the attached wire, and when that extension is dialed, the PBX "knows" that the phone at the end of the wire for that extension must ring. The PBX computer can also be programmed to make a record of calls to or from every extension number.

In determining the external network configuration for a PBX installation, the number of trunks of various kinds necessary to carry incoming and outgoing calls to the public switched and other wide-area network services are calculated based on an analysis of each user's telephone traffic history and perceived future growth. An appropriate modeling reveals the best probable configuration of local trunks, WATS, Sprint, and other services for each user.

Figure 4.13 The modern digital PBX offers to an organization or other group of telecommunications subscribers far more telecommunications capability than is available from a telephone operating company. (Courtesy of Northern Telecom International, Inc.)

DATA COMMUNICATIONS OPTIONS

The PBX can also be equipped with options such as an X.25 packet-switching device for long-distance digital communications or a modem pooling device for conversion of digital to analog signals. Multiplexers with codec chips and frequency multiplexers can be installed to provide links with microwave, satellite uplink, or fiber optic cables.

COMPUTER-ASSISTED CALL MANAGEMENT

To manage all these lines, trunks, and other transmission opportunities, the modern digital PBX uses a microprocessor-controlled computer which has been programmed to recognize incoming and outgoing call signals and to know how to handle each call, according to the features assigned to its extension to fill each user's need. Outgoing calls may be automatically assigned to lowest-cost routes such as WATS, SPRINT, or other lines. An extensive amount of user programmability is provided. Depending on the access rights given to the user of each extension by higher-level programming, a user can redirect calls to another phone, have calls screened by a receptionist, or forward calls to a "voice mailbox." Calls can be set up to include a number of parties at the same time. Calls can be transferred to extensions within or outside of the system. Calls can be made through the system from lines outside of the system to other lines outside of the system.

CALL DETAIL RECORDING

Software for call detail recording is used to drive a storage device (tape or disk) as a means of recording the data about every call which originates in the system. The extension from which a call was made, the time of the call and its duration, and the outgoing trunk or other connection used to complete the call are indicated. Computations can be done with this data for billing, accounting, or departmental cost control.

TECHNICAL LIMITATIONS

Although many voice and data communication needs are satisfied by the PBX, its dependence on twisted-wire pairs and telephone-related switching techniques cause the same limitations for data communications that occur in the public telephone network to occur in the PBX. Connections between the PBX and the external switched network at present limit data transmission speed to 9.6 kb/s. Internally, the use of twisted-wire pairs limits data transfer speeds to 56 kb/s. This means that many implementations of state-of-the-art computer technology—for example, the high-speed, high-volume requirements of applications such as electronic mail and file transfers between computers and intelligent terminals, retrieval of large amounts of data from distributed databases, and transmission of high resolution graphics—will not be supported by state-of-the-art PBX technology.

The PBX is a centrally controlled system and is therefore subject to total system failure if a major component of the PBX were to fail. Protecting the reliability of this major component becomes the source of great expense in applications of any size. The statement is sometimes made that the integrated voice/data PBX will eliminate the need for rewiring for data communications since existing phone lines can be used. This is not usually the case. For a number of reasons, an additional wire pair is needed to implement a state-of-the-art voice/data PBX system. Because of this, it is common in new installations to run triple twisted pairs to each extension.

ESTABLISHING COMMUNICATIONS CHANNELS—PACKET SWITCHING

A transmission path must be established between users on a network before messages can travel to their destinations. Up to this point, we have been dealing with the telephone network's method for this, which is known as "circuit switching." The alternative is known as "packet switching." In circuit-switched networks, every time a call is placed, an electrical path or circuit is established and switched in to provide the connection between the caller and the called. The long pause that occurs between completion of dialing and the first ring in a telephone call is the time it takes to establish the circuit—the call set-up time. After the connection is established, it is exclusive and continuous for the duration of the conversation. When completed, the circuit is disconnected. Every time a call is originated a totally new path is established between two points as calls are automatically directed by the most readily available route.

The set-up time required to establish circuits is not a problem in telephone conversations. However, data communications are often "bursty" transmissions lasting only fractions of a second. Once the circuit is established, the connection is ideal; however, for short transmissions which require the total channel capacity of a T1 connection (a standard adopted by AT&T for a circuit with bandwidth sufficient to transmit 1.54 Mb/s), circuit switching is slow, expensive, and inefficient. More time is spent waiting for a connection than is required to transmit data.

PACKET SWITCHING

Packet switching provides a more efficient means of exchanging messages between computers. Except for parallel communications between component parts of a computer system located in close proximity—such as processors and peripherals—packet switching is the predominant means for digital communication between intelligent machines.

Unlike voice transmissions, which require only a small portion of a channel's total capacity, computer communications often require the total capacity of a high-bandwidth channel to transmit brief bursts of data. This is especially true in networked, distributed, and interactive environments where there are many users and there is a need to pass files of information between many machines. Whereas circuit switching was a solution for the temporary connection of channels for continuous transmission of voice conversations, packet switching was designed to meet the intermittent, high-volume bursts of data characteristic of computer processing speeds.

"Packets" are whole messages which have been broken into discrete units of data. In most systems, they have a specified maximum length, measured in bytes of data information. The packets are constructed by software in the computer and contain bits for synchronization, control information, message number, number of the current and the last previous packet, destination and source addresses, acknowledgment, error checking, and data, all arranged in a very particular order or "protocol" set by the engineers who designed the system.

Packet-switching protocols determine the method by which packets are placed on a communications channel and travel to their destinations. Unlike circuit switching, where the channel or transmission technique is independent of the message carried, packets contain the address of the sender and the receiving destination. Packets travel through a network in a manner analogous to the travel of a railroad train. As the packet passes each intersecting node on the network, its addressing information is read and the unit is either received, read, and acknowledged or passed on to the next node. The path is established as the packet moves on and is disconnected as soon as the packet reaches another node, allowing the switching of other packets (see Figure 4.14).

The channels are used only when packets are transmitted; at other times, they are available. This makes packet switching efficient for bursty data transfer. Depending on the routing priorities on the network, packets are sometimes held by nodes for periods of time because of traffic; consequently, packets that make up a message may arrive at their destination out of order. They are reassembled in accordance with network software protocols at the receiving station. In some network routing schemes, the packets are broadcast over the medium. Only the destination nodes identified in a packet's address bits will intercept a packet. The others simply let it pass by. This technique eliminates the need for delays and is common in local area network architectures, which will be discussed in more detail in Chapter 6, Local Area Networks.

Many firms with data communication requirements subscribe to a public packet-switching network, such as GTE Telenet, or build their own packet-switching capability. The protocols of packet switching allow for faster rates of transmission on public telephone lines (56,000 b/s) than circuit-switched line standards support (1200 b/s average). In the public telephone switched network, packet switching is a technique for sending packages of digital information over telephone company switched circuits. The user must have equipment which breaks the communication into packets of defined size, encoded with appropriate addressing information. The standards (protocols) used to describe the order in which this information is organized in the packet has been established in a published standard adopted by an international standards organization—the CCITT X.25 standard.

CCITT X.25

In the X.25 public switched networks, the packets of many users are streamed serially (one after another) over T1 (around 1.5 Mb/s) lines or satellite or terrestrial microwave relay. Each T1 circuit can simultaneously connect a large number of users for digital communications. Packet switching cannot accommodate voice traffic, though it is expected that someday it may. Packet switching is limited in the volume of interactive data or video transmission that can be accomplished over time, and its chief value lies in the fact that data can be easily sent long distances through the public switched networks at the rate of 56,000 b/s, which is substantially faster than the voice-grade transmission maximum of 9600 b/s, though much slower than the 1 to 50 million b/s speed with which computers need to communicate for multiple user, interactive services.

BYPASS AND PRIVATE NETWORKS

A survey conducted by the National Regulatory Research Council in 1985 indicated that though users felt sure the Bell System services were

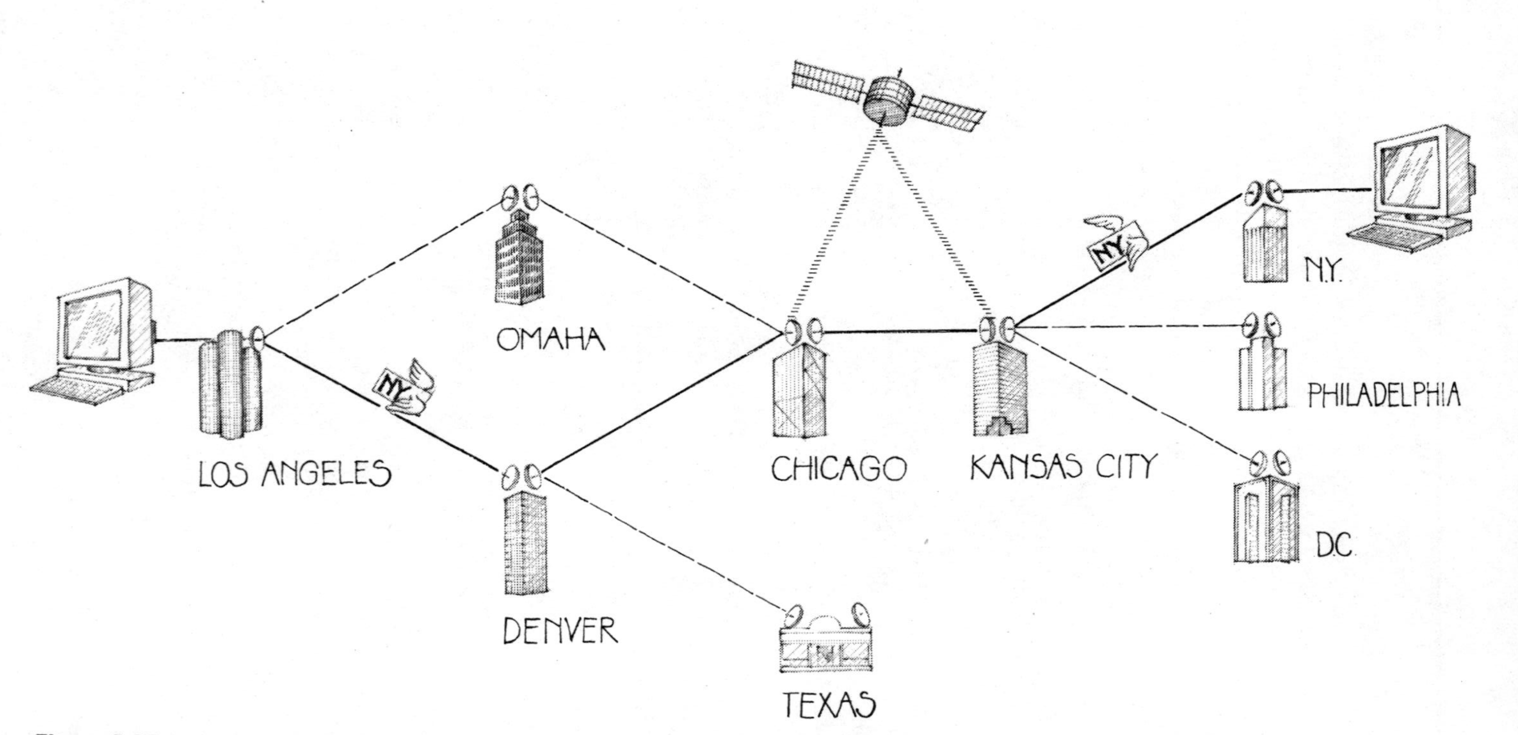

Figure 4.14 Packet switching allows the most economical use of a transmission medium. Each communication is sent across the network while bearing the address of its recipient. Transmission time is thus reduced to just the microsecond length of time it takes for the user to transmit the packet signals.

more reliable than those of its competitors, 87 percent of the corporate users surveyed declared they would invariably choose an alternative vendor when cost savings were in excess of 10 percent and 35 percent of the surveyed group said they would move when savings were in excess of 5 percent. None ruled out the possibility of alternative services.

Aside from the large number of competitive common carrier businesses which have begun since divestiture, many corporations and public agencies have found it cost-effective to install their own proprietary communications facilities. By installing its own microwave or satellite transceiving antenna, a company can interconnect a network of production and administration facilities with improved security, efficiency, and flexibility and at far less cost than by using the public switched network. Many companies lease cable or unused portions of the bandwidth of coaxial and fiber optic cable on CATV networks for interconnection of their facilities.

After cost (relative to public switched service cost), the main reasons for bypass are requirements for special methods of transmission for different communications purposes. Depending on the kind of traffic generated, a firm with several thousand voice lines in a headquarters building and at several remote locations may be satisfied with public switched services, except for cost. On the other hand, a company which requires the interconnection of a few mainframe computer centers would require the capability of private optical fiber transmission. Because of the rapidly evolving potential of telecommunications technologies, it would be a mistake for a company to limit a new telecommunications system by taking a minimalist approach.

Firms developing new facilities are well-advised to install provision for fiber optic media. The voice-grade line user in the example above may gain only slightly in terms of service reliability and quality from fiber optic technology. But the implementation of fiber optics would pave the way for many new time- and cost-saving techniques that are not possible with copper wire. Fiber allows high-capacity transmission over extended distances without loss or error. This ability will accommodate the implementation of a state-of-the-art local area network for distributed-processing computer services. It will also allow long-haul companies such as SBS, MCI, ITT, and AT&T to offer services that are competitive with those available from a local telephone company.

EMERGING TELECOMMUNICATIONS SERVICES—TWO-WAY VIDEO

Once fiber optics have been fully implemented, the technologies available on the public dial-up network are limited only by the quality of software available to discern, encode, and manage high-speed signal transmissions. Software designs using artificial intelligence are making possible many new uses of technology limited only by the ability to acquaint users with the values of the new applications. Many new possibilities may at first seem as strange as radio and television did when they were introduced to earlier generations. Video telephone and teleconferencing, for example, are regarded by people today as frivolous and expensive. Their value has not been recognized because the potential user cannot imagine that value. In terms of reducing the need for travel to accomplish the purposes of meetings, consultations, and conferences (telecommuting), it certainly cannot be thought frivolous. Since a purpose of telecommunications is to enable communication between people in locations remote from each other, the important value of two-way video is that it enhances and extends human communication across cultural and language barriers.

Taking the most extreme example, a purely voice telephone conversation is virtually impossible between a person who speaks only Japanese and one who speaks only English. Such a pair could have a "conversa-

Figure 4.15 The possibilities offered by two-way video are not yet fully realized by the public. Most people think of video conferencing as an enhanced kind of telephone service. In reality, the sense of intimacy provided by two-way video produces an effect that is more like personal presence than telephone conversation.

tion" if there were visual as well as voice contact; more succinctly, they could begin a human relationship. In a less extreme example, conversations between people who speak the same language may be facilitated by the potential for establishing a relationship that two-way video affords. Many business activities are conducted on the telephone. Having visual contact—and an experience of the person with whom one is doing business—can add to the effectiveness and integrity of communication. As of this writing, the Department of Defense has contracted to equip all Pentagon offices with video telephone service.

The technology for two-way video will be affordable for general public use when the digital technology for this function is made available on chips. Chip manufacturing technology is only cost-effective when there are large volumes of chips to be produced. Large volumes are required by large market demand. Because the market for video telephones has not been developed in the United States, the technology of inexpensive production lags. The situation is reminiscent of the early years of aviation, when commercial landing fields were few. In those days, Charles Lindberg barnstormed extensively around the nation and the world demonstrating the reality of powered flight and inspiring locals to build and standardize air fields. The presence of local airfields opened the possibility for the air transportation industry. One wonders what might have been the outcome had airport operations been given over to the exclusive domain of a single firm to develop, as was done with AT&T.

Local voice transmission does not require the bandwidth potential of coaxial or optical fiber cable, but two-way video does. AT&T, the Bell operating companies, and independent telephone companies have not been in a hurry to install fiber optic facilities. The prices of all wide bandwidth services are still high because of the lag in the state of the art of public telephone network technology. Following the introduction of fiber optic transport, a reduction in the costs of fiber optic cable and of signal conversion and switching equipment will be followed by growth in the demand for two-way video transmission. The manufacturing costs of optical fiber equipment and cable and of the circuit management required for video call switching will then move much lower relative to the cost of maintaining service.

The capability for video transmission to and from subscribers' homes via telephone connections indicates that eventually the activities of cable TV and telephone operations will merge. This not only creates problems with the present regulatory law but is also in conflict with the stance of AT&T and the Bell operating companies to preserve market share. There is no reason why the CATV infrastructure may not provide a more cost-effective means of signal transport than the telephone network. The sale of technologies which support private bypass of the public switched telephone network is incrementally absorbing some of the telecommunications market. Although the giant size of AT&T far outweighs any competitors, AT&T is literally being dragged backwards, kicking, into the competitive twenty-first century telecommunications environment.

SDN AND THE STRATEGY OF NEW AT&T TARIFF REQUESTS

As a response to the shift of market interest toward alternative methods to the established Bell System network, AT&T recently announced a service called the "software-defined network" (SDN). To the user, the software-defined network gives the appearance of providing services similar to an in-house PBX with a private long-distance network. In reality, the AT&T SDN is a service that maintains a set of instructions in a computer program so that whenever a call is made from or to any of the user's registered telephone lines, through the AT&T exchange, the call is managed according to user-defined criteria. In this way, a company's remote locations can be assigned direct line connections and extension numbers just as if the telephone system were owned and operated by the user over dedicated lines leased from AT&T. The user's data terminal equipment and processors can be interconnected with special authorization codes, access security, and automatically assigned data-grade lines. The user's own staff can program and control the SDN network, limiting access and defining call management and the location of extension numbers in a manner similar to the programming of a digital PBX.

Services available on the SDN are otherwise no different from services available through normal dial-up procedures. The pricing structure follows the format of WATS services rather than retail transaction pricing. The SDN service is not a new technology as much as a new rate-structuring method. Instead of leasing or purchasing set amounts of transmission capability (private lines) and organizing a proprietary bypass system, the user places network organization in the hands of AT&T network consultants. Services available are the standard set that is compatible with the current AT&T network offering. The SDN is aimed at preserving AT&T's market share of high-volume corporate users of services. The largest market for information management services, that of small- to medium-sized businesses, is not addressed by this rate plan.

ISDN

In the not-too-distant future, a "telephone" customer will be able to send and receive voice, data, and video images from a single console connected to an ISDN network fiber optic cable. The name "integrated services digital network" (ISDN) was coined to describe a system architecture that provides telecommunications services wherein all kinds of transmission (voice, video, and data) can be carried on one transmission medium (see Figure 4.16). One could connect a computer, voice or video telephone, television set, plotter, printer, or other device to the medium, and any type of communications service is possible.

TECHNOLOGICAL REQUIREMENTS FOR AN ISDN

The technological requirements for ISDN present no problem that cannot be solved by state-of-the-art technologies. The elements for an ISDN network are currently available at affordable prices. More efficient, higher-quality (higher-bandwidth) transmission is required for

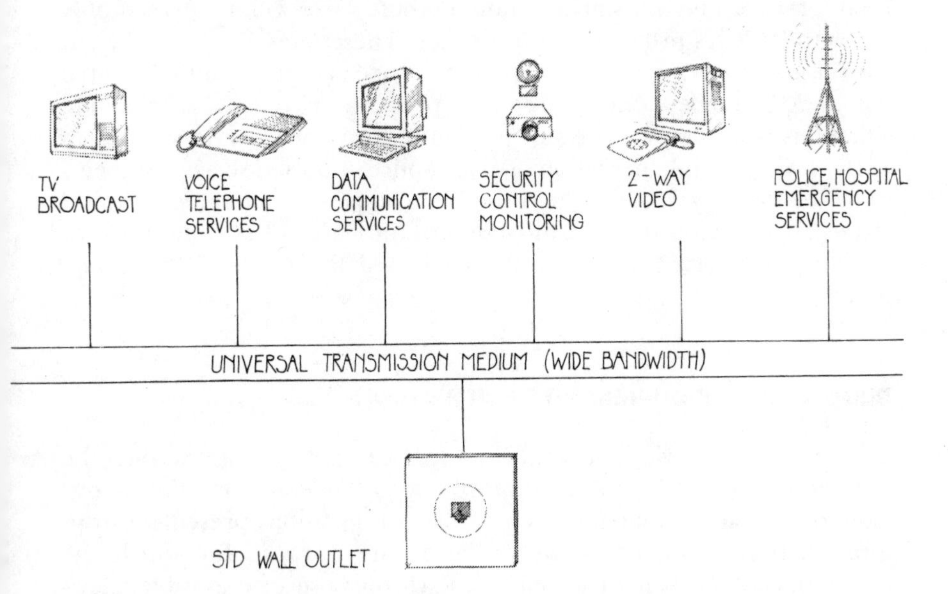

Figure 4.16 The most sensible concept for a state-of-the-art telecommunications network for public use will have a bandwidth capable of supporting every kind of communications. Unfortunately, the present telephone infrastructure is not a good place to start from to arrive at an integrated services digital network, which requires a high-bandwidth digital signal rather than an analog-based narrow-bandwidth signal.

ISDN. Fiber optic transmission offers a cost-effective means for meeting this need. A cost-effective total system designed with fiber optics by Fujitsu, of Japan, has been implemented in a beta-test site in Singapore. In California, the Grass Valley Computer Co. is manufacturing equipment for the switching of fiber optic analog signals capable of providing ISDN services for voice, video, and data transmission for private companies. Pacific Bell has currently installed a Grass Valley system in Los Angeles to provide transmission capability for television production and broadcast corporations.

STANDARDS AND PROTOCOLS OF ISDN

One factor important to the use of ISDN is standardization of digital signals and protocols so that users can naturally and inexpensively interconnect with each other and over the network systems of long-haul carriers. The regional Bell operating companies and AT&T have been test marketing "pre-ISDN" services utilizing standard telephone twisted-pair wiring. They are using the standards of the existing telephone network to overcome the problem of interconnection with long-haul and local services. The transmission rate on these wires will not exceed 56K b/s, with 9.6K b/s provided for most uses. These rates are not sufficient for full-motion video or interactive data conversations at any substantial volume. The telephone companies' purpose in these experimental situations is to discover ways of marketing profitable services using an ISDN prior to implementation of fiber optic supported service. It seems to be the strategy of AT&T and the Bell companies to pursue technical strategies based on the 56K-bit standard, at least unless some form of competitive service becomes available which delivers true ISDN characteristics.

REGULATORY REQUIREMENTS FOR AN ISDN

The ubiquitous service potential of an ISDN may require revamping the regulatory approach to telecommunications. Federal Communications Commission and public utility commission regulations presently distinguish between utilities on the basis of the purpose for which the communication is being transmitted. Each purpose such as cable television, radio and TV broadcast, and local area telephone exchange has been treated as if it were a different industry. In an ISDN network, the services of all of these industries and many other services can be supported on the same fiber optic cable. Bandwidth on a cable can be allocated to TV or radio broadcast, to public packet-switching service, to voice transmission, to video conferencing, and so forth. It is possible that the fiber optic cable itself may become the utility that needs to be regulated by means of standardizing access to established segments of bandwidth on a fiber optic cable, in a manner similar to the management of radio signal bandwidth in broadcast technology.

ISDN MARKETS

A study conducted by Pacific Bell revealed that 15 percent of California residents had home computers in 1984 and that 14 percent of the nation's installed residential personal computers are in California. The study further indicated that 16 percent of California's home computer owners use their computers for telecommunications. Pacific Bell expects this last figure to escalate sharply over the next few years as new applications are created and more people and businesses buy and use computers. The studies revealed that making full use of telecommunications from the home can increase discretionary time by an average of 4 hours per day. Based on statistics of this kind, the savings in time and costs associated with "telecommuting" (getting there by phone instead of in person) as the result of ISDN service may be enormous.

Aside from the home markets, the opportunities for ISDN services in business are bullish. Most business communications purposes will be better served with ISDN services. ISDN opens the door for the next generation of computer to computer compatibility. Many possibilities offered by artificial intelligence and "expert systems" become realities through the facile interconnection of intelligent devices. The ISDN will provide a new ability for such machines to monitor each others' activities and to receive reports from each other about conditions in real time. This facility will provide the ability to produce a great number of new and useful services. For instance, one will be able to perform any number of medical diagnostic procedures "on the telephone." A dial-up film service could be initiated to provide subscribers with a video copy of the film of their choice, instantly. A dial-up reference library could provide a lawyer or other professional with research services. A subscriber could dial up access to foreign media broadcasts.

CUSTOMER SERVICE

ISDN represents a departure from traditional telephone industry marketing. The way in which telephone subscribers use the telephone requires no training or support from the service provider. Customer service departments in the telephone industry have been limited to order taking, complaint processing, and bill adjustments. Typical ISDN applications—such as video teleconferencing, or connecting groups of remotely located computer-driven devices—will require extensive close support by the service provider. Much closer customer relations and more interaction with the service provider characterize the ISDN situation. Aside from technological changes, the idea of contact with the customer is revolutionary in the telephone service industry. It is easy to understand why firms such as AT&T and the Bell operating companies are struggling so valiantly to maintain their hold on the telecommunications industry in the United States. It is also possible to see the tremendous value to the public of releasing telecommunication technology from the grip of this group.

The next logical extension is direct public access to the global telecommunications network. At this writing, a T1 signal (minimum service capability required for two-way video or ISDN) connecting Los Angeles with London via satellite is priced at nearly $2000 per hour. This pricing structure is the result of yet another monopoly—Intelsat. Given the level of communication that we require for the care and feeding of people and the maintenance of peace as populations grow, we can no longer afford to be hampered by such feudal philosophies as monopolies like Intelsat represent.

5

The Public Telecommunications Utility

PUBLIC SUBSIDIZATION OF TELECOMMUNICATION SERVICES

The granting to a corporation of monopoly control for an entire industry as a means of protecting and supporting development of a public service has proven counterproductive in the long run. In hindsight, we can see several reasons for this. The primary reason is that in the day-to-day realities of business, the economic priorities of a privately owned public utility are motivated by a drive to increase profits, even if this is not in the interests of the public.

We are now entering a new era in telecommunications. With microprocessor-controlled transmitters and receivers, we soon may be able to have telephone service with a virtually wireless local network. We will still use fiber cable to interconnect points with high-volume traffic, such as between localities and regions. We will be able to carry voice, video, and computer signals within the same system. We are approaching a time when the user's terminal will become the most intelligent and sophisticated part of the telecommunications network and will determine the kind of services to which the user can have access. For this reason, telecommunications service providers will soon be concerned with managing a more sophisticated array of services tailored to fit the needs of a smaller number of users who represent a vertical market segment within the total industry.

The vertical marketing scenario does not require a monolithic telecommunications company. With modern technologies, in a competitive telecommunications market, very small-scale operations (such as a shared service for a campus or single building) can provide services to relatively small groups of users and offer more benefits and less cost because of economies of scale. Larger scale operations can produce no greater benefits for the user. There is no longer a justification called "the natural monopoly." Present advances in telecommunications technology have been available for many years. It is a moot point whether there ever was any justification for the Bell monopoly. It is important to understand how the present situation developed so that plans for future development will be based on the subtle realities of technology and the needs of society.

BACKGROUND OF BELL SYSTEM POLICIES

Dating from January 1900, the archives show that the expressed position of the Bell System companies has been to use whatever means are available to accomplish their ends regarding absolute control of the market. This company began by forcing competing franchisees out of business and has continued through several decades to pervasively invade industrial territory and to attempt to exclude all others from participation. In the 1940s, the policies of AT&T led to an antitrust action against the Western Electric subsidiary regarding its presence in the film industry, and the result was the limitation of AT&T to the telephone business in 1956. In the 1960s, AT&T attempted to exclude others from CATV, and in 1968, the Carterfone decision was the result of the Bell System's attempt to keep others from selling telephone equipment that connected to the telephone network. A lawsuit, settled very recently, began in the 1970s as the result of predatory practices intended to restrict MCI's entrance into the telephone business. In 1984, by settlement decree, the Bell System has been artificially separated into supposedly financially independent parts. This enforced separation is regarded by AT&T insiders as just another skirmish in their battle to incorporate 100 percent of the market share. Depending on whose figures are used, 2 years after divestiture AT&T still controls between 85 and 95 percent of the long-distance revenue market.

THE RESULTS OF MONOPOLY CONTROL ON TECHNOLOGY AND SERVICE

It is the nature of monopoly operations that management decisions are dominated by the need to conserve the monopoly and increase profits, even if this means a decrease in the quality of service. Many problems we are now experiencing in the implementation of high-speed digital communication are the result of the way the Bell System monopoly artificially restricted the implementation of technologies essential for the public benefit in order to protect its monopoly and increase profits.

Decisions to restrict the flow of newer technologies to the public have been wise decisions for management to make, relative to corporate policy, which management is obligated to uphold. The problem is therefore not caused by faulty management by the monopoly. It is a flaw directly attributable to the priorities of monopoly operation as conceived by Theodore Vail and his associates and carried out over several decades. Like a political dictatorship, a monopoly places power in the hands of a privileged group, and the results depend entirely on the character and wishes of this group. The history of lawsuits and antitrust activity associated with the Bell System provides a clear demonstration of the problem. If the leadership of the Bell System could be relied on to view competition with good will and seek to reduce market share in favor of better consumer economics, we could expect different results than we have seen. Such an expectation is ludicrous.

We need to analyze conditions realistically and admit that it is not possible for the public to exercise control over a monopoly operation with much success, even when the public owns the monopoly. We need to address afresh the issues about public utilities directly and develop regulatory procedures that are consistent with the realities of state-of-the-art-technologies and the needs of individuals and communities. The fact is that much more technology is available today—and with far greater economies—than is at present being offered by the established telephone utilities.

WHAT IS A PUBLIC UTILITY?

Granting monopoly privileges to a private company for the purpose of providing a "public service" is tantamount to public subsidization of business. Businesses which qualify by dint of offering basic services have acquired the status of a "public utility." That name places a business in a protected category whereby the company is granted a franchise to operate in a geographical territory safe from competition. The logic used to justify the practice of awarding exclusive franchises is that there is a need for standardization of service. When electrical and telephonic technologies were in their infancy, the issue of standardization was perceived as a major difficulty. People had nightmares of multiple competing wiring schemes weaving the sky in urban areas into black and ugly webs.

By now, we have mastered telecommunications technologies to the extent that we can determine standards to allow the best possibilities for future development and efficiency. We have technologies today that use visual and infrared light, radio signals, and other techniques for signal transmission while software-defined systems can be arranged to define systems, direct calls, and limit access with little difficulty. It is a new ball game.

THE STATE PUBLIC UTILITIES COMMISSION

Whenever the public subsidizes an activity, it becomes the lot of the bureaucracy to ensure that the subsidy is used on behalf of the public. The Public Utilities Commission (PUC) was conceived to evaluate the status of public utility operations and to determine whether rates, profits, and levels of service are fair.

Since any profit-motivated business must subordinate criteria about public benefit to criteria about profits, it is fair to assume that the job of the PUC and the public utilities negotiators becomes mutually antagonistic. Given that all the information the PUC has about the operations of the utility is generated by the utility, the process of rate evaluation has come to be regarded as lamentably inconsistent and unreliable. As a result, for many years people have felt that, regarding rates, they had to take what they got and like it, because that was all there was. People were not very happy with this situation; since 1984, they have shown their willingness to support the alternatives made possible by divestiture of the monopoly, even when there are risks involved.

DEREGULATION AND THE MONOPOLY

Despite divesture, a de facto telephone monopoly remains in operation. Start-up costs for new telecommunications companies are not the major obstacle to development of new service companies. The major difficulty is building a subscriber base for a new network that is large enough to distribute costs sufficiently to produce profitable services at low enough rates. This in itself is not an insurmountable problem. One of the major difficulties at this time is the state regulators' ambiguous stand regarding certain issues the resolution of which could severely hamper or tremendously support entrepreneurism in the field of telecommunications. For instance, small local companies could do very well if they were able to compete freely for the user's business by offering a total range of services without having, by regulation, to depend on the local Bell or other operating unit or to charge an artificially set cost for a service. Investors in start-up companies are also threatened by the fact that the multibillion-dollar Bell system has displayed methods of competing which are heavy-handed.

THE HIGH COST OF THE MONOPOLY

There are three significant reasons why state regulators need to focus on entirely new regulatory schemes and to support the retirement of the system of monopolistic operation of public telecommunications utilities. The monopoly has proved to be a handicap to the development of telecommunications technology, but there are even stronger reasons to be considered related to the affordability of service. The first has already been described above: the Bell System slowed the development of new technologies in order to profit even if at the public expense.

The second reason is more significant. There is no way that a small state agency could hope to regulate just one utility company, let alone two or several. Only a very knowledgeable and enormously efficient regulatory organization could hope to be effective in dealing with the pricing of complex telecommunications services. The result has been that rather than lower rates as technology costs were lowered, telephone companies operated without concern for expense and simply requested rate increases to cover expanding operating costs. The regulatory organization capable of keeping tabs on just one telephone company with a few thousand subscribers would require a supercomputer with expert system software capable of rendering moment-to-moment decisions about communications traffic patterns. This is because telephone companies are able to make substantial charges for calls outside what is called a local dialing area. Thus, even though the so-called basic service rate is kept to a minimum, the calling patterns of most families and small businesses require extensive use of measured rate services within a local geographic area.

An insidious reminder of this fact is the Bell operating companies' recent attempts to have tariffs approved to allow limiting the number of free calls available for "life-line" or basic rate service to 130 each month. It would take a detailed analysis of the calling patterns of individuals in local areas to accurately determine the fairness of the local calling area districting. However, it can be assumed that the Bell operating company is striving to arrange rate structures to maximize income. The personnel necessary to program a system for the necessary analysis could be found among the brightest stars in the telecommunications firmament, but they and the requisite software would cost the state far more than the PUC budgets allow.

The third reason for retiring the concept of protected franchise monopolies suggests the direction which public telecommunications regulation must take in order to chart a course away from the futile attempts at regulating monopolies. This has to do with the establishment of technical standards. Through the establishment of specific technical standards, the public can be assured of universal service in a much more manageable fashion. Because of the nature of state-of-the-art telecommunications technologies, it is possible for the public to be given access to local telecommunications capability at prices which are low relative to the charges we have been used to paying. In such an environment, telecommunications service providers can be free to compete without regulation for the more sophisticated service market. In this kind of market, there is no advantage to giant size; given equal access to a competitive range of long-distance carriers, the real values of local technology support groups would allow them to compete favorably against the national marketing orientation of larger corporations.

IS THERE A NEED FOR PUBLIC SUBSIDIZATION OF COMPETING UTILITIES?

The difficulties and problems associated with initiating the cycle of business for new telecommunications services such as affordable two-way video transmission indicate a possible need for some form of subsidization of competitive services. Without guarantees of exclusive ownership of a utility, it is difficult to interest investors in a business where there has never before been competition.

Were states to support signal transmission highways in the same manner as we presently support automobile highway construction, no further need for subsidization would arise. If standards were set within urban communities and the nation, specifying the nature of signals to be used for various communications services, companies that manufacture and support terminal, switching, and program production equipment would find a rapidly expanding market and continue to advance the state of the art for many new telecommunications technologies.

The blessings of software-defined techniques make it possible for a state agency to deal with the construction and maintenance of communication channels as we now deal with the building and maintenance of highways. Licensing vehicles for transportation on publicly owned thoroughfares is a more complex job than assigning bandwidth rights on a fiber optic cable system. This is not an esoteric or idealistic thought but a compelling argument on behalf of public welfare that state governments may take more responsibility for living in the age of electronic information management. People who are themselves intimidated by high technology presume that a state might complicate the management of high-technology utilities. Such fears are groundless. It is the natural simplicity and reliability of telecommunications technology which has made possible the enormous growth of the Bell System and not the possession by AT&T of employees and management with higher than average intelligence or ability.

PRIORITIES OF GOVERNMENT—THE ISSUE OF SUBSIDIZATION

The most important source of public subsidization of U.S. technological development has been motivated by the needs for economic growth and defense. Defense Department contracts have been *crucial* to the development of aviation, satellites, computers, television, and other technologies. The development of resources that are considered to be of strategic importance, such as highways, popular education, housing, hydroelectric power, and petroleum, have all been supported by both direct and indirect forms of local, state and federal (tax benefits) subsidies. In any of these cases, there has been an argument of emergent need sufficient to justify the use of public funds.

TELECOMMUNICATIONS DEVELOPMENT IS ESSENTIAL FOR ECONOMIC GROWTH

If growth of the economy is justifiably an urgent need, it is apparent that communities increasingly need to support trade with businesses in other communities and other nations. To support economic growth in the emerging world markets, we will need to develop, as rapidly as possible, the means of communicating from small, local businesses directly into the international market for our goods and services. And we will also need to develop more efficiency and cost-effectiveness in producing and managing services of all kinds. Not only is information management a service we may be able to sell to others, but our own implementation of state-of-the-art information management technology is crucial to economic growth.

IT IS NOT A FEDERAL PROBLEM

For a number of reasons, we should not now look to the federal government for solutions to our local problems of economic growth. Local problems require local control. The federal government has its own problems. As an example, government use of computer-assisted audit procedures has revealed enormously expensive abuses by both the Pentagon and defense contractors that have virtually destroyed the public trust in these institutions. Public opinion is likely to become more critical of federal government spending policy as the financial impact is felt of the $340 billion of loans we have made for military assistance of "developing nations," and the depletion of social security funds for the purchase of war bonds during the Vietnamese War.

LOCAL SUBSIDIZATION AND CONTROL

As an alternative to federal subsidy for technologies of public benefit, a combination of business interests coupled with local government subsidies can result in substantial new technology implementation. For example, a city might work with land-use planners to develop commercial centers supported by state-of-the-art services. This approach was tried recently in a high-technology building development in Virginia and in a development project called Teleport, which involved the Port Authority of New York and New Jersey, New York Telephone, and a commercial development company. Other alternatives include awarding local franchises to small local firms to operate specialized telecommunications services in urban areas in direct competition with established cable and telephone companies.

VIDEO TELEPHONE TECHNOLOGY, A GUIDE TO THE FUTURE

The promise of video telephone technology has been cited in this discussion because it has recognizable and immediate applications in such activities as the management of police work, court department work, hospital services, medical conferences, and polling activities of all kinds. The economic advantages offered by two-way video communications services exist because of increased opportunities for trade and commerce, design and development, library and archival access, education, and even psychotherapeutic applications. The technology opens possibilities which are unexpected. Video telephone service will reshape every aspect of civilization including mass media, political accountability and business. The technology for affordable transmission of two-way video signals have many practical applications. This is because the transmission technologies for two-way video require a bandwidth which is also suitable for digital transmission. There are literally hundreds of technologies which are too expensive for most firms to purchase and support, but which could be shared by groups of users who could use intelligent terminals to communicate with a central facility operating on a high-speed digital network.

THE NEED FOR LOCAL SUPPORT OF TECHNOLOGIES

Digital signals have very naturally become a kind of de facto standard. Digital signals are inherently simple, consisting of two operating levels equivalent to 1 or 0. Through the logic of the binary numbering system, a series of 1s and 0s can become code for any kind of a statement. Since all digital signals are alike in this respect, we have created not only the possibility of a planetary language system but also the means by which any language may be translated into any other language. The result of this is that the use of digital signals to transmit voice, video, and data is changing the economic geography of the world. More advanced means of communication, for example, the simultaneous transmission of voice, picture, and data signals, are becoming necessary to the development of local trade and development opportunities. Yet the need for technical support for the use of such technologies is experienced locally, where the signals originate.

Because of the complex and specialized nature of data-processing and telecommunications technologies, the installation of data communications systems creates a need for local technical support personnel. A key to high-technology implementation is the availability of highly responsive local support to install, maintain, and assist in the operation of customer-tailored, sophisticated facilities:

- A business needs to be able to support its staff with adequate engineering and educational assistance.
- Telecommunications and digital information-processing and terminal equipment require day-to-day maintenance management in order to guarantee reliable service through peak-load periods.

The current and future requirements of businesses make clear the need for highly skilled local technical support personnel for telecommunications services. The growth of the telecommunications services industry depends on the availability of a base of efficiently managed, well-trained professional support personnel.

THE NEED FOR TELECOMMUNICATIONS UTILITIES TO BE LOYAL TO THE SUBSCRIBER

In theory, AT&T and the Bell operating companies should have the advantage when it comes to training high-technology service personnel. However these firms are restricting themselves because of the self-serving priorities of their corporate structures. To compete with more cost-effective, smaller firms, these companies will have to greatly improve the sensitivity of their user policies.

Subscribers to highly sophisticated business services have to invite the telecommunications and computer technicians into the hearts of their businesses. The technicians become privy to trade secrets and private financial information. Service professionals must consult with executives, managers, and business owners and be cognizant of their concerns. It is arguable that smaller local concerns can provide a more vital, concentrated, and personal relationship with customers. This is particularly true in connecting local customers with wider network services, where accountability must be to the user rather than the provider and where there is opportunity to provide more cost-effective technology by dynamically choosing between different vendors.

Subscribers to advanced telecommunications services will always require engineering support in order to effectively utilize such capabilities as packet-switching networks, optical fiber transmission, and the kinds of services which can be purchased from long-haul carriers (MCI-SBS, GTE-Sprint, etc.) and packet networks (GTE-Telenet, ITT, and others). Users wishing to implement new information management technologies will also need local support in their access to wider area transmission facilities and to other telecommunications, computer-driven, and data-processing services.

Support by a staff of in-house data processing or telecommunications specialists is too expensive an alternative for most firms. Telecommunications consultants may be hired to help purchase, install, and stabilize a system, but a telecommunications system often needs to be tuned, modified, or corrected. An optimal solution is a local network staff acting as a value-added service to users. Since the Bell operating companies are committed to proprietary scenarios and have substantial overhead costs, this level of support may be provided most cost-effectively by smaller, leaner organizations that are able to be more loyal to the customer. The comparatively small size of a local community network, as contrasted with the wider distribution responsibilities of local telephone companies and long-haul carriers, provides a more conveniently manageable environment for supporting a broader range of technologies and services which will be in growing demand; these include sending high-speed data, interactive video, and voice messages.

One argument often used in favor of shared tenant services (discussed in detail in Chapters 7 and 8) is that shared tenant service (STS) customers can benefit from the economies of scale created by sharing the expanded technical and management expertise of an STS provider. The STS can also be more responsive to users' needs and is free to purchase technology and services from the offerings of a number of interconnect and service companies such as Northern Telecom, IBM-Rolm, Xerox, Siemens, Burroughs, Erickson, Fujitsu, Grass Valley, Nippon Electric (NEC), United Telecom, Allnet, DEC, MCI-SBS, ITT, and many others. The lower overhead costs of small local operations can make community integrated service digital networks (ISDN) affordable for individual homes and small businesses.

TECHNOLOGY DEVELOPMENT—THE NEED FOR LOCAL FIBER NETWORKS

The technologies for transmission of signals and for telephone, data, and video call management have changed more during the past 5 years than in all of the previous 50 years combined. The technology in current use represents the most cost-effective compromise involving the minimum possible investment in user-owned equipment coupled with use of telephone company "public switched" facilities. Observation of the technological capability under development makes it possible to predict the direction in which telecommunications should be heading. Within 10 years subscribers should have access to video telephone and advanced digital services by direct connection to fiber optic cables, by entering the system through dial-up connections from the local telephone company, or through access from shared PBX, microwave, radio diffusion, or satellite facilities.

FORECASTING COMMUNITY TELECOMMUNICATIONS NEEDS

To forecast development for a particular locality or industry, it is necessary to start with a set of wish lists representing the goals of the most interested parties including: (1) the body of corporate users, (2) the larger body of small- to medium-size commercial users, (3) the largest body, residential users, (4) the regional organization of local area telephone companies, (5) the body of long-haul carriers, except AT&T, (6) AT&T, (7) local government users, (8) the Department of Defense, (9) other federal government users, (10) the manufacturers of interconnect and telecommunications network equipment and software, (11) the manufacturers of computer equipment and software, and (12) other categories of business and government which are concentrated in the study area (such as media, manufacturing, high technology, entertainment, publishing, and agribusiness).

INTEGRATION OF OFFICE AUTOMATION SERVICES AND EQUIPMENT

The need for high-bandwidth transmission services for local transmission has been recognized by all technology manufacturers. Business activities already require integration of several office automation technologies. This requirement has been motivating major technology vendors toward design strategies for networked computer systems, software compatible with that of other manufacturers, and manufacture of machines that communicate directly with other machines. This trend enhances business opportunities for local networks that support a broad range of transmission speed requirements and bandwidth capability. The transmission media for such services must provide very high-speed, reliable transmission. Because of the problems of atmospheric interference and security, these characteristics are at present best met by optical fiber transmission.

The existing market for new state-of-the-art telecommunications service companies falls into two principal categories: larger companies (*Fortune* 1000) that require interconnection of their own facilities, and small- to medium-size firms that can benefit from the shared use of technological support systems for communications and data-processing services which they otherwise could not afford.

Many users of local fiber optic networks are already operating their own local area networks (LAN); they have a need to extend the use of on-line network facilities into remote sites. Most LAN users now rely on expensive and inefficiently slow public switched network lines to communicate between remote locations. A typical example of this can be seen in the computer time-sharing services that are provided to users on a dial-up basis to telephone network subscribers. Dial-up computer services currently must operate at 1200 to 9600 b/s. The telephone networks propose to increase this rate to a maximum of 56,000 b/s, which is still far too slow when one considers that state-of-the-art computers are now operating at speeds of 17 billion decisions per second, and even microprocessor-driven personal computers can handle rates in the megabit range.

Given a high-speed data link, equipment for many useful business automation applications is suitable for time-sharing with substantial cost savings for users. A small, local business communications network can offer highly specialized services tailored to the needs of businesses in the community as well as more cost-effective connection to long-distance and packet-switching networks.

QUANTIFYING THE SMALL-BUSINESS COMMUNICATIONS MARKET

The demand in any community for intensively supported small- to medium-size business communications services can be calculated by studying installed telephone company lines and telephone costs for representative companies within a locality. Such information is not to be expected freely from Bell, so that market surveys are the best source of this information. The information gained from a market survey would be vulnerable to two kinds of weakness: (1) many services which could be offered via an optical fiber network, such as low-cost interactive video transmission, will create entirely new markets that cannot as yet be quantified; (2) many costly methods of communication will be made obsolete by new technology (these include trips for meetings and presentations that could be eliminated by low-cost video and digital transmission of graphic material). However, projected demand for new services can be estimated from an appropriately designed survey. Information culled from surveys could help define an initial service offering of high technology communications.

In several cities (Chicago, Washington, D.C., Los Angeles) pilot business communication service projects are now being initiated to serve a small group of representative users of business and data link services. The market for these new start-ups has been quantified through three methods:

- Surveys and personal interviews with telecommunications or information service managers of representative organizations in the community
- Compilation of statistics available from the transportation-related studies conducted by the city, county, state, and regional quasi-governmental agencies
- Analysis of records of service charges paid by local firms to the

telephone company over a period of time in terms of the types of services used

The list below has been divided into three categories of typical users who can benefit from having access to an alternative business communications service: corporate clients, public sector organizations, and multiuser services.

1. Private sector commercial clients
   a. Banks and financial institutions
   b. Insurance companies
   c. Energy companies and utilities
   d. High-technology and software manufacturers
   e. Real estate development firms
   f. Sports and entertainment organizations
   g. Mass media broadcasters and producers
   h. Architectural and manufacturing design firms
   i. Medical service companies and hospitals
   j. Research and educational institutions
   k. Telecommunications companies
   l. Food service companies
   m. Transportation companies
   n. Import/export firms

2. Public sector organizations
   a. City, county and state agencies
   b. Educational facilities
   c. Legislative organizations
   d. Judicial activities
   e. Police and regulatory activities
   f. Halls of records and clerical services

3. Multiuser services
   a. Intelligent building services
   b. Business support shared services—electronic printing, data processing, training and education, and office support services

SERVICE OFFERINGS OF LOCAL SUPPORT NETWORKS

Services that can be made available to users of a local business communications network include a great deal of technological support. Services can be made available now using existing technologies: point-to-point transmission, T1–T4 graded services, and packet-switched X.25 transmission services.

POINT-TO-POINT TRANSMISSION

The term "point-to-point" refers to a service which connects two distinct geographical locations for voice, video, or data communications. This kind of service is distinct from "switched" services (which connect users with a central switching exchange through which the user's signal can then be routed to another subscriber or station on the network) and from "broadcast" services (which connect a user to a general broadcast signal-transmitting facility).

Point-to-point service has several values: The transmission speeds and formats can fit the user's specific requirements, with little or no need for modification of signals by the carrier system. Transmission quality is not affected by ambient conditions caused by other users. Security of transmissions is assurable providing that the transmission medium is itself secure. Users can more easily utilize the protocols of their own proprietary local area network software. Equipment and maintenance cost for transmission per bandwidth circuit–mile is relatively low. Sufficient bandwidth on fiber optic cables can accommodate simultaneous two-way video, multiplexed voice, and data transmission rates at speeds with which state-of-the-art systems can process data in real time.

Typical users of point-to-point services include:

- Banking institutions with data-processing centers at one location and branches or administrative offices at other locations
- Retail chain operations with data-processing and management functions in one location and remote pollable point-of-sale cash receipt and inventory-reporting stations
- Real estate brokering companies with central data-processing facilities for mortgage and loan evaluation and placement
- Telecommunications long-distance resale services for direct connection between subscribers and bypass technologies such as satellite uplink and terrestrial microwave
- Medical management organizations to provide health care facilities with records processing and remote access to hospital or laboratory analysis procedures, records, and reports
- Mass media producing and broadcasting firms that require wide-bandwidth one-way or two-way single channel or multichannel transmis-

sion facilities between program production and origination facilities and satellite uplink or local cable distribution locations

- Database resource and computer time-sharing service firms that require high-security dedicated circuits between processing locations and their customers' premises. This area includes many types of services which could be made possible through the economical use of a fiber optic data highway. These include electronic printing services, shared tenant services, building and property management services, business financial and banking services, high-technology computer-aided design, and engineering services.
- Telemarketing firms utilizing 800 or 900 dial-up services on the public network

T1–T4 GRADED SERVICES

T1, T2, T3, and T4 refer to AT&T adopted standard rates of transmission speed for digital information in terms of bits per second. T1 is the only standard available to subscribers at the time of this writing. Only T1 is available from local telephone companies direct to users' premises. It is equivalent to 1.544 Mb/s. State-of-the-art AT&T and local telephone services further divide the T1 channel into 24 subchannels of 64,000 b/s each, with 8000 b/s reserved for control signaling. This limits the rate of switched services to 56 kb/s, and sets the tariff for T1 as a multiple of twenty-four 56-kb channels. T2, T3, and T4 standards have been established as 6.312 Mb/s, 45 Mb/s and 274 Mb/s, respectively. These transmission rates are utilized only at present for transporting large volumes of multiplexed signals between distant points. There are also European standard rates of transmission which differ from the American standards. Typical users of T1–T4 services include:

- Users with PBX equipment can have a T1 connection to wider area networks and can multiplex simultaneous voice and/or data conversations for T1 transmission between very remote facilities, producing favorable economy
- A low-cost two-way video circuit can be made available on the public switched network utilizing T1 service

Many of the users listed under the heading Point-to-Point Transmission, above, could utilize T1 and other transmission techniques for differing purposes. Rather than repeat this information, only the kinds of activities that exemplify a new use are listed following each of these new service headings:

- Shared tenant services in "intelligent buildings"
- Users requiring high-volume multiple voice line connections between two or more points on the network (e.g., stock and commodity exchanges and brokerages)
- Users in campus types of locations (e.g., medical, judicial, governmental, educational facilities, and film studios) who could benefit from a multiplexed direct connection with long-distance carriers

PACKET-SWITCHED, X.25 TRANSMISSION SERVICES

Packet switching, described more fully in the previous chapter, is a data communication technique. Data to be transmitted is packaged in self-addressed bit streams, and the packets are sent out over a telephone network like electronic railroad trains. The address information, included in the packet, cues switches along the way so that the packet eventually finds its way to the recipient computer. The address of the packet also contains the sequence number of the packet so that the recipient computer can put all the packets together in the right order.

The advantage of using packet switching on the public telephone and long-haul networks is that the user is only charged for the actual time it takes to transmit packets of data, and not for conversational waiting periods. This is somewhat analogous to being charged only for the time you are talking on a voice telephone and not for the time when you may be listening or waiting for a reply. Many kinds of businesses can benefit from packet switching. They include banks, savings and loan and other financial associations, stock brokerage firms, news retrieval services, chain stores with electronic cash registers, catalog sales companies, credit card verification services, reservation services for airlines, hotels, and car rentals.

"X.25" refers to international standards for transmission of digital information in packet form which have been established by the International Telephone and Telegraph Consultative Committee (CCITT). The X.25 standard describes packets of a standard size and form as well as the standards for packet identification. Standardized packet transmission makes possible the interleaving and switching of packets from various users having varying equipment. This allows users to send and receive data to one another using standard dial-up lines of their local or long-haul telephone network.

To access packet service, users must have a high-speed connection between their own premises and the public switched data network exchange. The X.25 protocols allow users to easily, reliably, and trans-parently network computer systems in remote locations. The drawback of packet switching is that it cannot support voice or video communications and thus does not lend itself to ISDN support. The speed of packet switching is now limited by the 64,000-b/s limitation of telephone line channel capacity, of which 8000 b/s is reserved for control frequencies. The technology is capable of much higher speeds.

Typical users of X.25 networks include:

- Firms or public sector organizations which have remote locations with each location running a local computer system
- Travel, airline, and other reservation systems
- Firms or individuals that can benefit by sharing access to an X.25 packer access device (PAD), such as database resource services, libraries, batch processors, polling and accounting management services, and the accounting departments of large businesses

LOCAL AREA NETWORK SUPPORT

Local area networks (LANs) are described in greater detail in Chapter 6. Local area networks are most typically used as a strategy to interconnect users in a building or campus environment. The medium for transmission in a LAN can be anything from twisted-wire pairs to fiber optic cable. Most LANs can still have the drawback of not accommodating voice or video transmissions and requiring expensive gateways into the public switched network in order to communicate with users with terminals located outside the building. A local business communications network could effectively carry traffic between subscribers' LANs as well as providing the protocol conversion for integration with public network services. Applicable volume-discounted long-distance services can be supplied to LANs. With the implementation of direct network satellite uplink service, long-distance point-to-point, a range of local and long-distance services may also be made available in support of proprietary LANs, providing data transmission rates much higher than those offered through public switched services.

The advantages include high-speed, high-volume transmission services that may be offered to customers in place of the less efficient 56K b/s services of the telephone company; high-speed, high-volume connections can be brought to local network subscribers with less lead time, more economically, and on a transaction pricing basis.

Examples of typical users are:

- Larger organizations requiring the set-up and operation of proprietary networks in local buildings, with a need for communication between local and long-distance facilities

- Low volume subscribers who can benefit from volume-discounted service rates for extended distance services
- Date-processing and time-sharing services. Bandwidth on fiber optic cable may be allocated for communicating to and from a set of computers running software for many common business activities, ranging from word processing to relatively sophisticated accounting, records-filing, and other programs. Network subscribers could have the option to utilize these programs on a pay-for-use basis
- Firms which are organized to provide specialized data-processing and database services, such as ticket reservation, home banking, direct mail, and electronic printing services.
- Firms which provide software and support for business management and office automation services such as accounting and tax consultants, shared tenant services, property management, real estate listing, and loan processing
- Very small firms or individuals with little or no staff to carry out routine business activities, such as independently practicing professionals

CUSTOMER PREMISES EQUIPMENT SUPPORT

All of the services listed above require some kind of equipment installed on the customer's premises for utilization of a service. The cost of equipment on the customer's premises may be either calculated into transaction pricing, as for instance, is typical when providing a point-to-point communication service, or sold or leased to the user, as in the example of providing a data-processing and telecommunication workstation.

MAINTENANCE AND MANAGEMENT OF TECHNOLOGY

There are many arguments in favor of reducing the size of telecommunications networks in order to increase the service offerings of local telecommunications networks. Many high-technology service businesses could benefit from smaller, more intensively supported local telecommunications services. The favorableness of this is being demonstrated in the successful implementation of shared tenant service (STS) operations. In addition, businesses which are small and cannot afford to maintain specialized information technology technical staff are the most likely to benefit. (The use of state-of-the-art systems requires a staff which is not only familiar with installed systems but able to quickly adjust to rapidly changing technologies.) Businesses are becoming highly dependent on the quality and constancy of telecommunications technology support staff. A local network can provide management services so that subscribers need pay little attention to the maintenance of technologies.

Users of sophisticated, highly specialized technologies that require specialized support staff can benefit by subscribing to a local network that offers a technology support service. A bank, for instance, may own a relatively large mainframe system and may wish to integrate new technology such as new laser scanning devices for storing and accessing graphic images of transaction documents. The technologies involved in this will be distinctly different from the technologies for managing the information as it is contained in the mainframe environment. Existing personnel would not have the expertise needed for implementing the new technology. The software in the mainframe would not be amenable to modifications, and there would be a necessity for retraining of personnel.

Larger firms operating proprietary LANs could also benefit. In a LAN, information flows between users connected to the system and between computers and computer-driven machines that are connected to the system. In a local fiber optic network, bandwidth on fiber cable can be allocated to baseband applications (see Chapter 6) to provide a virtual extension of a firm's LAN to include information processors located at different remote locations. With protocol conversion, this service could be extended to support communications with processors outside the net, accessed through the public switched or packet-switched network. The potential users for such services include financial organizations, brokerages, electronic publishing companies, data retrieval services (credit reporting), and police agencies.

LOCAL VIDEO TELECONFERENCE AND BROADCAST SUPPORT

Video teleconferencing and other applications of two-way video can provide relief from the expense and time of much local traveling. At this time, the cost of transmission services for video conferencing is so high that there is virtually no demand for local applications. Were the cost of this service to become realistically competitive with the time and expense of physical travel, most businesses could benefit from graphic and image transmission services as well as teleconference.

Video teleconferencing and transmission requires a wide bandwidth transmission service, especially for commercial service applications. The public telephone network is approaching this problem by converting video signals to a digital format and packetizing the digital code on 56 kb/s channels within T1 lines; the packets are then transmitted through the public network at 1.544 Mb/s and switched as a collection of 56 kb/s channels. This situation has so far limited the growth of video conferences and other two-way video transmissions. T1 (1.544 Mb/s) lines are also not readily available. The process of digitizing video and utilization of 56 kb/s channels is very awkward, especially when one considers that analog TV signals, carried on fiber optic cable, can be efficiently switched by technology already available for analog signal switching. A local network could effectively allocate bandwidth to switched signals, whereas the public telephone networks need to be concerned with the limitation of signals so they are compatible with an embedded base of voice quality technology over a large domain. A more local network could provide local two-way video services to users immediately and could—via satellite transmission, terrestrial microwave, coaxial cable, and long-haul fiber—eventually extend long-distance ISDN services.

LOCAL POLLING OF DATA

An increased facility for data transmissions in a local, high-bandwidth network makes feasible many management and monitoring activities which at present require periodic polling of information. This facility comes into play whenever a person within a company periodically needs to ask another person within a company for information which could, alternatively, be sent in the form of automatically polled reports by a computer. Such a facility increases productivity by reducing the need for utilizing personnel time. It also reduces the load on the voice communications system, thus saving in costs for service and equipment.

PBX—VOICE-RELATED SERVICES

Voice mail is typical of recently developed new applications available as a result of the integration of telephony with computer services. It is representative of new voice-related technologies which take advantage of emerging PBX electronics and lowering of hardware costs associated with microminiaturization of telecommunications control equipment and circuitry. Voice mail allows an individual to leave or receive a voice message for one or more people. In the most sophisticated systems, a computer-driven device periodically redials the called party until the message is delivered or responded to. Most programs provide for response or acknowledgment to be recorded and transmitted back to the message originator.

COMPETITION AND THE PRICING OF TELECOMMUNICATION SERVICES

The intention of divestiture was to allow development of competitive telecommunications services. Competition is not too meaningful if it does not translate to more or better service per dollar. A possible obstacle to free market telecommunications services is the identification by regulatory agencies of these services as a public utility, rather than just as a business using the bandwidth of cable or other transmission medium. Telephone operating companies now claim that since they have lost long-distance revenues, and can no longer cross-subsidize to maintain residential services, they should be protected from competition. Although it is difficult to present evidence to counter these claims without a thorough examination of telephone company procedures, few people who are knowledgeable about the technology involved would turn down the opportunity to relieve telephone companies of the responsibility of providing residential service in return for receiving the revenues involved. State-of-the-art telecommunication services are remarkably simple to maintain. The accounting systems for telecommunications are managed automatically by software, and there is nothing which is not proceduralized and manageable.

When the pricing strategy of telecommunications network services becomes more influenced by competitive service choices, businesses seeking to link remote facilities may conceivably demand a wider range of service choices. In addition to the technical problems of maintaining a network facility and the need to be concerned with technological upgrading, etc., the Bell operating companies and independent telephone exchange group will need to adjust their management to less arbitrary rate structures. The start-up service companies need to be protected from the Bell operating and independent telephone companies and this is the only current need for regulation. So far, in the shared tenant services arena, the telephone companies in most areas have tried to obstruct and interfere with the ability of entrepreneurs to pursue this market, though the STS service offerings of the telephone companies are not substantially different from the standard telephone service and represent no new benefits to the end user.

At this time, there are very few alternative telecommunications services other than private bypass networks (which have been very successful). Those that exist are too new to have produced any spectacular results. However, several very promising entrepreneurial projects are in development, and their success should lead the way for others. In theory, a wideband local network's facilities, like the shared tenant service's, should be more cost-effective to install and operate than the telephone company's hybrid mixture of part conventional twisted copper wire and electromechanical switches and part fiber optics and digital circuitry. There should be more efficiency in the total wideband network coupled with a reduced need for costly signal amplification equipment. The cost of installing conduit for new alternative ventures may also be mitigated by coventure contracts with CATV franchisees, power companies, and others for the joint use of conduit space and bandwidth on jointly used cables.

Pricing of telecommunications should eventually be based on return on investment over time, mitigated by competition. Given the lower overhead of more easily run, smaller organizations, pricing of alternative services should become more favorable in competition with the public switched telephone networks over the long run.

CHAPTER 6

Data Communications and Local Area Networks

IMPORTANCE OF DATA COMMUNICATION SERVICES

Development in the workplace and changes in job procedures parallel the evolution of computer processing technologies. Recently, new techniques for business management have been made possible by the evolution of communication between intelligent machines. These new techniques have both extended the usefulness of computer-driven machines to new areas of business and made it possible for the different departments of a business to work together on projects with more independence and reliability. Communications between the computers of different departments helped to make possible the expansion of large organizations in the 1970s.

The modern workplace is filled with intelligent machines that assist in carrying out day-to-day tasks. These include computer systems, telemetry devices, scanners, monitors, copiers, printers, plotters, terminals, telefacsimile machines, security devices, telephones, word processors, personal computers, and many other specialized workstations. With many different kinds of data-processing equipment being interconnected, the communications capabilities of the voice-oriented telephone system have been surpassed. Data communication within the local work environment has become essential. The demand for interactive communication between machines has led the way to new technologies for connecting systems together in what has come to be called a "local area network."

In order for groups of people in organizations to function as efficient and well-integrated members of a team, the machines on which they depend also need to communicate and exchange information quickly, easily, and reliably.

RATIONALE FOR COMPUTER COMMUNICATIONS

The databases, programs, files, and other information assets of a company are created, maintained, and refined at locations close to the production or business activity which generates the data. Most jobs have grown more sophisticated in their use of information management technology, which enables people to perform with more autonomy. In 1985, surveys concluded that 35 percent of employed people used computers in their jobs. More is being demanded from the information that workers need and more from the systems that deliver it to them.

Users at computer terminals, word-processing workstations, and personal computer workstations must now be able to routinely exchange data between terminals, send messages via electronic mail software, access common database files to input and manipulate data and generate reports, share application programs and other computer utilities such as storage devices (disk and tape drives, scanners, etc.) and output devices (copiers, high-speed printers, telefacsimile machines, graphics plotters, etc.) and exchange information with other local and remotely located parts of a job team.

THE NEED FOR LOCAL AREA NETWORKS

Local area networks were first implemented to allow people to perform their internal departmental jobs using intelligent terminals more effectively and to make better use of management. The LAN enhanced the communications within the department. The integrated departmental units allowed much quicker response to information needs in organizations and proved invaluable to the larger network to which the departmental job belonged.

EVOLUTION OF LANS

The evolution of modern-day LANs beyond the original departmental support concept can be understood by tracing the history of the earliest methods of networking and data communications. LAN development was motivated by the need for information exchange in local work environments. This was influenced by the evolution in the kinds of information that are exchanged.

Development of LAN technology for data communications closely paralleled the evolution of computer technology, in particular the growth of distributed processing techniques (see Chapter 3). Because of the demand for data communications of higher speed and reliability to support distributed processing, LAN engineering opened the door to many new developments in the telecommunications industry.

EARLY COMPUTERS—BATCH PROCESSING

The first computers were large, expensive, complicated machines requiring lots of power and special isolated rooms. They could be operated only by experts. They were expensive to maintain and support. In the 1950s, people who used computer services brought their jobs to the machine to be run in a batch. The information had been previously punched onto cards or paper tapes by data entry operators using card- or tape-punching machines. The cards—or stream of paper tape—were then fed into a computer's reading apparatus. The computer stored a program for a task, and as each card or tape record was read, the machine did a computation involving that transaction until all the records were processed. People did not interact directly with their programs while they were being run on the computers.

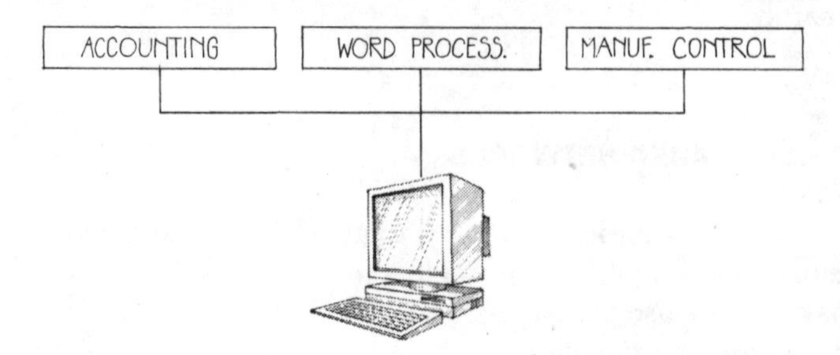

Figure 6.1 Multitask work stations require instantaneous access to several programs, databases, telecommunications, and other computer-driven utilities.

TIME-SHARING

It became common for a number of different users to run programs on the machines. They could be charged for the time during which they used the machine, and in that way shared the cost of maintaining the system. Each user brought the job to the machine as a stack of punched cards or a stream of paper tape, and the processing for all of each user's needs was done in a batch. There was no direct communication between the user and the computer.

TIME-SHARING USING INTERACTIVE TERMINALS

Interactive access to computers came about with the sophistication of time-sharing technology in the 1960s. "Time-sharing," in the computer field, refers to the way in which people could use time on a computer and pay for the cost of the time they used. Time-sharing allowed many people to use the same computer and benefit from it while sharing its cost. Batch processing with punched cards or paper tape was superseded by data entry on magnetic cards or tape coated with a metallic oxide similar to that used for sound-recording tape.

Soon, a means was developed for converting the digital signals to analog signals so that the electrical signals recorded on magnetic tape could also be communicated over telephone lines. Users with keyboards and video display screens, connected by dial-up telephone connections to a central computer facility, could type data directly into the computer system's active memory. Programs were then developed which gave the appearance that the user was in active conversation with the computer. Prompting questions would appear on the user's screen requesting the next required piece of information. Not only was it unnecessary for a computer data entry operator to have any knowledge about computers, but also, relatively untrained people could carry out complex jobs.

Soon the computer programs were operating in real time; each job was being done immediately in response to an operator's data entries. This kind of communications required the transfer of bursts of data back and forth between the computer and the user—referred to as "interactive" communication. Applications for interactive use of computers multiplied as computer programs became increasingly easier to use, or "friendlier." Engineers and scientists found they could use the central computer for complex computational problems; business managers could obtain status reports on key control measures of their businesses; educators could use the computer for automated training;

government agencies were assisted by the computer in everything from asset management to aerospace design. The expansion of the use of computers in all areas has been supported by a parallel development of telecommunications procedures, equipment, and software. Teletypewriter and data transmission technologies were combined to produce the so-called "interactive computer terminal."

COMMUNICATIONS WIRING STANDARDS

The typical interactive terminal consists of a standard typewriter keyboard and a video display screen. Initially, the interactive terminal was connected to the computer by a multistrand wire, the standard for which became the 16-strand wire "interface" adopted by the Electronic Industry Association (EIA)—the EIA RS232C connector. The RS232C standard is used to define the I/O bus (input/output function) wiring standard for interfacing computers with printers, terminals, and other devices. (The I/O bus on a computer is the mechanism within the computer for carrying data *into* its processing functions and back *out* to the terminal—see Chapter 3.) Each communications "port" on a computer consists of the circuitry and software for managing the conversation between an external device and the programs which the computer is running. The physical connector often uses the RS232C protocol for the interface with external devices (see Figure 6.2).

The operating system of the computer assigns priorities so that the

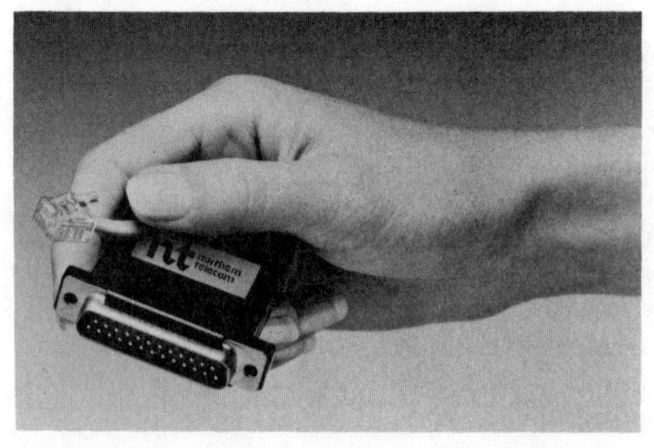

Figure 6.2 The most common physical interfaces for connecting computer-controlled devices are the 25-pin connector and the 4- or 6-wire modular telephone jack.

computer can quickly manage communications between a number of ports in sequence. In a situation where there may be several ports all contending for attention simultaneously, preset priorities can be determined so that certain programs will be done while others are waiting. Protocols for communication are established in software so that a computer can recognize the nature of requests and information it receives from each port and know which program to use in order to process it appropriately.

COMMUNICATIONS BOTTLENECKS—PORT CONTENTION

The use of the computer has expanded to include more and more jobs and greater numbers of users. In the process, the number of terminals contending for access to computer ports produced a bottleneck. Although the computers are very quick and able to process the requests of many more users, there are always a limited number of ports available. Multiplexing techniques were developed which allowed each port in the computer to manage communications with several users simultaneously. Through multiplexing, the signals from the terminals of many users can be sent to the computer on different frequencies. A computer can switch back and forth between frequencies quickly enough so that users will not experience a delay in the processing of their requests. This permits an even greater expansion of use and further development of new application programs. The bottleneck then moved into two new areas: one was the ability of the central processing unit (CPU) of the computer to handle the increased volume of requests, the other was the speed with which communications could be transmitted back and forth between the CPU and other parts of the computer system.

CPU OVERLOAD—"THE INTELLIGENT TERMINAL"

To help relieve the central computer of the burden of new requests, interactive terminals were developed that incorporated a degree of computing power on their own. Programs such as word processing could be off-loaded onto these "intelligent" terminals, leaving the central system free to manage other processes. This distribution of processing power was aided by the parallel development of microelectronic circuitry which miniaturized formerly cumbersome hardware into packages the size of a fingernail. This made possible the manufacture of very small and inexpensive workstations with substantial built-in processing capability. On their own, these terminals could manage record entry, financial calculations, word processing, and many other tasks such as monitoring a manufacturing, design, or laboratory procedure. When a task was completed, the operator could send completed data files or a report to the central system, where it would be included in files accessible to others in the organization for other purposes. This development changed the requirements of data communication from transmission of individual characters and short bursts of data to exchanges involving large volumes and whole files containing millions of bits of data.

THE PERSONAL COMPUTER SPIN-OFF

The development of the "personal computer" (PC) was a marketing spin-off of the technology for miniaturized circuitry and stand-alone processing capability. The personal computer contains all elements, in miniature form, of the largest computer system. In many situations, personal computers are used as a form of intelligent terminal. Depending on the job being done, or the "application," a computer user requires either a "smart" or a "dumb" terminal. The data transfer requirements between the terminal and the computer are much greater for smart terminals and personal computers than they are for the dumb terminal.

DISTRIBUTED PROCESSING—MINICOMPUTERS

The next step in the progress of interactive communication was a larger commitment to the concept of distributed processing. Instead of one large computer system running all the programs for an organization, smaller systems were designed to be dedicated to specific programs for the tasks of each department. Each of these systems can serve a cluster of interactive users, numbering in the tens or hundreds. A need then arose for some users to access programs running on the systems of other departments. Computer users are no longer computer specialists. They are not concerned with the technology behind their desktop workstations. It would have been difficult to implement systems if users had to know communications procedures to route their requests to the appropriate system for processing. Procedures for managing the exchange of information between computer systems had to be automated. Systems are now designed so that the user never needs to know how or where a task is being done or which computer is working to get the job done.

During the 1970s, versatile and inexpensive minicomputers became preferable to mainframe installations as users demanded computing power located close to the area in which the work was being performed. (Minicomputers are substantially large computer systems capable of running programs to manage calculations, word processing, accounting, and billing for a large business.) For a range of applications, minicomputer users are able to easily share files, programs, processing capability, data storage facilities (disk and tape drives), high-speed electronic printers, and other "peripheral" devices. In a distributed processing situation, using minicomputers, users often can easily exchange data across departments, as well as over long distances. A new and increased need for communications from computer to computer emerged with the intensive use of distributed minis. The data exchanges required more high-speed capacity than did the connection of dumb terminals to computers.

The most important argument for distributed processing on minicomputers is the difference in the design approach of minicomputer systems—the way in which programs are executed. Mainframes process whole screens of information. Minicomputers keep programs active and switch back and forth between users and programs so that the communication between users and programs happens with much quicker response times.

In many large organizations, distributed processing on minicomputers has been used to off-load the central mainframe. Rather than try to modify a large mainframe set-up, very often a corporation has established new applications on separate minicomputer systems. When connected to each other in a network, minicomputers can sometimes be used to entirely replace a central mainframe computer. By doing certain applications in specially assigned minicomputer units, minicomputer networks handle many distributed processing loads more economically than mainframes can. Collectively, a network of several minicomputers provides more interactive processing facility than the comparatively cumbersome techniques of mainframe computers.

The design of distributed processing networks is geared to individual jobs that make up the work environment. Minicomputers are placed where the work is being performed, with each processor serving a clearly defined job set. Neighbor processors and applications communicate via the network. The network can be expanded and reconfigured fairly easily to meet growing and changing needs. The modular nature of the network is such that failure in one part of the network has a very limited effect or no effect at all on the operation of the rest.

There are many reasons which explain why distributed processing grew to dominate the market for business-purpose computer-driven technologies. A very important one is that very few mainframe computer systems have been successfully implemented for business management. A system of programs which incorporates all departmental tasks and communications of a large organization is very difficult to design. Implementation of such a system requires simultaneous adoption by the entire organization of procedures which may be customary in some departments and totally foreign to others. Program modifications to correct errors or provide for new tasking for one department may disrupt the way another department uses the system.

The incremental implementation that is possible with distributed processing systems allows an orderly evolution of a business or other activity from manual, paper-based methods to the procedures of electronic data processing. Hardware and software tailored to the needs of each department can be separately implemented, allowing integration with the systems of other departments. People who actually use the systems can also become involved in system design as well as implementation. This is not a feature typical of larger systems. Many mainframe systems which have been attempted failed because, by the time they were put together, they were out-dated by changes in the jobs they were intended to serve or by the development of superior processing technologies. Others have failed because of the difficulty in modifying parts of large programs or because the implementation proved impossible to interface with personnel, with established office hierarchy, or with client relationships.

The demands of distributed processing—and the need to connect both smart and dumb terminals to computers for interactive processing—pointed the way to more sophisticated data communications techniques and the evolution of the local area network (LAN).

During the 1980s, the advantages of distributed processing and networking computer systems were recognized for office, factory, and laboratory environments. Network users were seen to gain commercial advantages from the efficiencies of sharing distributed resources—equipment, computational power, databases, and specialized software—which give them computing power equal to that obtainable from most mainframes. It is now commonplace for parts of distributed systems to be located where the job is being done, providing such services as data processing, database management, manufacturing process control, typesetting, word processing, and electronic mail. And it is commonplace for these distributed systems to communicate with one another over limited distances using a LAN. Longer-distance communications still primarily use standard long-haul telephone technology, provided by carriers such as GTE, MCI, and AT&T.

REQUIREMENTS FOR DATA COMMUNICATIONS

A substantial difference in the requirements for data communications and voice communications explains why the voice telephone network is not suitable for supporting data communications in local applications. Other than private long-haul systems, which only a few giant corporations can at present afford, there is no alternative to the use of telephone long-haul networks for long distances. Developments in currently available technology make it predictable that within a few years these networks will go through radical changes. There will be more lower-cost communications services available to users; these will be comparable to the services now available only on private networks.

ELEMENTS OF DIGITAL COMMUNICATION

Binary Bits

The building blocks of computer languages are binary bits of information. In a binary system, there are only two numbers: 0 and 1. All computer data can eventually be distilled to a series of 0s and 1s. The 0s are indicative of a switch *off* condition and the 1s indicate a switch *on* condition, within a circuit array.

Computer Words

A series of eight 0s and 1s makes up the smallest standard word of computer language. This series of eight 0s and 1s can be used as an equivalent symbol for a character of the alphabet, a number, or any kind of value. The sequence "01011011" may be a word of meaning to a computer program. The meaning is determined by the sequence in which the word is received and the software being run at the time. Word-processing software assigns a binary "word" value to each character of the alphabet, enabling the computer to store alphanumeric characters as a sequence of binary numerical equivalents. Thus, "01000111, 01001111, 01000111" spells DOG in the American Standard Code for Information Interchange (ASCII). If I wanted to send the message "dog" from one computer to another, I would need to transmit this streamof 0s and 1s, called bits, and include some other bits to indicate the order in which to read the bits and instructions that would reveal, among other things, where each binary word began and ended.

Alphanumeric Standard Codes

The above data communication example presupposes that the communicating computers are running the same software or using a common standard for sending alphanumeric code. The most prevalent standard for alphanumeric code is ASCII. In ASCII code, a specific numerical value is assigned to each alphabet character and function needed, including lowercase letters, uppercase letters, numbers, commonly used punctuation and mathematical notations (+, −, =, etc.), carriage returns, graphic symbols, and symbols common to computer programming. For instance, when a computer using ASCII code needs to send the lowercase letter "d," it simply transmits the binary number equivalent of decimal number 68.

DIGITAL VERSUS ANALOG COMMUNICATION

In digital communications, only two possible states need to be transmitted: 1 or 0. The nature of the digital signal is consequently like a pulse rather than a complex wave. The speed of the pulse can be very fast since the I/O bus on a computer is designed to handle high-speed, high-volume traffic and operates at speeds measured in millions of bits per second. Voice communication is quite different. An analog voice signal is more complex. It is an electrical signal which changes in a way that is analogous to fluctuations in the timbre, pitch, and spacing of sounds in human speech.

There are several differences between voice and data technologies that require consideration: voice transmission is more forgiving of errors; voice transmission is very slow (relative to requirements for computer transmissions); voice conversations require long and continuous channel connection, whereas computers get it over with quickly. Telephone systems have been optimized for voice transmission and do not provide enough channel capacity or speed for optimal transmittal of data. The call set-up time (the time it takes to establish a connection between two points) with the telephone network averages 17 seconds. We have grown accustomed to this long period between dialing and call answering for voice conversations, which are typically long. The long set-up times in the voice network become a problem in data conversations, which may last only 2 or 3 seconds. Whereas voice calls require long continuous connections, data calls require short bursty transmittals of signals with long periods of waiting in between.

I/O BUS COMMUNICATIONS

Prior to the development of standards for local area networks, data communication over very short distances was done with an extension of a computer system's I/O bus. The I/O bus is normally used for communications within a computer system, between processors and peripherals. Data transfer on an I/O bus occurs at high speeds (at rates of 1 to 10 million bits per second). The I/O bus can vary in length from a few inches to several hundred feet, subject to several restrictions:

- I/O bus cables are very expensive and sensitive; there are electromagnetic emission restrictions requiring substantial insulation, and errors become prevalent as length increases.
- The I/O bus is designed to connect dependent components within a system rather than for connection of autonomous systems; I/O bus protocols are designed for intrasystem communication.
- An I/O bus of one manufacturer is unlikely to be compatible with machines of other manufacturers.
- The I/O bus is easily subject to catastrophic failure as the result of one component's failure.
- If the volume of traffic overloads an I/O bus, the most typical resolution is a hardware or software change.

LOCAL AREA NETWORKS

A local area network (LAN) is traditionally a private communications system designed to support the transfer of data between machines within a building or group of buildings. A principal distinction for the LAN is the distance through which LAN signals must travel. LAN technology is aimed at providing communications over relatively short distances, ranging from a few hundred feet to a few miles. "LAN" is therefore a symbol for a type of telecommunications system which may integrate various types of signal transmission technologies. The primary purpose of a LAN is to provide a primary link between machines. This link operates independently of long-haul or public telephone company networks, PBX systems, or the hardware structures of any particular manufacturer of computers. A LAN may be specifically designed to provide communications capabilities that fit the needs of a users' organization and computer system.

CHARACTERISTICS OF LOCAL AREA NETWORKS

LANs use many kinds of media and transmission technologies used also by voice telecommunications networks (fiber optic and coaxial cables, microwave radio relay, etc.). Whereas a voice network always needs to provide a large number of discrete 4000 Hz channels, a LAN may need to deliver 1, 10, or 30 million bits per second (Mb/s) using all or most of the capacity of an entire cable. LANs are typically used to provide very high speed and high bandwidth transmission capabilities over relatively short distances. The transmission speed and other characteristics of any particular LAN are determined by the nature and volume of traffic that needs to be handled in the user's organization and the kinds and manufacturing standards of the machines connected together by it.

THE NEED FOR HIGHER TRANSMISSION SPEEDS

Most information exchanged within a department of a business has little relevance outside the department. Consequently, there is more information exchanged within a department than between departments and less routed outside the business premises. The exchanges within departments are usually fast and bursty interactions with a working file or database. For example, users may be transferring files from one system to another, as when dumping the results of processing jobs to a storage device or sending screen graphics to an electronic printer or plotter. These activities require the transmittal of large, accumulated files of data. In order to avoid having people sitting in front of blank screens waiting for a response, higher rates of data throughput are necessary, requiring a large bandwidth capability and a minimum of time spent in establishing communications channels.

The transmission speeds of LANs come close to the speed of a computer's internal I/O bus. LAN capacities are great enough to be used for internal communications between components of very large computer systems. Unlike voice networks, in a LAN it is critical that the network management and routing procedures do not introduce delay. The methods for connecting users and nodes with each other, determining access rights, and allocating channels must allow equal, immediate access for all purposes.

LANs frequently need to be equipped with devices which allow a user or computer to communicate beyond the parameters of the LAN—through the public telephone network into other discrete LANs or to remote computer-driven devices. This "outside" communications utility is provided by a device which, in LAN terminology, is called a "gateway" (Figure 6.3.)

Gateway devices can provide access to public telephone transmission services to any node on the network. T1 and X.25 services may be incorporated to provide private dedicated computer lines to remote places through the public telephone net or a public packet-switched net. (These technologies have been discussed in detail in Chapter 4, Telecommunications Technologies.) Communications from one LAN can be routed by gateway devices through the public telephone wires directly to users on another discrete LAN.

DESIGNING LANS TO SUPPORT OFFICE AUTOMATION

Although the state-of-the-art LAN may one day support voice and video traffic as well as data communications, the words "local area network" were originally put together to make a distinction about the way in which a group of electronic, computer-driven devices, within the area of a single building or group of buildings, could be interconnected. The object in wiring these devices together was to provide the means by which a number of people, in different locations, could use a number of computers and devices capable of doing various kinds of office automation jobs—filing, printing, calculating, and so forth.

Usable knowledge about LANs must therefore include background about applications: office systems and office system technologies

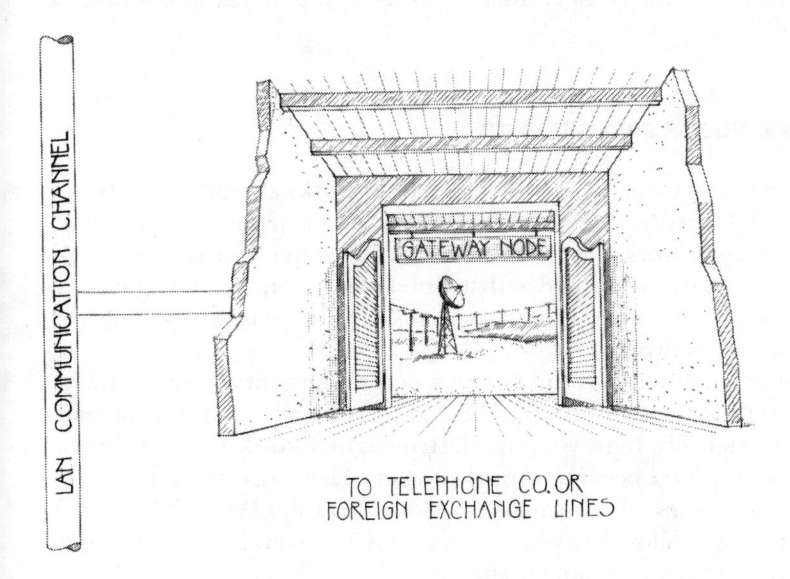

FIGURE 6.3 The node which routes communications out of the local area network to the outside world is called a "gateway."

Changes occur within businesses when they begin to use LAN technology. When a business has committed its administrative or production management procedures to LAN technology, the resultant office system becomes less tolerant of delays. The office becomes 100 percent unproductive if the flow of data stops.

Data processing and other information management tools have revolutionized the way in which offices and businesses are run and the way that most office jobs are done. Office automation has had an impact on every aspect of business management, communications, and facilities planning and on the performance and productivity of office personnel. The LAN has provided new possibilities for running a business, further changing business management procedures. How and why this has come about can be seen by studying the way a job is handled using the services of a distributed network of shared computer tools.

LAN DESIGN ELEMENTS

In LAN jargon, the methodology of a communications network is referred to as its network "architecture." The physical distribution and location of the network resources, including workstations and computer-driven devices that provide electronic data storage, filing, printing, electronic mail, and other utilities, is referred to as the network "topology."

NETWORK NODES AND SERVERS

Devices connected to the network, such as workstations and network utilities, called network "servers" (e.g., file server, print server), are all referred to as network "nodes." The user's access to resources on a LAN is usually via a node equipped with an intelligent computer terminal that includes a video screen, a keyboard, and software to manage communications on the network.

The most common server nodes on a network are for electronic filing, printing, and communications. The file server node traditionally consists of a relatively high-volume electromagnetic disk storage device. Disk storage is used because it provides very fast access to 10 to 600 or more million bytes of information. More recently, laser disk storage techniques have allowed even faster access to several billion bytes of information on disks of similar size.

The print server nodes of a large network may utilize electronic printing devices capable of printing documents of near-professional publishing quality at the rate of over a hundred pages per minute. Smaller networks use character or line printers or small laser printing devices.

NETWORK MANAGEMENT NODE

A key element of a network is network management and control. This is provided by software loaded into a computer which then acts as a network management node. The names, addresses, and access privileges of every node on the network are stored in the files of the network management node. When a user on a LAN wants to print a document, the print request may employ several different nodes of the network, each accomplishing a certain set of tasks.

The request is first transmitted to the network managing node, for security and access privilege authorization. Next, the node which drives the printer (print server) requests that a copy of the print file be sent to

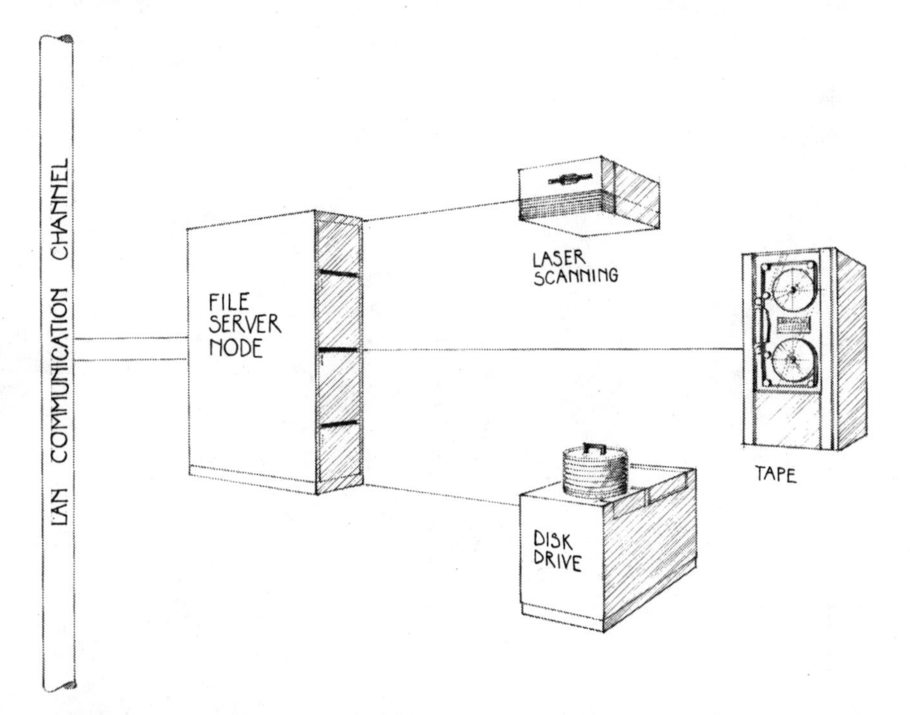

Figure 6.4 On a local area network, users economically share a number of specialized computers for certain functions. The file server is a node which provides storage for any kind of data.

the printer from a node which stores files (file server). If the requested file is stored in the domain of another network, a communications server might be employed to send the request through a gateway converter out through the public telephone network. When the request reaches the remote network, the network manager node of that LAN will have to approve the access rights of the request by examining its database of network users and passwords. After the file has been sent to the print server and the printing is completed, the print server must notify the network management node and the user that the job is done. A high degree of reliability is required, given the complexity of procedures involved in executing a relatively simple request such as printing a file. The communication processes in all of the above routine interactions need to happen in nanoseconds.

Not only do LANs provide user access to the services of a range of shared computer-driven tools, but they also become a primary means for communication between individuals who have access to terminals. The

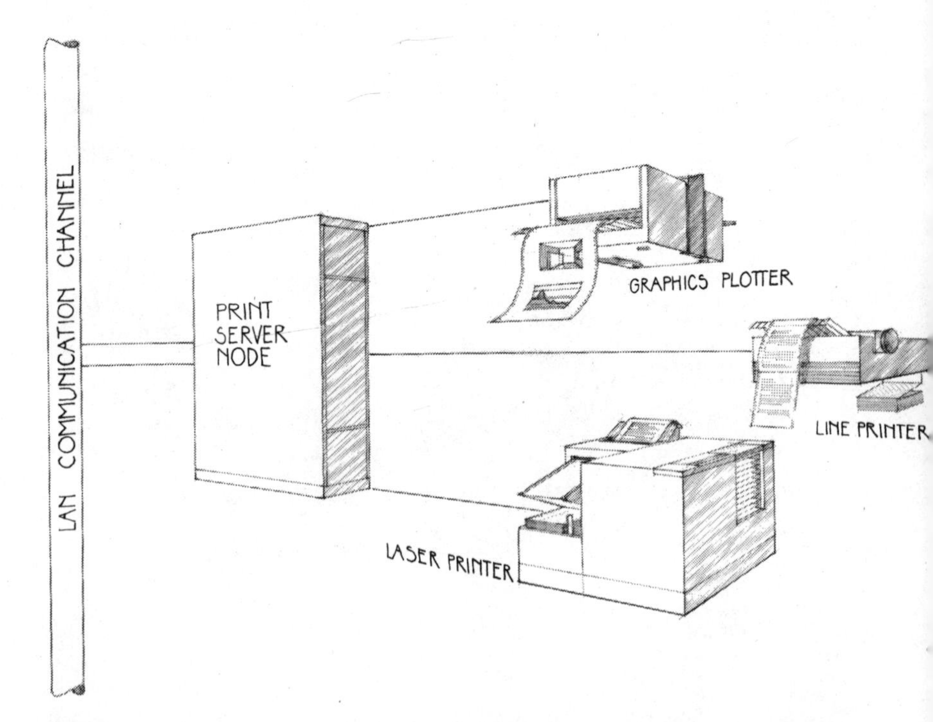

Figure 6.5 Print servers are nodes which provide users with hard copy when required. They may provide any kind of output ranging from color graphic plotters or high-volume laser printers to line or character printers.

entire structure of formal requests and promises that compose the manageability of a business may be committed to software.

To use a LAN, an intelligent machine is connected to a transmission medium such as a coaxial cable, a fiber optic cable, or a radio transceiver tuned to a particular frequency range. To communicate, a machine transmits a signal in an appropriate frequency. The transmitted signal includes coded information which identifies the sender, the recipient, and the nature of the communication.

LAN METHODOLOGIES

The procedures by which the communications signals of various machines are directed across a LAN between different machines and terminals vary with the design of the network. Several standard methodologies of networking have evolved in recent time. In addition, many

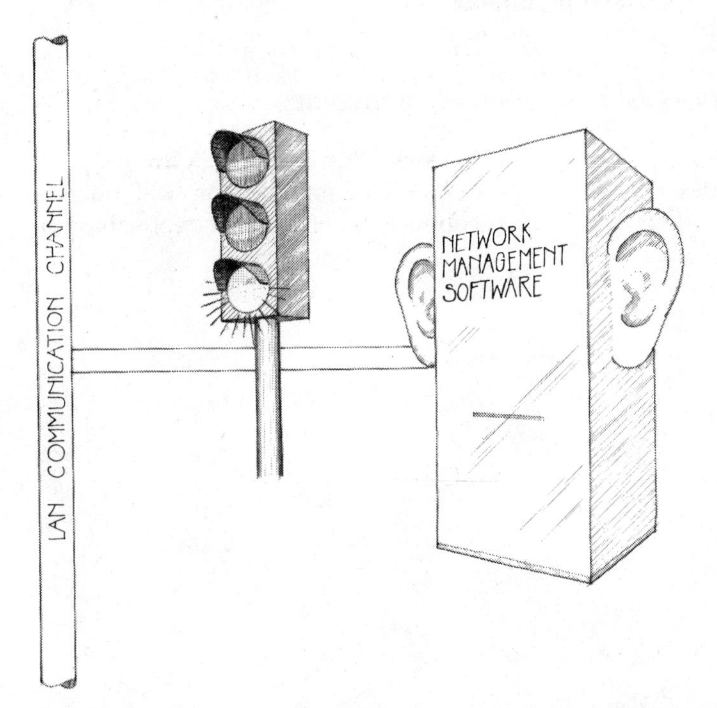

Figure 6.6 The network management node keeps a record of all users on the network and where their files are kept; it may also report when users have logged on, what files were accessed, what print jobs were ordered, etc.

networks being implemented use the techniques of all of the common forms of network architecture.

NETWORK TOPOLOGIES AND CONTROL

The topology of a network results from the physical arrangement of the links between nodes (end points or junctions on a link). Nodes communicate with each other over links. Connections may be physical or logical. Physical links are electromechanical circuits between nodes. They are "hard-wired," either permanently or through physical switching. In a logical link, two nodes are able to communicate with or without a direct, mechanical connection.

In Figure 6.7, there is no physical link between *A* and *C*. If node *B* could "route" (pass messages to adjacent nodes), then all nodes could be logically linked and *A* could send a message to *C* through *B*.

Two kinds of physical links can make up a network topology: point-to-point links and multipoint links.

POINT-TO-POINT AND MULTIPOINT TOPOLOGIES

In a nonrouting point-to-point network, illustrated in Figure 6.7, only adjacent nodes can communicate. Full communication will only be possible when there is a physical connection between every possible pair

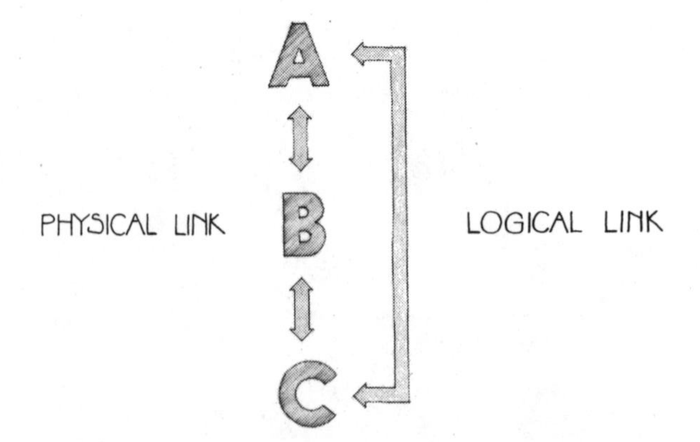

Figure 6.7 A physical link is provided when one machine is "hard wired" to another, even if through a telephone circuit. A logical link is established when one machine communicates with another by means of routing communications through an intermediary machine(s).

of nodes. The wiring scheme for such a network becomes expensive and difficult to manage. If routing were permitted, full communication would be possible when all the nodes were operational. However, nodes must include capability for making routing decisions in addition to recognizing and receiving messages, and communications between many nodes will depend on the operational status of intervening nodes.

Multipoint links (also called multidrop links) are communication links shared by more than two nodes, as illustrated in Figure 6.8. Multipoint links greatly reduce the number of links necessary to connect nodes, reducing link costs, especially in complex systems with large numbers of users. Nodes are more complex in that there must be a method of controlling access to the channel to avoid usage conflicts.

CHANNEL CONTROL AND FREQUENCY ALLOCATION

Depending on the user's needs, the resulting number of participating nodes, and their kind of participation, a network can be designed including both point-to-point and multipoint connections. This configuration can then be used to determine the optimum strategy for control and channel allocation.

Strategies of Centralized Control

In some network topologies, control resides in a master node, as illustrated in Figure 6.9. All messages are routed to the master node and retransmitted to the recipient. "Broadband" network topologies often utilize this procedure. In the broadband application, messages are transmitted by nodes on specific discrete frequencies and messages are

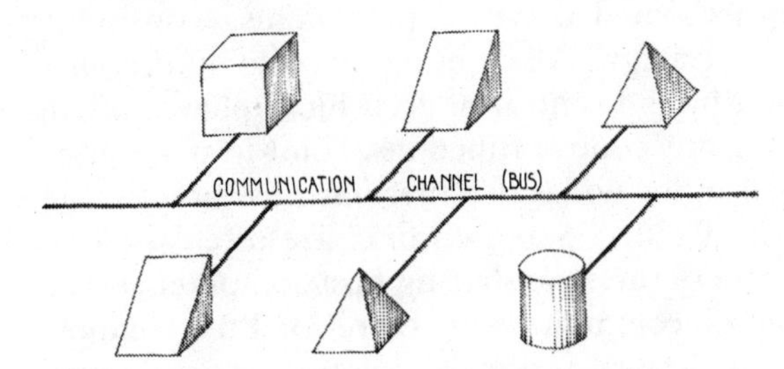

Figure 6.8 Multipoint links are physical lilnks between machines which allow the connection of several machines, with any machine being able to communicate with any other machine.

received by nodes on another set of frequencies. A master node, called the "head end," is the only node that can receive signals on transmission frequencies. The head end determines access privileges and converts the signal to a receiving frequency corresponding to the addressee's receiver before retransmitting it. In another centralized control scheme, called polling, a master node determines which node will transmit by querying each node in an order established by a prearranged scheme of traffic priorities.

Distributed Control Strategy

Alternatively, network control can be distributed so that rules are set for the behavior of nodes. According to preset mechanical procedures, nodes may broadcast their traffic on the medium for limited periods of time in the absence of other traffic. If two nodes broadcast simultaneously, preset varying holding times are established for each node to reduce the possibility of repeating the simultaneous transmission.

TOPOLOGICAL STRUCTURES

Most LANs are based on one or a combination of three types of topology—star, ring, and bus—which have been found most successful in meeting the design goals for LANs: high-speed transmission, immediate and equal access for all users, and cost-effectiveness. Depending on the number of connections required and the volume and kind of traffic produced, one or another of these structures will be best suited to the needs of the user.

Star Network

In a star network, all nodes are joined at a single point. This is consistent with a centralized control strategy. All routing of communications between users is performed by the central node, which relieves other nodes of the need for having any control functions. Point-to-point lines connect the central with all other nodes. Connections are simple and may be inexpensive to manufacture. Star networks are often used in time-sharing applications, where the time-sharing host computer serves as the central node. It is also a common architecture for PBX technologies and small clusters such as word-processing centers or accounting departments that share the resources of a central processor.

Star LANs are best suited to situations where most of the traffic on the net is between the nodes and the host, and there is very little traffic between nodes. When node to node traffic grows, the switching burden for the central node can block communications and inhibit its ability to perform other tasks. In some star networks, such as the Micom Data PBX, the control function is given over to a node which performs this task exclusively. The capacity of a star network is determined by the power of the control node. It is a useful, cost-effective technology in environments with a limited number of users. Systems like the Micom are reliable when not overburdened. A characteristic of star networks is that the entire network goes down if the control node fails. Since the network management functions of other topological structures (ring and bus) are typically centralized, this is to some extent true for every LAN. (Network management includes the controls by means of which access to network resources is granted to nodes.)

Ring Network

In ring networks, each node has the ability to pass messages not intended for it along to the next node along a single pathway called a "ring." A point-to-point connection connects each node to the next adjacent node, forming an unbroken circular configuration. All nodes are provided with a logical connection in the ring. When access control in the ring is distributed, rather than controlled by one of the nodes on the network, any node can transmit freely and directly to any other node.

Loop Topology. When a central control node is employed in a ring, the topology is often referred to as a "loop." When a node is granted access

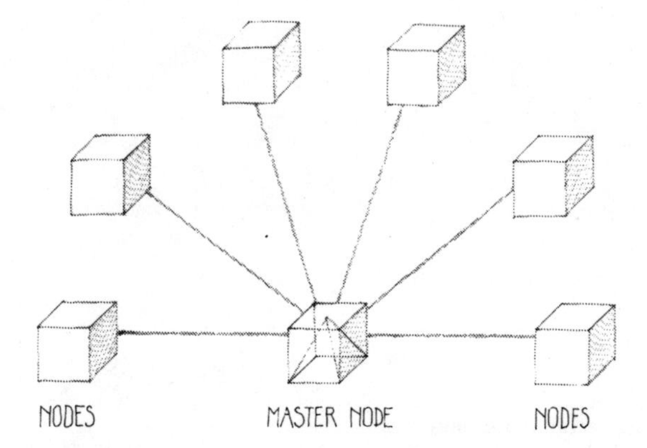

Figure 6.9 Star topology network architecture is characterized by a master controller node through which all traffic must be routed to any other node.

in a loop, the message can travel around the loop to its destination rather than traveling through the central, access-granting node. (If the control requires that the message must pass through the central node, the performance of the loop is similar to that of the star network.)

The network functions of ring nodes are not complex, since the message route is determined by topology. Messages always travel in one direction, to the next node on the ring. This reduces the complexity and expense of the nodes. Failure of a node in a ring or any break in the line, as well as failure of the central control node, would lead to total network failure. This vulnerability may be managed by strategies for bypassing failed nodes or circuits; however, this adds complexities to components and requires repeaters. Because rings must be physically arranged so as to be fully connected, lines have to be placed between a new node and two adjacent units if the system is expanded or added on to. (It is difficult to prewire a building for ring networks.)

Polling Techniques for Control of Channel Access. To avoid contention by nodes for the use of a ring network, several control methodologies are based on polling techniques. Polling techniques determine the order in which nodes can access the network, thus avoiding conflict. Methods for control include token passing, slotted rings, and a polling list.

Token passing. In token passing, a bit pattern called a "token" continuously travels around the ring. A node gains access by "holding" the token and transmitting the message. After the message is read and

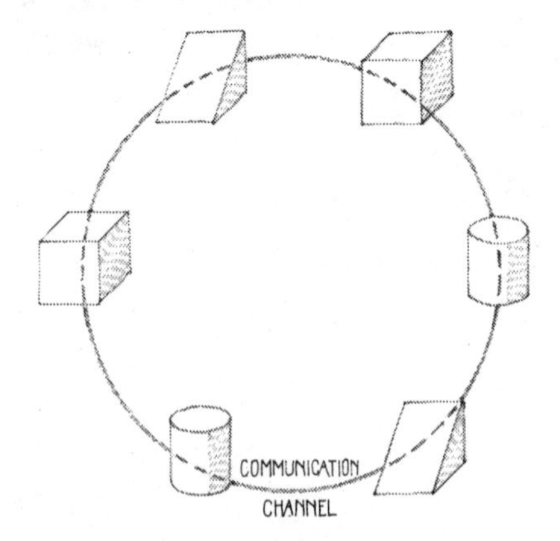

Figure 6.10 In ring topology architecture, machines are linked together like lights on a Christmas tree. Messages are routed around the network by each machine in sequence until they reach their addressees.

acknowledged, the token is released and is ready for the next node that needs to communicate.

Slotted rings. Slotted rings are similar to token-passing techniques. In slotted ring polling, "frames" of a fixed size circulate around the ring. A frame is a series of bits which identify a message signal field. A message of a fixed or limited length may be placed between a specific series of bits in the frame (see Figure 6.11). To send a message on a slotted ring type LAN, a transmitting node takes the first available frame passing by, puts data in the appropriate field, sets a bit to indicate that the frame is in use, and changes other bits in the frame to identify the source and destination.

Polling lists. Polling lists (Figure 6.12) set up an order in which nodes may communicate (A, B, C, D, etc.). The order can be adjusted to reflect priorities (B, A, C, B, B, D, B, A, C, etc.). The length of time a node may use the channel is usually set by a limitation on the size of messages. A polling list scheme may also employ a form of time division multiplexing (TDM). When TDM is employed, a clock is used to regulate the transmissions of all nodes according to prearranged priorities. There are specific time periods during which each node has the right to transmit.

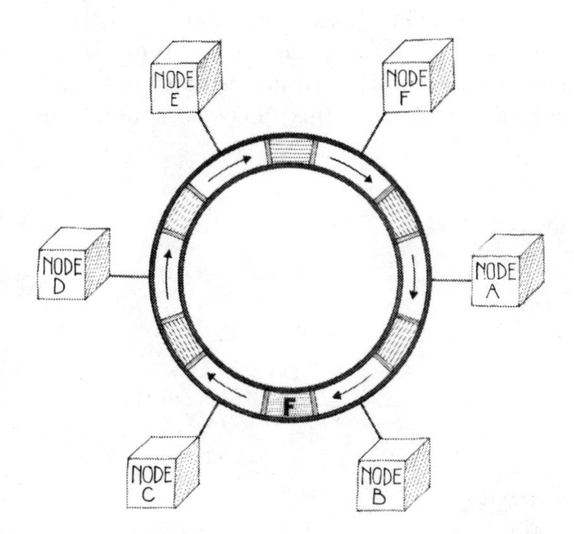

Figure 6.11 Token-passing architecture is a modification of the ring topology. Data frames called tokens are circulated around the network. To communicate, a machine fills an empty frame with a message and an address as it passes by.

Bus Network

Bus topology typifies the concept of the multipoint line—a single open medium shared by a number of nodes. Whereas star networks use point-to-point connections to a central switch, and rings consist of point-to-point links between adjacent nodes in a circle, bus nodes share a single channel which can be tapped into at any point. Traffic can travel across the bus from any node directly to any other node. Nodes are passive, as they are in a star network, but they do need the ability to recognize messages addressed to them. They must also possess sophisticated technology for listening to and avoiding contention with traffic on the line. Any medium can be used for the bus topology, including coaxial cable, twisted-pair wire, fiber optic cable, or unbounded media. Individual node failures will not interfere with any other network operations, with one exception: the functions of network management and access control will reside in one node location.

Channel Access—Contention Techniques. Unlike the ring and star networks, which employ a "polling" process to control access to the common channel, bus networks use a "contention" technique. In polling techniques, nodes are given an exclusive right to use the channel through a process such as token passing or a previously established order such as a polling list. Since only one node can transmit at a time, there is no possibility of collision of messages from different nodes that are transmitting at or near the same time. Whereas bus nets use contention

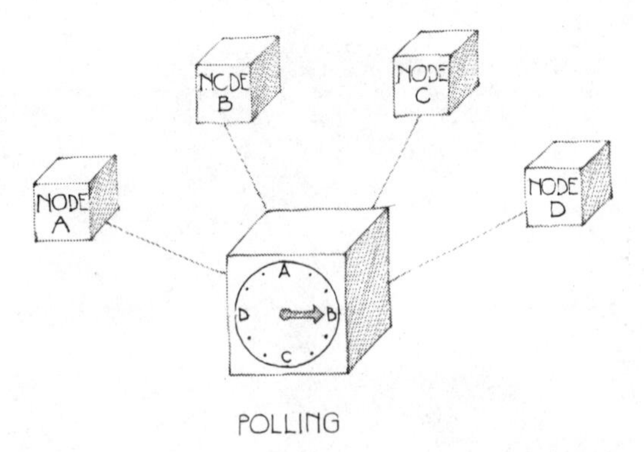

Figure 6.12 Polling techniques use a clock to allocate access times to each node in turn. Based on preestablished priorities, each node has a limited period of time in each second during which it may transmit.

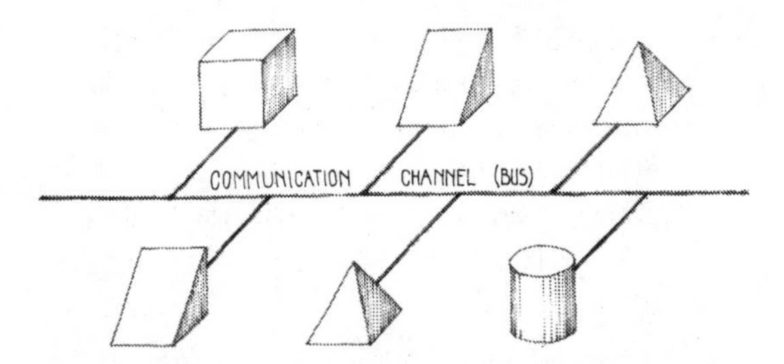

Figure 6.13 Bus topology networks resemble the internal communications systems of computers.

techniques that employ data collisions and conflict as part of the design for controlling channel access.

Carrier Sense Multiple Access with Collision Detection (CSMA/CD). Under the rules of CSMA/CD, any node can transmit whenever it senses there is no traffic in the channel (carrier sense). There is no need to wait for a token, slot, or polling process. However, because of the time it takes for a signal to travel across the network (called the propagation delay), two or more nodes could begin transmitting at or near the same time. A collision will then occur between messages; it will produce an energy level in the channel that will be sensed by all nodes, including those which are transmitting, and interpreted as a collision (collision detection). When a collision occurs, all nodes stop transmitting for a period which is equal to a multiple of the propagation delay time which varies for each node according to the distance the node is from the termination point of the network. The delay period is thus different for each node, which gives one of the nodes the opportunity to begin transmitting before any of the others. At this point there will be no possibility of a collision since the other nodes will detect traffic and defer to the transmitting node. (See Figure 6.14.)

Although the technology of CSMA/CD is complex, it provides very high capacity transmission and is very economical of transmission time. It has proved to be a successful means of networking in high-volume traffic situations, allowing through-put in the range of several million bits per second, with few delays even at peak channel capacities.

THE NETWORK MANAGEMENT NODE

A level of security of files and limitation of access to the use of devices in a network is provided by the node equipped with software for network management. This node becomes the network controller which is programmed by a system administrator to prohibit requests and messages without authorization. The database of network passwords, routing information, and the ability to monitor and record the traffic on the network then reside in this node, and it becomes a critical part of the operation of the network.

LAN EXAMPLES

Transmission media and control technologies have already been discussed in detail in the previous chapters about telecommunications. Certain technologies have been refined by manufacturers to produce some attractively priced off-the-shelf solutions for data communications networks. There are now several manufacturers of off-the-shelf LAN systems, and several firms specialize in designing and installing custom-tailored networks which utilize a blend of LAN technologies to provide optimal private network solutions. Cost per node is the priority with which most firms evaluate a choice of network technologies. The LAN methodologies to be described next are being utilized in the product offerings of major manufacturers such as DEC, IBM, AT&T, 3M Interactive, SYTEK, and Ungermann Bass.

BROADBAND LANS

Broadband local area networks use frequency division multiplexing to divide a single physical channel (such as a coaxial or fiber optic cable)

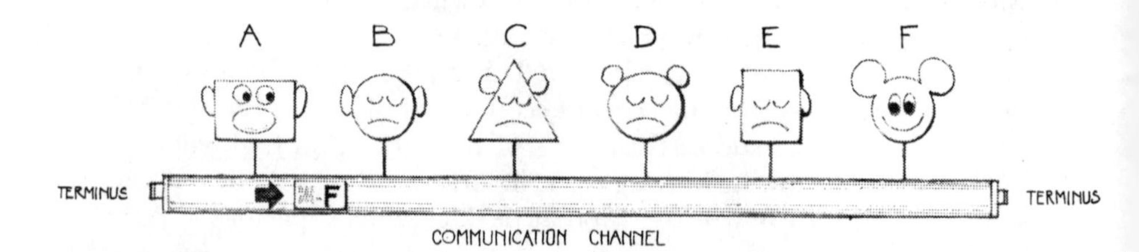

Figure 6.14 Carrier sense multiple access with collision detection (CSMA/CD) architecture. All nodes constantly listen on the network for messages with their address code. They can transmit at any time providing that they do not sense a signal already present on the line. If two start transmitting simultaneously, the energy level cues the transmitting stations to withdraw and start again after a clocked interval prioritized according to distance each node is from the terminus of the network.

into a number of smaller independent frequency channels. Each of the smaller frequency bands may be assigned a specific use. Several separate networks can thus operate on the same physical channel simultaneously. Voice signals can be carried on one set of frequencies and video signals on another. The topology of broadband networks is that of a bus with branches and subbranches, like a tree.

Transmission Media and Components of Broadband

The standard transmission medium used in most current broadband implementations is 75-ohm CATV coaxial cable because of its availability, low cost, capacity (300 to 400 MHz), and performance (error rates of one bit in a billion). Nodes use a modem to connect to the network. The modem is equipped with a connector to the terminal and a physical tap

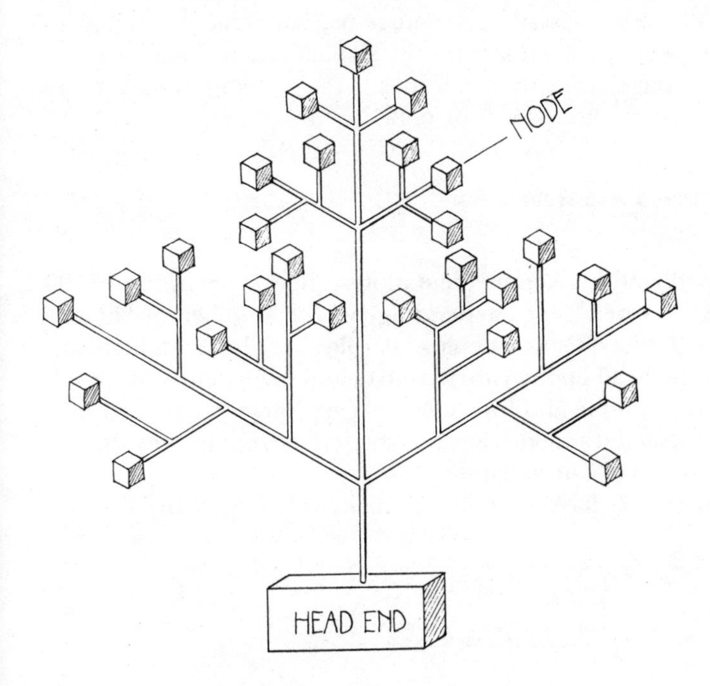

Figure 6.15 Tree topology network architecture allows the signal carrier to branch off in any direction. There are problems associated with keeping the level of a signal equally balanced in all parts of the system, and as each new branch is added, the signal level needs to be amplified in places.

into the coaxial cable. A sophisticated frequency-multiplexing unit is required; it is programmed to establish frequency allocation. The balance and strength of signals on broadband LANs must be properly adjusted and supported by signal attenuators and repeaters which rebroadcast signals to maintain constant levels throughout the network.

Channel Allocation for Broadband

Many channels of different bandwidths can be assigned to provide for independent voice, video, and data signaling. In broadband LAN applications, channels are established for each direction of communication with a node (transmit and receive). All transmissions outgoing from a node are on one assigned bandwidth. The node receives transmissions on a separately assigned bandwidth. The assignment of frequencies and channel allocation is managed by a unit called the "head end." The head end receives all node message transmissions, converts the signal to receviing frequencies, and retransmits the signal. This is done independently of the message content, which makes the system usable for any type of transmission: voice, video, or data.

Cost-Effectiveness and Reliability of Broadband

The cost of broadband LAN implementations ranges from around $500 per node to $1800 per node, depending on the number of stations implemented and the type of technology employed. There is a high cost associated with the head end network control and management technology, but the cost per node and for cabling is very low. If there are many nodes to be connected, these designs are cost-effective; but they may be too expensive for smaller installations.

Broadband networks have been in use in citywide CATV installations

Figure 6.16 Broadband networks divide the bandwidth capacity of a cable into several channels. In single cable systems, transmissions by nodes are always in one set of frequencies and a head end node converts these signals into another set of frequencies for reception.

since 1949. In 1982, there were 21 million CATV subscribers using these networks. The technology is relatively simple and easy to maintain. CATV networks are one-way systems, however the technology for frequency allocation and transmission does not change in LAN implementations using broadband. The essential difference is that nodes on a LAN can transmit as well as receive signals. Because data communications require that signals be in digital rather than analog form, the transceivers on a broadband LAN also incorporate frequency modulator/demodulator (modems). Modems are a stable, inexpensive technology for converting digital signals to analog signals. Because of the inexpensive technology available, broadband is a cost-effective methodology when traffic volume requirements are moderate and where there is a large number of users. Maintenance for signal balance is costly when nodes are added to an existing net or when the configuration of a network is changed. Prewiring for a broadband LAN is reasonable, though the cost for coaxial cable is high and the system will need to be electronically balanced each time a node is added later.

BASEBAND LANS

Baseband LANs are direct applications of the bus topology structure. They are the most efficient means of providing data communications within limited distances. With the advent of optical fiber transmission, however, the distance limitation of baseband has jumped from a limit of 1500 meters to one of several miles. In a baseband LAN, the entire bandwidth of a channel is used for every message (Figure 6.17).

Instead of frequencies being assigned for different purposes, CSMA/CD collision detection is used to avoid contention on the network. Because only one user transmits at a time, using the full capacity of the channel, baseband networks can support transmission speeds well in excess of 10 Mb/s. Transmission speeds in the gigabit range (1 gigabit =

EACH MESSAGE CAN USE
FULL BANDWIDTH OF
THE CHANNEL
BASEBAND CHANNEL ALLOCATION

Figure 6.17 Baseband networks provide the fastest transmission speeds because they allow the transmitter to use the entire bandwidth capacity of the cable for each transmission.

1 billion bits per second) have been attained using fiber optic cable. Unlike broadband technology, in baseband there is no need for a head end processor to convert and retransmit signals. Nodes transmit directly to recipient nodes, which increases throughput speed and eliminates the cost and complication of the head-end unit. This savings, however, is offset by an increase in the complexity and cost of each node—to include the intelligence for CSMA/CD.

Transmission Medium for Baseband

For low traffic capacities, a coaxial cable similar to that used for broadband transmission may be used in baseband. The emission problems of baseband and its greater sensitivity to radio frequency (RF) and electromagnetic (EMI) interference require multiple shielding techniques which greatly increase the cost of cable. Where traffic volumes are very high, requiring higher bandwidth capacity, heavier cables may be used to provide additional capacity. Because of the way baseband uses the total capacity of a cable, compatible simultaneous transmission of voice and video signal components has so far not been successfully implemented on a baseband LAN. If sufficient bandwidth can be allocated, a baseband channel can also be established within a broadband system for some applications. When this is done, baseband signals are transmitted within an assigned frequency range which is not used by the broadband components, nodes, or the head end unit.

Baseband Components

Baseband nodes must have circuitry and software for intelligently managing communications—including intelligence for carrier sense, collision detection, transmission, and receipt of messages. Communications functions are necessary to format and address data packets for transmission, as well as to hold packets in buffers during transmission and receipt of messages, recompose the received packetized messages into their original form, and so on. These functions are provided by software that is usually programmed on read-only memory chips (ROM) on circuit cards called transceivers (see Figure 6.18). Transceiver hardware and software are sometimes built into circuit boards that plug directly into a computer system's I/O bus.

In some cases, the transceiver unit is contained in a separate box into which one can connect one or several nodes. The transceiver incorporates connectors for the terminals or computers in the form of a serial type interface connection and a shielded tap which is literally screwed into the coaxial cable. When a fiber optic transmission medium is employed, signal converters are used in place of the physical tap to convert the electrical signals to light wave signals and vice versa.

Network Management in Baseband

Whereas broadband utilizes a head end unit for network management, any node on a baseband network can be equipped with software to provide network security, control, maintenance, and monitoring functions. Such functions are necessary to the administration of a network but are not necessary to providing the facility for any machine to communicate with any other machine.

Cost-Effectiveness of Baseband

The cost of the transmission medium is the same for every network architecture; the other costs associated with baseband communications include node components for packetizing, transceiving, carrier sense, and identifying messages. A network management node is also needed

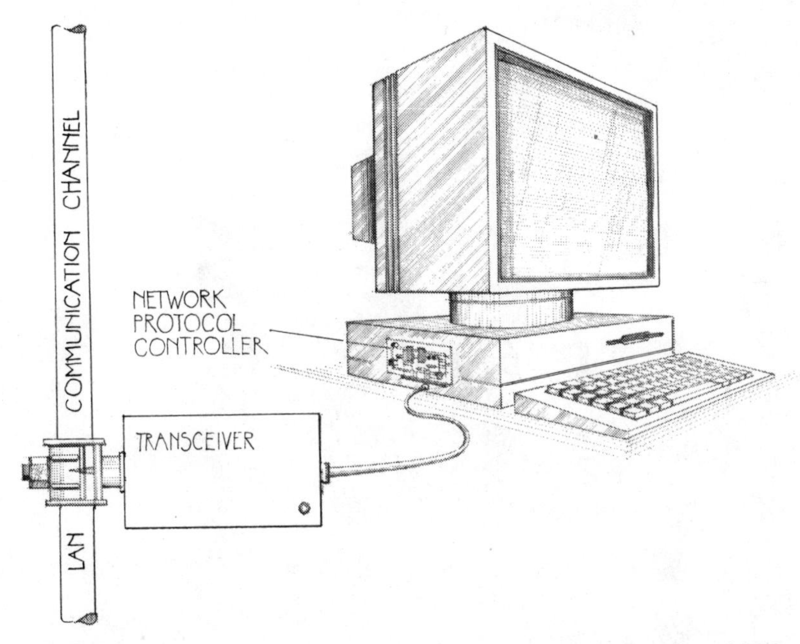

Figure 6.18 Baseband nodes are significantly more expensive than are nodes of other networking schemes. They require several intelligent components to process, transmit, and receive messages. As the prices of these components move lower owing to the use of VLSI (chip) and fiber optic technology, baseband may emerge as the preferable network architecture for most applications.

to perform maintenance, monitoring, and security functions. Because of the intelligence that needs to be built into each node, baseband is more expensive per node than is broadband. The total cost of setting up a baseband LAN is therefore dependent on the hardware and software costs associated with the particular node equipment.

Using a baseband LAN, a group of personal computers or minicomputers can be networked at a cost of around $800 to $1200 per node; this includes circuit boards for each node, equipped with transceivers and software for network management, communications, file serving, and print serving. The cost of placing a minicomputer (DEC VAX, TI 990/X, HP 3000, etc.) on the LAN can be much higher, depending on the applications software involved. Although the baseband methodology is the more expensive at this time, the throughput rates achievable with baseband have sometimes exceeded the speed of an I/O bus in a computer, making baseband an indispensible part of many distributed processing situations. Baseband installations have been especially valuable in situations involving computer-aided design and manufacturing

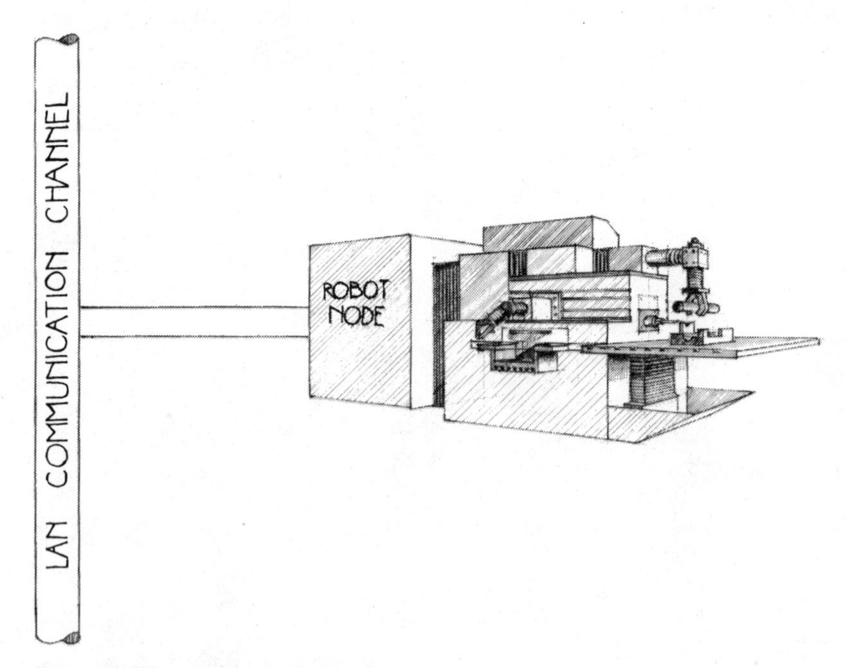

Figure 6.19 Computer-aided engineering and manufacturing are an emerging industry of enormous potential. Current technology allows the nodes for manufacturing and robotic machines to be monitored and programmed directly from engineering workstations.

(CAD/CAM), where network nodes may include computer-controlled robotics and sophisticated engineering applications.

Reliability of Baseband

Baseband LANs, particularly the Xerox-DEC-Intel-3COM product called Ethernet, the Network Research Corporation product called Fusion, and the Ungerman Bass Uninet product, have been in active service for several years with excellent reliability. In throughput and peak-load performance tests, they have outperformed all expectations and all other LAN techniques. Baseband has become a preferable means of interconnecting systems when there are substantial volumes of traffic to be carried between large computer systems.

PART 3

The Intelligent Environment

Because of the publicity and promotion surrounding the recent use of computer-driven devices to help manage the environmental systems of new buildings, the phrase "intelligent building" may evoke images of systems that control heating, ventilation, elevators, security, and other "life support" services. The thought of intelligently designed commercial buildings may also call to mind the inclusion of an infrastructure to support communications such as telephone services, electronic mail, and other information management technology. However, commercial buildings are environments that support people doing relatively specialized business activities. Interpretation of the term "intelligent," when applied to buildings, must therefore imply the availability of high-technology systems that support business and information management, including telecommunications and the various other computer-assisted services for modern business needs, as well as the support of a physical environment which emphasizes the *creative value that the human presence brings to the business task.*

The information revolution is just beginning to have an impact on the operation of businesses and professional firms. Very little is known in the fields of architecture and interior design about the way new technologies and their applications affect space planning and building design. The social impact of system science on the workplace is most extraordinary. New freedoms are emerging in the workplace, and with them new questions arise about the design of the structure where creative work is to take place. The largest portion of the working population (those who work in small businesses) has yet to be directly confronted with computers on the job.

Of the approximately 7 million businesses currently operating in the United States, the overwhelming majority (86 percent) employ fewer than 20 persons. Very few of these firms (5 to 10 percent) are at present using computer services. Most of the few who are using computers rely on the rudimentary kind of general purpose software commonly sold off-the-shelf for personal computers. Many of these firms would be ideal tenants for multitenant commercial buildings if such buildings were to offer a significant technological and economic advantage. These relatively small space users (1000 to 10,000 gross square feet) are also often the typical clients of shared-use technology systems. Individually, these firms could not afford the high costs of supporting elaborate technology and the cost of technologically expert support personnel.

Small Business Information Technology Market

Most specialized, industry specific, information technologies that are currently offered by value-added resellers focus on the needs of small- to medium-sized firms. Telecommunications companies are also making a concentrated effort to offer enhanced services to the great body of smaller firms. The combination of new products and services offered by just these two industries produces the potential for a breakthrough in productivity for small firms. Software and expert systems make possible administrative efficiency; capability for creating and transmitting communications; and management techniques for enlarging a customer base, improving customer service, and generally increasing the time available for use of any firm's or professional's special value-added expertise.

Certain key requirements must be satisfied for small businesses to realize the potential of new technologies. They need to have adequate hardware and software at affordable prices. They need a relatively simple means of accessing knowledge about new computer tools. For these reasons, there have been significant changes in the marketing of computer products and services:

- There has been phenomenal growth in the activities of contract labor services. Contract labor involves "leasing" groups of employees to a firm for the purpose of setting up and operating computer services. Sometimes the entire department is a contract operation.

- Value-added-resellers (VARs) of computer services are surfacing as the leading edge of software and systems marketing. In 1985, there were 1700 VAR system businesses, serving 10 percent of the computer market. By 1990, the number of VAR services is expected to reach 7000, absorbing a 24 percent share of the total market for computer services.
- Shared tenant services, driven strongly by the needs of commercial real estate marketing, are offering the advantages of volume purchase discounts for groups of building tenants. Telecommunications products and services are purchased for all the building's tenants, which makes for better leverage in dealing with vendors of equipment and services.
- Intelligent buildings may, in the long run, provide the most cost-effective potential for all these services and may eventually become a primary means of delivering state-of-the-art technology to users everywhere. Before this can occur, building owners will have to recognize the need to invest in technology systems for their tenants. Familiarity and confidence must be established with potential information system users, and shared information utilities must be capitalized to endure a start-up period consistent with new building occupancy and development in a locality. Vendors of technology will also need to enhance the communications capabilities and compatibility of their products with equipment manufactured by other vendors.

CHAPTER 7

Shared Tenant Services

Ideally, a shared tenant service (STS) makes it possible for a business tenant to move into a space with nothing but a good idea for a business, some capital, and time. The STS unites the hardware and software necessary to handle the essential tasks that every business requires of computer-driven machines. These include the most cost-effective means of providing many specialized tools and services such as design graphics or statistical resource files. Affiliation with a shared tenant service should make available to the tenant the consultation support and on-site education needed for the business to use such services.

STS AS A DERIVATIVE SERVICE OF SHARED TELECOMMUNICATIONS

An STS service is implicitly connected with state-of-the-art telecommunications services, since it must utilize a digital PBX networked with an array of computer-driven devices, including peripheral equipment, which are conveniently located in the building. To be of value, these devices must be accessible by terminals or telephones placed in the individual offices of building tenants. To accomplish this requires using the highest state of the art of telecommunications and local area network management—a service capability which exceeds, by far, the kind of service that a public telephone utility can support.

Tenants who subscribe to a sophisticated STS service would have the benefit of expensive data-processing systems, sophisticated software, security systems, and the applications training and personnel assistance necessary to manage and maintain sophisticated information technology systems.

COST-EFFECTIVE TECHNOLOGY

The costs of STS services are distributed among all users of the STS building's network. Tenants need pay for services only in proportion to the use they are able to make of them. Each tenant company can have access to all the network services but need pay only for the part it uses, as it uses it. Each tenant company can either access the network from workstations in its own offices or use facilities owned by the network, located in common space outside its own offices. Companies can be supported by on-site computer and telecommunications managers and an on-site educational service. Applications and program support personnel may be available from the STS network personnel pool or provided through agreements with value-added resellers arranged by the STS management on behalf of tenants, possibly with favorable volume discounts.

With the advantages of an on-site staff of specialists trained in computers and telecommunications and a program in technology education for tenants' employees, the STS concept addresses the problem of introducing businesses to new information management technologies. The trends in current computer development promise more networking capability and communication between computer systems. The favorable economics of sharing computer resource centers should become more important as businesses and professionals become more able and knowledgeable about the use of computer-assisted information processing.

STS CUSTOMER PROFILES—THE TENANT AS END USER

Ultimately, an STS must support applications for a tenant's business specialty. Consequently, STS staff must be not only computer-trained but also familiar with applications of automation techniques to a number of businesses, the subtleties and realities of which they must understand.

An example of a favorable STS situation using industry-specialized application software might be a group of architects and engineers, operating cooperatively or as separate businesses, in a large business campus setting or in adjacent urban buildings.

STS networking can make hardware, software, and training available so that the design professional has access to state-of-the-art design workstations. Unlike the situation in remote time-sharing, they can have the security of creating their own electronic files. Plotters can be located in their own spaces. Automated accounting software, word processing, document printing, and other general business services can be provided with or without drafting, clerical, or secretarial assistance.

Some of the many businesses that can be profitably served by an STS network and support staff are described below.

Architectural and Construction Firms

Accounting and statistical software can assist tenants with specialized bid computations, production management, graphic design, and structural analysis. Graphics workstations can be made available at a reasonable cost to assist tenants with automated drafting, illustration, engineering, and design tools that increase productivity in design and construction professions, with commensurate labor-cost savings.

Law Firms

A network can provide services such as time and billing and general ledger accounting. A word-processing service can store a firm's set of standard forms and allow an attorney to order the viewing, storing, editing, or printing of documents. Word-processing and electronic file software can allow attorneys to access or enter information without assistance. Enhanced telecommunications services can assist tenants with access to private sector statistical, electronic legal library, and governmental database resources. Software can be provided to support the accounting and management needs of law firms and assist legal staff in using state-of-the-art technology for the law business.

Property Management

Network software may provide graphic display of property so that furniture, utilities, telephones, and other details about space under management can be accounted for, located, and instantly identified. Software should provide for tenant billing, accounting for improvements, and financial reporting. This particular software can be provided by the system that is used to manage the STS business.

Medical and Dental Offices

An electronic filing system can store and provide remote access to privileged hospital medical records and other files so that physicians can personally enter data or get information instantly about a patient, laboratory report, medications, and so forth. A physician's staff can be assisted with software for medical insurance records completion, general accounting tasks, and other business tasks.

Accounting Firms

The STS network can provide data processing for general accounting services as well as a telecommunications service to help integrate the databases of a firm's client with the accounting firm's own record keeping. Network office automation equipment is able to facilitate tasks that require batch processing and the generation of reports during periods of seasonal overload at year end and during tax-reporting periods. Network staff can assist accountants with the preparation of reports for clients, including preparation, printing, and mailing of tax returns, checks, vouchers, statements, financial reports, bills, and invoices.

Media Production Companies and Advertising Agencies

In addition to standard business and text-editing processes, a producer may require access to daily status reports about production management and auditing data. Information management software should include word processing designed for script writing, script printing and duplication, production budgeting, payroll accounting, and the automated computation and disbursing of royalties, license fees, and assessments common to the performing arts industries. Network electronic print servers can deliver quantities of collated scripts and shooting schedules, incorporating daily input. Workstations and personnel assistance can be available to projects on an as-needed basis to provide staff and services according to current production requirements. Enhanced telecommunications services could provide media production and distribution companies with a means of shipping their product by means of direct satellite transmission to remote places, or via fiber optic, coaxial, or microwave relay to local broadcast facilities.

Real Estate and Mortgage Brokers

In addition to general business support services, special software features may include preparation and printing of loan and mortgage documents and the automatic updating of records and procedures in accordance with changing state and federal regulations. Mortgage companies may also find a use for software for batch processing of loan payment data and periodic printing of statements. Mortgage brokers may require access to dial-up financial databases and electronic real estate appraisal records and listing services.

Marketing, Import-Export, Wholesale, and Retail Firms

STS network staff can assist tenants with setting up software for maintenance of catalogues, automatic pricing adjustments, and printing of orders, invoices, statements, and other forms. Workstations can be provided for the composing of graphics for printing, publishing, and updating of catalogs, price schedules, sales reports, and advertising materials.

Consulting Firms

Software can be provided to assist tenants with preparing reports from statistical computations based on stored, researched, or reference data for the purpose of doing projections using specified formulas with a relational database. Such software and enhanced telecommunications services can provide the ability to rapidly produce current reports using remote electronic databases. Network word processing and electronic printing can be used to facilitate proposal and report finishing. These services should be available on a temporary project by project basis. Network communications servers should be available to facilitate access to remote computer services or databases of the Patent Office, Labor Department, Commerce Department, or other statistical sources.

SHARED TENANT SERVICES—THE TENANT'S PERSPECTIVE

The contemporary business or professional person operates in an international community of suppliers, clients, and investors. Most of the network of technological resources on which a firm relies in day-to-day business are not apparent to the user. When a business person in Los Angeles orders a stock item from a supplier in New York, the telecommunications service seems to be provided by a telephone set, behind which is a mysterious aggregation of human and technological elements that one is more comfortable not knowing about. Shared tenant services promises to provide a broader range of technology support for businesses and individuals in just such a manner—so that the technology itself is transparent to the user. Shared services offer support for company information and office system management as well as providing more cost-effective access to city and wider area telecommunications. These services include many that are at present available only to very large firms.

ACCESS TO TECHNOLOGY IS LIMITED BY KNOWLEDGE LEVEL

To a great extent, the user's knowledge level determines the technological resources that he or she can access. For example, the simplest technology understood by all users is the standard telephone wired directly into a local telephone company's central office. It provides access to dial-up voice communication anywhere in the world. Beyond this level of access is a universe of expanded opportunity. Services already available range from telemarketing and teletraining programs available from AT&T, instant delivery of documents available from MCI, remote connection with computer-based reservation services available from GTE's packet-switching network, Telenet, and access to governmental and private sector databases. A user must be educated about each of these services and many others in order to use them. At present, the educational process forces a user to interrupt business, attend seminars, and try to evaluate the benefits of different services offered by a variety of manufacturers, consultants, or value-added resellers.

In the medical service industry, simple compliance with standard procedures already requires using a sophisticated array of technology. The hospital is an early form of shared tenant services which is industry specific. Imagine the difficulties that the medical care industry would face were it necessary for physicians to be concerned with the technological equipping of a hospital. The idea of STS is to provide other professions such as lawyers, accountants, and marketing representatives with access to more advanced technical resources about which they, like the doctors, can remain happily ignorant. The STS differs from other time-sharing schemes to provide this support in that the STS network must support users in the practical application of sophisticated technologies, on the firing line.

BENEFITS TO BE DERIVED BY TENANTS FROM STS OPERATIONS

Location

The only alternatives to shared tenant services for most small- to medium-size firms is subscription to a remote computer time-sharing service or the purchase of a small self-owned, self-run, self-supported personal computer or larger system. Neither alternative can equal the practical value of a state-of-the-art, well-managed, on-premises network of distributed processors with state-of-the-art software designed and staffed to meet the specific needs of the business.

The opportunities available through access to the widest geographic network of resources begins with local, on-premises technology and support. For this reason, STS is a solution made possible by the evolving standards for machine communication. The location of STS equipment and support personnel in a user's building makes service and support more accessible. As compared with remote time-sharing services, data transmission rates are more rapid and errors less frequent on the STS local area network. Also, the software available from an STS may be more specifically tailored to the user's needs; lack of pertinent software is a frequent user's complaint in remote time-sharing services. STS users will also experience more local and direct control of their own data.

More Powerful Technology

A network of distributed minicomputers and peripheral devices allows STS clients such as professionals and executives to enter files, get reports, order jobs, print records, do accounting tasks, and even create publications and other documents without reliance on the time or availability of others. This frees people from dependence on others and eliminates the need for menial labor.

More Technology for Less Money

A shared network of local resources has the added advantage of leveraging the buying power of users. STS services can be economically maintained at state-of-the-art levels as new technologies become available.

Ease of Access to Sophisticated Technologies

Possession of an STS network terminal can provide a user with most services of a fully automated office. These include laser printing of custom-designed forms, electronic mail, data-processing, and electronic file systems. STS users should be able to easily gain access to sophisticated telecommunications services such as telefacsimile transmission of documents and access to sophisticated computer tools including design and engineering graphics software, high-capacity batch processing capability, personnel training services, on-site custom programming assistance, and various forms of applications support.

Low Entry Cost

The expense of setting up a company-owned "turn-key" system of hardware and programs for general business is ordinarily very expensive. The STS local area network (LAN) allows new users to become familiar with automation products affordably.

Compared to remote time-sharing operations, an STS network can deliver interactive computer software with shared-use economics. This is made possible by the use of LAN technology in an STS. The LAN's characteristics of extremely rapid data transmission rates plus the luxury of on-site applications support produce an optimum environment for data-processing technologies of all kinds. These are further enhanced by the inclusion of users in a campus type of setting, forming a local community of users who can share knowledge about new practices and methods.

The cost of connecting a user into an STS network, including purchase, rental, or lease of one of a variety of workstation terminals, can range from as little as a few dollars per month for a terminal with limited stand-alone intelligence to several thousand dollars per month for some types of computer-assisted design and manufacturing (CAD/CAM) workstations. The total package of services that can be provided by an STS network, if purchased as a stand-alone system by each firm separately, would cost an individual or firm as much as 1 to 10 million dollars to purchase, not including the cost of education and ongoing system maintenance and support. In an STS situation, this cost may be reduced to as little as $200 per month, depending on the user's needs.

More Usable Applications

STS networks can address all the important information-processing needs of individuals and businesses; these include general ledger accounting, time and billing record keeping and reporting, high quality document and forms preparation and printing, customer and product information record keeping, and cost-saving management of telecommunications services. The STS staff of applications support personnel can cost-effectively offer support that is essential to implement new software. STS maintenance personnel can also provide responsive service for sophisticated automation equipment on which users must frequently depend.

TECHNICAL REQUIREMENTS FOR COMPREHENSIVE STS SERVICES

Hardware

The STS LAN network must provide a high-capacity digital communication utility that is capable of interconnecting users' terminals with a variety of devices that are shared in common.

In their private offices, tenants may have video display terminals and keyboards, plotters or printers, scanners, local data file media (tape, disk, or laser disk drives) or other peripheral equipment.

Common equipment available with access to the STS network may include minicomputers to support software for electronic file service, document printing, telecommunication, and other services such as word processing that are common to the needs of all businesses.

The hardware of the ideal STS may include laser print servers, high-capacity copiers and duplicators, optical character readers, scanners and digitizers (which scan printed matter and record text for editing on word processors), communications servers (through which network users can directly access data processors and data resources in remote locations), telex, telefacsimile equipment (for transmission via telephone lines of graphic, printed, or written matter), a secure data media storage vault (for safe storage of users' archival data on disks or tape), several workspaces with desktops, cabinets, computer terminals, and appropriate lighting and seating (for as-needed use and for purposes of training staff), supplies, training manuals, software guides, and spare equipment to replace hardware when repairs are required.

Software

By employing a network of distributed minicomputers, the STS can provide tenants with a number of independently operating computer programs that each perform an important set of business functions. When interrelated , such systems can allow an individual, who may have little or no particular experience or knowledge about computer programming, to record and access files, to order and print reports or letters, to enter or access accounting information about the business, to obtain summaries of stored information, and to do many time-saving computational jobs.

STS AS A FUTURE MAINSTREAM MARKET FOR COMPUTER SERVICES

Providing integrated total information management services is the goal of value-added reseller services and many vendors of turn-key business automation software and hardware. An STS brings to this task the unique asset of on-site support, which is equivalent to providing users with their own data-processing staff. Although significant problems need to be overcome before the STS concept is fully realized, a close examination of the problems of bringing technology to the great majority of small businesses clearly indicates STS as an important direction. The greatest difficulty encountered at this time is a lack of experience with technology on the part of building developers, designers, owners, and managers as well as among the prospective tenants.

STS TECHNICAL FORMAT—THE TENANT SERVICE CENTER

Within a building supported by STS information utilities there must be rooms available for the core equipment of the network and the network's management. This facility may occupy as little as 700 to 1200 square feet of space. It may include common workspace for users and provide secure storage for users' data and supplies. Minicomputer equipment, including peripheral devices, needs to be installed in a clean, climate-controlled environment, allowing easy access for operation and maintenance. Space, clean power, and flexible climate control must be available for the unusual requirements of high-tech machines such as laser printers, file servers, plotters, digitizers, and workstations. Network management stations for monitoring the tenants' use of services must be provided along with cabinets for storage of forms, tapes, books, disks, and other supplies. Telecommunications equipment, including a PBX and accessory devices, will usually be best located in a separate space where there is access to the building's wiring distribution system and which is securely isolated from intrusion by unauthorized persons.

TENANT WORKSTATIONS

An STS must provide a LAN cabling system by means of which tenants can access the tools of the STS tenant service center from anywhere in the building. Depending on the LAN architecture implemented and the number of users to be served at peak periods, this system may be a coaxial cable similar to that used by CATV, a fiber optic cable, or multiple twisted-wire pairs similar to those used for connecting standard telephones (see Chapter 6). User terminals located anywhere in a building must be able to connect to this cable network in order to communicate with the public telephone network and outside data resource services.

STS users should be able to use their terminals either on the LAN or off the LAN to connect via dial-up telephone with resources outside their office building. Tenants should be able to have their own printers, disk drives, plotters, or other devices located in their own offices, rather than sharing the use of the equipment in the tenant service center with others. The LAN software must provide security that effectively isolates the privately maintained equipment in tenants' offices from access by the unauthorized.

A key feature of a good STS network design is its ability to support a variety of terminal types and qualities. The selection of microprocessors, minicomputers, business workstations, and peripherals must depend on the ability of devices to support software which is compatible with the network.

The STS technical services should also be able, as much as possible, to adapt every modern computer or peripheral to the network, per a user's specific request. Such a request could be the result of a user's previous substantial investment in an existing system or software.

An STS network should make it easy for users to order fulfillment of jobs by STS personnel. For instance, high-technology graphics terminals and plotters for architectural or technical illustration, publishing, and other applications may be made available to designers or other users who require such tools.

A SAMPLE STS

The distributed processing system described below is an example of an early STS design. In actual situations, the technologies employed must be specified to provide the hardware and software necessary for simultaneous access to computer services for a number of users, as determined by the expected tenancy and volume of users during a start-up period. As the use of service expands, more devices can be linked into the network as required. The example below is for a model with an expectation of 20 to 40 initial users, with an expansion capability of service for 400 users.

Hardware

1 Minicomputer (examples: HP3000 XX, DEC VAX 750/780, DG MV8000 or TI 990 Series)

2 Laser printers (40 to 120 pages per minute—example: Xerox 2700, 5700, or 8700)

3 Electronic file servers (three 300-Mb to 600-Mb disk drives)

2 Tape drives (accessory to file servers)

1 LAN cable distribution system (broadband or baseband—examples: Xerox Ethernet, SYTEK Broadband Net)

25 Workstation terminals, with software and interface to LAN

2 Line printers

1 Digital PBX and accessories including ISDN capability, a call director, call-accounting software, and network management terminals (example: Northern Telecom SL1 system)

1 Voice message system (accessory to file server)

1 PBX multiple twisted-pair (three pair) telephone wire distribution system

Test and installation equipment to connect network users with the LAN and PBX wire system

Software

General business applications software should include business accounting systems, a word-processing system, an electronic mail system, database management and electronic filing systems, and network management software.

Support equipment must include a technical library of user program guides and software documentation manuals, supplies, workstations, and high-speed, high-volume copy equipment.

STS EDUCATIONAL SERVICES

The STS is an ideal employer for entry level people who are interested in career opportunities in computer applications support and data-processing equipment management. An opportunity exists for the STS industry to support people in having satisfying and rewarding employment serving others with technologies through STS networks.

APPLICATIONS SOFTWARE

Among the hundreds of software and equipment options available for different businesses, here are some that may be expected for general business activities. Choice of options should depend on the kinds of tenants in the building:

General business systems accounting services—an accounting management program that can be set up by accountants and operated by users.

Text editing and output formatting—word-processing software and workstations that help make typing and editing enjoyable and efficient. Tenants should be able to use either document printers in their offices or the higher-volume print and copy services of the network.

Database Management—software that allows a professional or executive to enter his or her own files and create a report or document without assistance. Tenants should be able to accomplish routine sorting or computations on internally generated, stored data; this should allow them to extract information from data, based on operator-entered selection criteria, in the form of sorted reports, the format of which has been specified by the input operator.

Filing—a rapid access system that uses rigid disk storage of files so that users can scan indexes and locate and call up files or parts of files very quickly and with very little training. The option of hard (paper) copies of any information brought to a user's screen should be available. It should be unnecessary for users to keep extensive paper files of letters and memoranda.

Optional software services

- Typesetting and electronic printing direct from data or word-processing equipment
- CAD/CAM and graphics software and equipment
- Calendars and personal suspense files
- Multiple access to a single database, allowing a group of independently operating individuals to extract information or reports from the same database

Enhanced Telecommunications Services are an essential part of an STS. They are needed to provide access to dial-up data-related services such as commercial electronic research libraries (Lexis, West Law, Dow Jones News Retrieval Service, The Source, Compuserve, General Electric Information Service Co., etc.), data-processing services (EDP, ADP, TRW, etc.), and public data resource services (U.S. Patent Office, Labor Department, Bureau of Commerce, etc.).

The technology supporting enhanced telecommunications centers around a digital PBX equipped with features such as software-defined services including:

- Automatic least-cost routing service, which routes calls from users' extensions automatically via the least expensive routing and renders a coded billing of calls for each extension
- Access to credit information from services such as TRW, Telecredit, and Trans/Union
- Access to cash management reporting by connection to users' banks

STS MANAGEMENT TASKS AND PERSONNEL

Because the kinds of applications support personnel depend on the kind of businesses located in the building as well as the kind of services customers demand, STS networks are best when operated as independent profit centers, managed by on-site personnel in a building or business park. Network management and STS business administration requires qualified personnel to manage the tasks described below.

Billing and Accounting

STS users must be billed by the network for the services they use during each monthly period.

Technical Maintenance

The technical system, including the hardware, software, and all other components, (such as user terminals) must be serviceable by STS-trained staff, supported by service contractors and vendors.

Network Administration

STS personnel must monitor the network to ensure security of files and to flag unusual conditions or attempts at wrongful access to data, guaranteeing user security. Network electronic monitors can provide data for accounting reports and records for billing, planning, and management purposes. However, personnel are required to supervise word- and data-processing services. This is in addition to the monitoring, supporting, supplying, and maintenance of the LAN. Under the network administrator's supervision, the STS staff must do preventive and remedial equipment maintenance, load tape and disk drives and printers, and also assist and educate tenants so that they get maximum benefit from the network.

Telecommunications Management

The STS must manage the installation, management, and maintenance of tenants' telephone systems, a job of ongoing complexity. The STS telecommunications manager must provide the interface between tenants and vendors' sales and repair people, engineering technicians, and the representatives of both local and long-haul telephone networks.

Industry Specific Software Services

The STS technical and user education support staff must include both on-site staff and on-call consultants. Support personnel must include software system designers and applications specialists with expertise in fields for which automation services are to be provided. These personnel must be skilled as educators in order to provide ongoing training for users and STS personnel responsible for the operation, maintenance, and marketing of network services.

Users will also require assistance for database integration as well as software applications consultation. STS staff must be able to provide these services to tenants on a fee for service basis. Outside consultants should be available on request through the STS network.

STS PERSONNEL—DUTIES AND QUALIFICATIONS

Network Manager

The manager takes responsibility for the supervision of an STS profit center, including a job shop. The manager needs to be an excellent sales person who is familiar with the computer and its peripheral hardware, its software, and the system library and software guides. The manager will be able to operate the system and know when to call for assistance, whom to call, and what to ask.

Entry Level Management Trainees

Employees are needed who know how to operate network software and computers and who can handle the requisite materials and supplies.

They must have rudimentary knowledge of software and understand the logic and terminology of the particular systems being used well enough to accomplish jobs, answer users' questions, and train user personnel. They are trained to handle the activities of a professional office operation.

Applications Consultant

An STS needs established agreements with software and system contractors who have specialized in applying automation procedures to particular businesses such as architecture, engineering, law, accounting, media, and so on. Such contractors may alternatively be regular employees of an STS. Since they will be experts in a business or professional specialty, they may be retained permanently by an STS because of their familiarity with state-of-the-art applications of technology in the business of principal tenants. They may assist tenants on a fee per service basis in applying sophisticated software and may also assist with the training of STS network staff.

REVENUES—PRODUCTS AND SERVICES

Principal revenues for an STS come primarily from the sale of both services and equipment in connection with a network of computer-driven automation devices and peripheral equipment located in office buildings and business parks, with direct cable connections to the workstations of tenants located in users' own offices. Income may also be derived from a contract with a building owner providing a margin of profit from the rental of space in professional suites and buildings where STS services enhance value and allow a building owner or master lessor to charge more for such space. The following list identifies many sources of revenue that may be created in an STS operation:

- A monthly fee based on the kinds of equipment, number of terminals, and amount of services of various kinds used by each user of the network during a monthly period
- Consultation fees charged per hour for applications assistance, including fees for software modifications and specialized applications programs
- Sale, lease, or rental payments for terminal equipment used in the offices of tenants or in the STS's service center
- Profit margin from space rental in professional suites, in accordance with special contracts with building owners and master lessors
- Program modifications for individuals or groups of users
- Batch processing

- Sale of custom-designed forms and other supplies
- Digital document printing and duplication services
- Sale or lease of special purpose systems or equipment for tenants' offices
- Temporary personnel services to support tenants for job assignments on an as-needed basis
- Sale of training media, staff education, and related consultation services and systems to tenants and other users
- Connection to remote data-processing resources
- Form preparation, mailing, and fulfillment services
- Telecommunications services
- Telephone call screening and automated answering services, coupled with message delivery
- Sale and programming of user-owned and -operated (turn-key) systems to firms or public agencies
- Consultation services for software and applications needs of users other than building tenants
- Sale of hardware, software, and training aides to tenants for home use or travel
- Licensed sale of software and remote resource services
- Commissions from real estate leasing and fees for management received from building owners or master lessors
- Commissions from sales of vendor-provided order fulfillment services of various kinds associated with professional suite service management

Case Study

THE OLYMPIC PLAZA STS PROTOTYPE
WINN INFORMATION NETWORK (WIN) MANAGER'S REPORT

WIN set up an STS prototype by designing, building, staffing, and operating, in cooperation with a building developer and the Xerox Corporation and Northern Telecom International, a shared resource service center, suite, and voice data networks within a business framework known as the Top Executive Suite. Space in the suite and building was leased to small entrepreneurial businesses such as paralegal services, construction companies, executive search firms, financial consultants, attorneys, accountants, investment firms, and advertising and direct mail companies. These firms had available to them the kinds of support that are usually found only in *Fortune* 1000 firms.

In the prototype STS project, prospective tenants were sold by the fact that they could literally walk in and have everything comfortably set up for them without much planning, concern, or expense. They simply had to move in their furniture, pick up their pens and pencils or telephones, and go to work. They could store records, order time and billing to clients, access accounting and spread sheet software, and send out correspondence in a way that forwarded their own particular businesses. The services included a phone-in dictation facility that allowed tenants to call in their work from any public telephone. The service center kept a supply of the tenants' own stationery to facilitate this service.

Services Available in Prototype

The shared resource suite was rented to a mix of tenants who used supervised services for a multitude of varying needs defined by the nature of their own businesses. These services included:

Word processing

Mailing services

Dictation services

Copy and duplication services

Optical scanning

Rental of workstations

Accounting services

Records processing

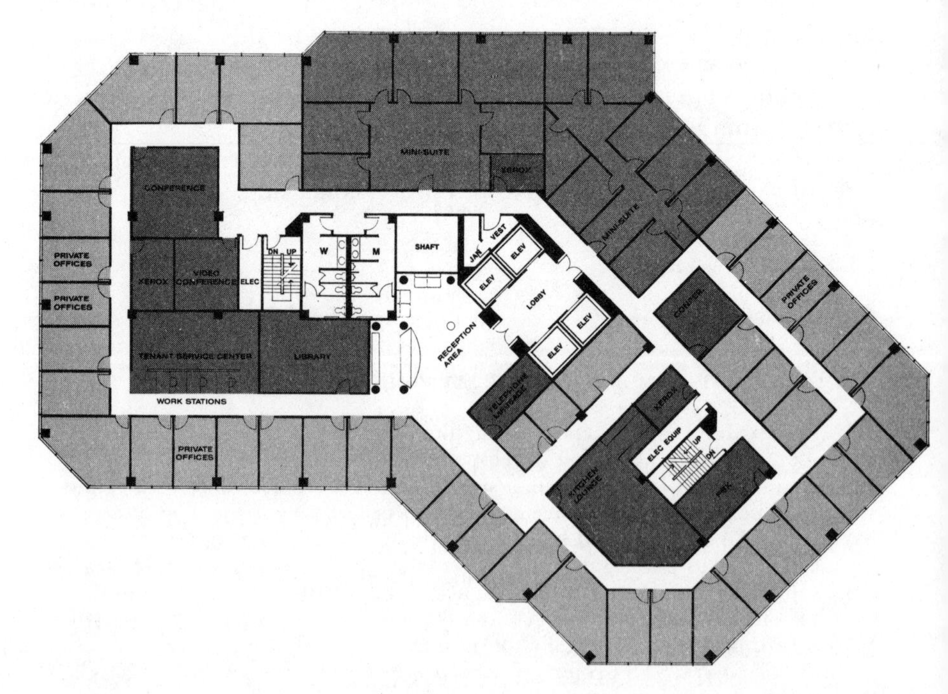

Figure 7.1 The earliest form of the shared resource suite was designed to provide common amenities for independently operating attorneys. Today, many different small businesses and branch offices of large organizations rent offices already equipped with state-of-the-art information management systems which the tenants share. The trend is toward incorporation of this concept in entire buildings.

Graphic enhancement of word-processing documents

Message taking and forwarding

Physical Facilities and Systems

The location was a five-story office building of approximately 235,000 rentable square feet. Ethernet cables were initially installed throughout an area of 25,000 square feet, comprising about half of the fourth floor of the building. This area was built into a "shared resource suite." The space was finished with 103 private offices, some of which were grouped in "minisuite" configurations of 2 to 5 offices each. Included in the common area spaces were furnished conference rooms, a reception area, a law library, a lounge, copy and duplication rooms, telephone message and equipment rooms, and an office automation service center.

Tenants of the suite or the rest of the building could rent or buy workstations which were able, via the Xerox Ethernet or the Northern Telecom PBX SL1 system, to command computing and peripheral equipment in the centrally located automation center. They could use workstations located in the service center or order services from the STS staff.

The following items of office automation equipment were available to users on the LAN:

- Electronic (laser) printers (2 Xerox model 2700, providing 24 printed pages per minute)
- Electronic (rigid disk) file servers (2 Xerox 600 Mb rigid disk find servers)
- Communications servers
- An optical character reader (Kurzweil device)
- Word-processing, graphic, and microprocessor workstations (various)

Telecommunications Equipment and Services

The Northern Telecom SL1 PBX system, expandable to include capability of serving the entire building, was installed to provide tenants with state-of-the-art telecommunications, including simultaneous voice and data transmissions. Within 6 months of installation, the SL1 was providing service to 70 percent of the building's occupants and to 100 percent of the occupants of the shared resource suite. Features available to users of the telephone services included:

- Immediate connection of phone service on move-in
- Advanced technology services including call forwarding, transferring, conferencing, speed dialing and redial features, automatic call timing, call code accounting, multiline sets, call directors and consoles, least-cost routing, call detail reporting, and access to a range of long-haul carriers
- A range of telephone instruments included phone sets with built-in data communications ability and electronic logic phones programmed for the level of service specified by each tenant

Other Amenities

In addition to the usual technology, the STS tenants could avail themselves of a complete federal and state law library and a Westlaw electronic library terminal. Other amenities of the suite included:

- A receptionist and telephone console operators who provided mail, message, and concierge type services

- A fully equipped kitchen and lounge with complimentary coffee and tea service
- Luxuriously furnished conference rooms and boardrooms
- A complimentary amount of copy, dictation, and word-processing services for each tenant, each month

Marketing Results—Office Rental

As of 6 months after opening, the shared resource suite was 84 percent leased, a statistic that surpassed the projections of the business plan by 100 percent. The rapid leasing rate of the shared resource suite has been attributed by management to the promotability of the STS services offered to tenants; these included many services that they could not find all together elsewhere.

For example, tenants who moved into the shared resource suite had immediate access to telephone service that was already installed and was instantly programmable to meet their needs. An instance that dramatically demonstrates how this affected leasing is the case of a large savings and loan institution which rented space temporarily and then remained for a year. Thirty-four percent of the shared resource suite was leased, at a wholesale rate, to four divisions of a large savings and loan company. The decision of this firm to move into the suite was based on two important factors:

- They could move into a suite that was already built, and they needed to move four divisions to the area immediately.
- They could have phone service within 10 days of signing the lease, including operable phone numbers which they could have listed in the phone book.

Although the discounted rates were still substantially above market, the above two factors influenced the decision to locate in the suite rather than move into space in another building at a lower rate. In that case, they would have had to then buy and install a phone system, wait longer for other support services, and deal with many other problems involved in providing work space for more than 40 professional personnel.

Although the savings and loan was a special case, other tenants cited the same features as contributing to their decisions, and none mentioned location as a deciding factor.

The prototype STS taught much about what doesn't work in the interior design and operation of an automated office. The prototype revealed a strong market for minisuites within the shared resource suite, with most desirable sizes ranging from 850–1200 square feet. There was more demand for conference rooms than expected at first, and there was a substantial interest in equipment for presentations. Interior offices were found to be aesthetically undesirable but still marketable for most business activities. However, they do not rent as well as outside space. The executive office sizes were acceptable to tenants in sizes smaller than the 150 to 195 square feet as designed in the prototype plan.

The rental rate of executive window offices ranged between $3.50 and $4.50 per square foot, depending on the size and the location in the suite. The interior secretarial offices, which were prefurnished, averaged about $3.00 per square foot. The overall effective rental rate for the suite, including common areas, was $3.25 per square foot. Table 7.1 gives the posted rent schedule.

TABLE 7.1 Posted Rent Schedule

Offices	Dimensions, feet	Size, square feet	Rent*, dollars/month
	Individual Offices		
438	Odd shaped	301	900
402	14.5 × 19	275.5	875
440	Odd shaped	230.25	875
441–448	15 × 13	195	850
428–437	15 × 13	195	825
403–409	15 × 13	195	800
421–417	15 × 13	195	800
426	13 × 11	143	775
437	13 × 13	169	750
439	13 × 13	169	750
418	14 × 10.5	147	600
425	12.5 × 11	137	600
All interior offices	12.5 × 10	125	600
Secretarial offices		62.5 per station	350†
	Minisuites		
445	Odd shaped	1,052	3,100
437	26 × 32.5	845	2,700
441	26 × 32.5	845	2,700
450–453	Odd shaped	771	2,300
424–427	21 × 13	373	1,000
410, 411	21 × 13	373	1,000

*Rents based on size and location.
†Two secretarial stations per office at $350 per station.

Marketing Results—Office Automation Services

The original marketing plan asserted that it is difficult to operate a business properly today without some form of office automation. Earlier research indicated that by 1983, 1 out of 10 white collar workers would be using desktop terminals, and the industry projects now that this ratio will move to 1 in 4 within the next 2 years. Market studies found experts claiming that small business computers priced at $6000 to $10,000 cost a business user 3 times this amount by the time they are programmed and installed with software (including the time and expense needed to integrate data-processing techniques with traditional business procedures). It was comprehendible that small businesspeople, independent sole practitioners, executive search firms, paralegal firms, and other entrepreneurial endeavors such as those who located in the prototype building could not afford to spend $20,000 to $30,000 in 1 year of business and financially survive. The validity of these assertions was borne out by the emergence during 1984 of a sharp decline in the sale of personal computers.

At the prototype STS, small businesses were given the opportunity to have a competitive edge without spending large amounts for hardware, software, and personnel support. Since operations commenced, it has become clearer that these services have more than a luxury value, and in fact are essential. Table 7.2 shows telephone equipment rates, while Table 7.3 shows the automation services available and their rates.

TABLE 7.2 Telephone Equipment Rental Rates

Equipment	Rent, dollars/month
SL-1 Telephone	30.00
SL-1 Plus speaker phone	35.00
Guest phone (2500 set)	15.00

The quantity of office automation services sales in the prototype was interesting but insubstantial. This was due in part to the low occupancy level of the suite and building during start-up. Marketing efforts were started with 22 businesses in the suite; 17, or 82 percent of them, used the office automation services at various times. After analysis of the various problems, opportunities, breakdowns, technologies and many other factors influencing profitability in the prototype STS, a marketing plan was developed which produced results that exceeded the projections of the original plan. The projections of income for the prototype were based on an aggressive use of a detailed results-oriented marketing plan, coupled with a plan for investment in more industry specific application support software.

The prototype proved the concept of using the shared suite to leverage the introduction of shared services into a building. A private phone system installed within the suite provided an inexpensive telecommunication system to tenants located elsewhere in the building. To further enhance profitability in the telecommunications area, a plan was initiated to incorporate an automatic voice-messaging service and to add a facility for voice message storing and forwarding. Since commencing business, voice-messaging systems compatible with the PBX became available.

In the area of computer applications software, we discovered that the demand for support services quickly surpassed our ability to provide even very simple industry specific software services. Part of the problem resulted from the initial selection of equipment and software, which was oriented toward the needs of attorneys and law firms (i.e., word processing and document preparation). After the building opened, new software was made available to run on minicomputer systems which provided greater flexibility to integrate special purpose software.

Competition

The prototype demonstrated that the STS business has a competitive edge following from the unique strategy of locating support and services in the building and creating a community of common interest with the tenants. Although this was the conclusion from the experience in the prototype, the project remains at this time the only STS in the nation that has offered both office automation and telecommunication services in a shared resource environment. None of the larger firms presently involved in STS have fully exploited the opportunity which shared tenant services represents for marketing of real estate, systems, software, and support, presumably because of problems such as the prototype experienced in providing users with industry specific applications software and support. It is also difficult to plan and staff sophisticated STS facilities in empty buildings.

TABLE 7.3 Office Automation Network Service Center

Services offered	Price list
Word processing orders	
Double-spaced documents	$ 4.00 per page
Single-spaced documents	$ 6.50 per page
Statistical documents	$12.50 per page
Legal documents	$ 6.50 per page
Proofreading	$ 0.40 per page
Repetitive letters	
Set-up	$ 6.50 per page
Play-out	0.55 per page
Envelopes	0.25 per envelope
Dictation transcription	$25.00 per hour
Text editing and revisions	$25.00 per hour
Copy and duplication services	
1045 copies	0.08 per page
Laser printouts	0.50 per page
Kurzweil optical scanner	
Set-up	$60.00 per hour
Scanning	0.75–1.20 per thousand characters*
Accounting services	
Data entry/accounting and reporting	price by consultation
Software integration	
Software modification	price by consultation
Machine rental	
Xerox 860	$10.00 per hour
IBM PC	$10.00 per hour
Xerox 16-8	$10.00 per hour
Xerox Star	$10.00 per hour
Kurzweil optical scanner	price by consultation

*Charge is dependent on quantity of materials to be scanned.

Strategic Plan

The prototype plan was to provide a solution for marketing automation products and services to users who as yet have not been reached or educated to the use of automation, either by large system manufacturers or microcomputer sales. That is, users were to be small- to medium-size businesses, entrepreneurs, and professionals who could benefit from the shared resources of larger buildings. Of equal interest was the possibility, which arose in the prototype, of selling services to larger organizations such as the savings and loan tenant for whom the prototype provided substantial overflow service and supporting satellite operations.

The prototype model revealed an economical modular approach that is workable in a great number of smaller buildings. The plan is operable in buildings ranging in size from 40,000 square feet in gross leasable area to millions of square feet, and it can accommodate installations that are profitable in virtually any size of building in this broad range. This is not so for the plans of firms such as UT, EOCA, and AT&T. The high investment cost of their operations is prohibitive.

Conclusions

Firms were attracted to the prototype STS building because of the services available. The prototype had only just begun to market the office automation services to tenants when the building project experienced financial difficulties unrelated to the STS project. The building changed ownership and the project was abruptly ended. The shared resource suite with its automation service center and the building telecommunications services continued to operate and the suite is at this time still fully leased.

The office automation services and Ethernet LAN provided by the Xerox company proved to be an excellent tool for marketing. Prospective tenants recognized the Xerox logo as a mark of quality. However, the lack of an integrated set of business applications software for accounting and database management tasks inhibited business growth in this area and forced the prototype to move down a path dictated by limitations of the installed equipment, to wit, document production. In this regard, the installed Xerox equipment gave excellent support to the tenants.

In particular, the plan to use off-the-shelf microprocessor (personal computer) software proved untenable either because the variety of software was not supportable by prototype staff or this was not interesting to tenants.

CHAPTER

8

The Miniature Telephone Company and Telecommunications-Enhanced Real Estate

According to the terms of the decree requiring divestiture by AT&T of the Bell System operating companies, anyone can access any intra- and interstate long-distance telecommunications networks through telephone lines provided by the local telephone operating company. But people do not *have* to go through the local telephone company to get to long distance carriers and need not rent or purchase equipment from the telephone company which they use to access those carriers. The local telephone company is under no constraint to provide "inside wiring" for new buildings as they used to be, or to replace outmoded or unworkable wiring in existing buildings, or to provide telephone instruments for the customer's use. The local telephone companies are, at this time, prohibited by the FCC from directly supplying customers with certain enhanced services available through privately owned PBX systems.

Advances in the state of the art of telecommunications technology have made it possible for small, minimally capitalized telephone service firms to buy, service, and operate sophisticated telephone connection equipment. Locating such equipment within a building as in STS situations enables these firms to resell dial tone service to other tenants in the building, often with substantial discounts for the customer. By limiting connection to building residents, STS operators can escape the regulatory code which defines a common carrier as one who transports communications signals over public space.

Very compact state-of-the-art new digital PBX systems, driven by modern microprocessor computers, are capable of providing service to 500 or 1000 separate telephone lines at an installation cost to the service provider that ranges from $300 to $800 per line, including telephones, wiring, installation, and vendor warranty. Small firms can wire a building and provide tenants with telephone equipment and services far superior to those available from the local telephone company for far less cost than the telepone company can. Because of their lower total overhead costs and because they have the flexibility to install and support more modern equipment, they are able to save tenants money and still be profitable. Because they are able to aggregate all the tenants' use of long-distance services, they take advantage of competition among long-haul carriers and produce a profit from the resale of long-distance service. They buy a long-distance service at a flat, high-volume rate and resell the service at retail prices which are still lower than those available to the individual buyer. They offer discounts (20 percent or more) to customers, still providing a comfortable margin of profit for themselves. In addition, they are in a good position to furnish local bypass equipment to their customers. By installing microwave antennas on buildings, they can relay their customers' signals to remote locations without accessing the local network, with favorable economics.

Most intelligent building services now being offered are actually shared telephone services. For this reason, AT&T has chosen the term "telecommunications-enhanced real estate" (TERE) to describe this kind of operation instead of STS. The technology of TERE is relatively simple. Users of a TERE service are connected via telephone-type twisted-wire pair cable standardized by the Bell System. Through telephone sets and using low-speed data modems, they can share the use of a digital PBX through which they can access the public telephone network, long-haul carriers, and a limited range of computer-oriented services. The TERE business faces most of the technical and administrative problems with which telephone companies must deal, but on a smaller scale. For this reason, most telephone companies and many vendors of telecommunications equipment have become involved in TERE business.

In the time elapsed since the AT&T divestiture, many new companies have started up to exploit the opportunities offered by TERE operation. The Bell operating companies and the independent telephone companies, long-haul carriers such as Satellite Business Systems and United

Telephone have all seen STS and TERE as an opportunity to broaden their customer base. Local telephone operating companies see the opportunity as a threat of bypass.

Entrants into the STS/TERE field include some coventuring partnerships between building developers and telecommunications companies. These have offered to provide attractive and cost-effective telecommunications services as a building amenity, thus providing incentive to locate in multitenant buildings.

This chapter summarizes the history and development of the shared tenant telecommunications service industry and informs about the technologies used, the advantages offered to tenants, and the possible risks. It reveals the direction of new technological growth and industry trends as well as key elements that relate to regulation.

SHARED TELECOMMUNICATIONS SERVICES—DESCRIPTION

TERE services are primarily telephone services provided for tenants of a building or office park by a telecommunications service company. The services are rendered from a facility located within the building or complex. For the most part, TERE operates like an in-house telephone company for office buildings, industrial complexes, and shopping malls. Unlike telephone companies, TERE businesses do not usually generate dial tone; instead, they carry the dial tone of other telecommunications carriers to the end user. However, by using a more sophisticated modular digital PBX system, they are able to offer a wider range of telecommunications services than is available from the public telephone network.

The evolution of telecommunications technology will continue to support the technological gap between the public network and more flexibly adaptable smaller systems. An example of this is the foreseeable merging of local area network (LAN) technology with telecommunications service technology. The separation of these two technologies, prior to the Carterfone decision in 1968, was artificially created by the restriction which prevented the connection of any devices to the public telephone network except those sold by the Bell System. Local (in-house) communications, especially sophisticated data and video communications methods, thus developed apart from the telephone system. The telephone system's voice optimized technological standards were also maintained at levels which are not capable of supporting sophisticated uses. With the successful implementation of fiber optic transmission technologies in public telephone networks, there will soon be bandwidth capacity available sufficient to provide improved levels of service—enough to support two-way video transmission (video phones) and effective interactive communication between computers.

Even with the advent of improved transmission capability in the public telephone network, TERE operations are likely to maintain their competitive edge because of their confined size. They should be able to reliably and quickly implement new developments to utilize the fiber optic medium much more easily and rapidly than possible in the public telephone company network. This may result in generation of carrier signals for internal communication within a building, making the TERE more like a high-tech telephone company and providing cost-effective management for customers by integrating the service offerings of long-haul connections and the public telephone network.

The rental or purchase of telecommunications equipment is a difficult decision for businesses. Telecommunications consultants can provide cost-effective assistance for larger firms with regard to the selection of a privately owned system. However, the complexities arising from the ongoing integration of data, video, and voice signal transmission and the fluctuating rate structures among competing long-distance signal carriers make telecommunications decisions a dynamic issue. Although the cash outlay for a private system might average out to a lower total expense than would rental of equipment, there are unknown costs attributable to updating obsolete equipment and reinstalling because of business changes. The system buyer also has to bear the cost of managing esoteric technology. Because of their ability to distribute the cost of call management equipment (and the personnel support involved) over a number of users, TERE operators can provide telecommunications equipment and support services at prices which are lower than the cash outlay for individual purchase.

Small businesses cannot afford the costs of a comprehensive survey of their telecommunications needs and the services of a knowledgeable consultant to review the product offerings of interconnect and long distance vendors. They are, therefore, natural clients for TERE operations. Simply on the basis of substantial long-distance discounts, Electronic Office Systems of America has been able to sign up most tenants of the Apparel Mart building in Chicago to their TERE service. Although TERE operators begin to come into their own by meeting the key requirements of smaller businesses, they will eventually provide more sophisticated network capability than that which is at present available through a digital PBX telephone switch.

It is possible that the advantages, services, and benefits of TERE operations, as described below, may eventually influence builders, telecommunications, and data-processing entrepreneurs to provide state-of-the-art information management technology support affordable to the large number of small businesses and individual professionals in every community. The value of concentrated resources available in urban commercial buildings would thus be truly enhanced.

THE DIGITAL PBX

Today, the typical TERE facility centers around a PBX system, which is a high-speed switching device for interconnecting lines and trunks. On one side of the switch are trunks and dedicated lines that carry traffic to and from the building. On the other side of the switch, lines lead to the telephone extensions of individual tenants. The PBX automatically connects lines to outgoing trunks, and it connects incoming calls to the tenants' line extensions. The digital PBX provides a broad range of programmed services to telephone users, and the value of shared tenant services (STS) stems from the ability to share the expense of this sophisticated equipment as well as telephone trunks. The professional management of these facilities, provided by a TERE operator, is a more important value for users. It makes the service reasonable even for large firms that could afford to purchase private equipment. For example, it is imperative for an operator to manage the PBX so that less expensive trunk volumes can be shared in order to create profitability.

TERE ADVANTAGES

Cost Effectiveness

- Telephone trunk time is priced by carriers on a sliding scale—the more you use, the less it costs. The TERE operation aggregates the total volume of calls for multiple users and achieves a higher-volume use and commensurate lower trunk cost per minute of use.
- Certain kinds of telephone trunks and telecommunications services bear fixed, flat monthly rates. These trunks can also be shared, distributing the fixed cost between several users.

Superior Equipment and Better Management

In addition to cost savings, shared tenant services can more speedily and flexibly provide equipment and up-grade software-supported PBX features. Many state-of-the-art telecommunications services are not available from telephone companies. The size of a TERE operation permits a more easy adaptation of new technology as it becomes available.

TERE can provide tenants with a broader range of telephone terminals and other equipment. Although the console call-directing and station equipment of each PBX manufacturer will not fit with the equipment of its competitors, TERE can provide an interface between equipment items within a building. The product lines of the major PBX manufacturers include a selection of telephone terminals that are more advanced than those sold and supported by telephone companies.

Installation and service are immediate in shared tenant situations. The TERE operator has a definable range of clients, allowing more predictable staffing and technology installation lead times. The TERE operator also cannot afford dissatisfied clients and must deliver service benefits to keep clients from migrating to telephone company service. The TERE operator has the advantage of being able to create a staff of manageable size to suit the needs of a known group of customers. On-premises personnel can be carefully selected and trained to manage state-of-the-art equipment which has been engineered to provide the best fail-safe features required by customers.

EVOLUTION OF STATE-OF-THE-ART TERE SERVICES

Because the TERE industry is in a seminal stage, it is dominated by the influence of risk capital. Investors are reluctant to risk on service implementations for which consumer demand cannot be demonstrated, though it can be predicted. Over time, the services offered by TERE operators can be expected to grow and change, reflecting new customer demand. The features offered are available from a digital PBX, including a broad range of accessory devices. These features are available to individual users, just as though they were *Fortune* 1000 corporate executives with dollars to spend on state-of-the-art services and a telecommunications management staff. Many newer services offered by a digital PBX system are revolutionary tools that can improve the quality of business communications, resulting in higher productivity, more closed sales, faster delivery of product, and more effective business relationships. In addition to the typical features of call waiting, call forwarding, automatic dialing, and conference calling provided by local telephone companies, these new STS value-added services include:

Manned message centers. These provide professional telephone screening and answering services; telephone receptionists use video screens for call message information. An incoming call signals a PBX integrated message service to bring up a video display which details the called party's call-handling preferences and provides space for message taking. When the call is completed, a message that has been entered can be forwarded automatically to a file where it can be picked up later by the message operator or the call recipient.

Voice messaging. This feature offers callers an alternative to dealing with a call-screening operator. Voice-messaging equipment can be programmed to forward messages automatically to the recipient's telephone address and to store messages until they can be delivered.

Automatic least-cost routing (ACR). This feature automatically scans outgoing trunks in a PBX system and selects the least expensive route for outbound calls. Operators keep track of various carriers' rate fluctuations and program each user's routing priorities to provide the greatest economies. When the least-cost routes are busy, a calling party may be signaled that a more expensive route is being used so that there is an opportunity to cancel the call; alternatively, the call can simply be blocked with a busy signal.

Call detail recording (CDR). This service provides the tenant with monthly telephone records that include a coded report about outgoing calls for monitoring their use and, in the case of lawyers and other professionals, for billing clients. CDR programming can also provide billing for customers by 6-second increments instead of the 20-second increments used by many carriers, as well as a means of automatically monitoring a firm's use of telephone services and providing firms with means for controlling their telephone bills.

Point-to-point. A facility for high-speed data communications lines can be provided within the building to support data terminals within a tenant's offices. Modems and packet-switching equipment can be provided to support data communications on the public telephone network.

Video conferencing. Equipment and line connections and, in some locations, complete production and transmission facilities may become part of the service offering.

TERE facilities can also be implemented for building management, security, and environmental control.

TELECOMMUNICATIONS MANAGEMENT AND SUPPORT PERSONNEL

As business methods continue to be influenced by the use of new information management technologies, deciding whether to adopt the state-of-the-art technology distracts managers from the focus of business. Upgrading technology usually also results in a need to retrain personnel. And there is the problem of ongoing management and evaluation of the new service implementation. TERE operations do not eliminate these problems, but they do much to reduce the problems they cause. TERE management and staff have more to gain than their customers do in making the most cost-effective decisions about new technology, and they benefit by being able to support their customers' best and maximum use of the new tools. The greatest potential value of TERE may be the support staff available to assist tenants in meeting and managing their telephone and data communications needs.

HISTORICAL PERSPECTIVE

Bell Canada is reputed to have initiated the TERE approach to shared tenant telecommunications services through the development and implementation of the telephone exchange on customer premises. Bell Canada wished to provide telephone services more cost-effectively to tenants of large buildings. A solution was found by locating telephone switching gear in large buildings, which was initially done in Toronto. The existing call handling equipment was impractical because different groups of users wanted different groups of telephone features. Telephone switch gear at that time was mechanical, not intelligently driven by digital computer devices. Such mechanical devices treat every call in the same way. They cannot distinguish between calls and assign special attributes to incoming or outgoing calls, based on who is placing the call. In 1976, Bell Canada requested from Northern Telecom the development of a PBX switch that was "partitionable," to provide distinctly different services for separate customer groups. Northern Telecom had purchased the Danray company, which had invented the technology that pioneered the development of the modern partitionable digital PBX. The Northern Telecom PBX family is the evolutionary outgrowth of the original Danray patents, as are the systems of other manufacturers of digital PBX systems.

THE PARTITIONABLE SWITCH

A "partition" in PBX terminology is actually a set of programs for managing calls. Each partition of the digital-controlled switch provides a different set of call management instructions for an assigned set of telephone line extensions. All calls made by telephones included in the same partition are managed according to the same set of rules. Depending on the features ordered by a tenant, telephone extensions can be assigned to one partition or another, or a totally new partition can be programmed in. The simplest partitionable switch offered at present in Northern Telecom's family of products provides 256 distinct classes of service. The Northern Telecom switch became the forerunner of a large and rapidly expanding family of similar devices, now being made by several manufacturers, which are being exploited by shared tenant service operators in many buildings all over the country.

At about the time Bell Canada was implementing solutions with Northern Telecom, GTE in the United States initiated "Centrex CU" (Centrex customer premises) services. Centrex is a telephone company trademark for advanced call-managing facilities offered through the telephone company central office. In Centrex service, some programmable services of a PBX are offered to businesses through a Centrex tariff description. Centrex CU is thus the marketing label for locating an annex of telephone company switch gear in a large building in order to provide PBX-type services for the tenants. Centrex *CU* technology was developed as an alternative to "Centrex *CO*," which provides PBX-type services directly out of the telephone company's central office facility. Centrex technology is less sophisticated than the digital PBX type of facility developed by Northern Telecom for Bell Canada. With the advent of divestiture and competition from other vendors of service and equipment, Centrex must undergo a vast improvement before it is able to compete with STS offerings.

DIVESTITURE AND REGULATION—IMPACT ON STS/TERE

One basic premise underlying the concept of shared tenant services is that not everybody in a large building will be using their phones at the same time. Consequently, many customers can share a common group of private and long-distance lines. In 1981, the Federal Communications Commission (FCC), acting on the requests of companies such as MCI and Sprint, modified regulations to allow the resale of private lines. This change in regulations created the opportunity for entrepreneurs to profit by reselling the use of telephone lines. As long as no wires were connected into, over, or through a public thoroughfare, the service provider could also escape regulation by state public utilities commissions since it could not be defined as a common carrier. The necessary investment was modest, requiring only the purchase of a PBX (as little as

$150,000 at start-up) and the ordering of lines from local telephone companies. Trunk services on commonly used lines could then be sold to many different customers within a building. From this beginning, shared tenant services expanded to include the rental of terminal equipment (telephone sets) to customers. After AT&T restructured their rate schedule from flat to measured rates, the FCC allowed the resale of WATS and other long-distance services by shared tenant services. Today, a few shared tenant services offer voice and video terminals, connections to shared data-processing tools, electronic printing and filing, video teleconferencing, and other computer-driven tools.

One of the first entrepreneurs to enter the TERE business was Bernard Bishop, a former GTE executive who founded Electronic Office Centers of America, Inc. (EOCA), in Chicago in 1981, following the FCC decision to permit resale of private lines. EOCA is now a division of Westinghouse and at present has contracts to provide shared tenant telephone services in more than 15 million square feet of urban building space in several cities; its customers include the Apparel Mart and the Merchandise Mart in Chicago.

The FCC decision to allow resale of private lines was supported by AT&T and the Bell operating companies because it increased the total volume of existing network and equipment usage and revenue without further investment. Essentially, it was a marketing boost for STS. It was afterwards that AT&T restructured its tariffs from a flat rate to a measured rate to allow the resale of WATS lines.

The terms of the divestiture settlement with AT&T in 1984 further enhanced the opportunity for entrepreneurial activity in shared tenant telecommunications services. Under the principle of the requirement for equal access, telephone customers may specify—to their local telephone company—their carrier of choice for long-distance in direct dial service. A company such as MCI, SBS, ITT, GTE-Sprint, or Allnet may be specified as the carrier of choice, so that a user's calls automatically are routed to that carrier. Although equal access guarantees better sales among residential users to the long-distance competitors of AT&T, problems arise for the business consumer because of the difficulty in managing decisions about the rate structures of several long-haul carriers which vary depending on the routes, times, seasons, volumes of traffic, and classes of service. Shared tenant services add value for their customers by choosing the carrier with automatic "least-cost routing software." Since rates fluctuate frequently, the adjustment of programming requires constant surveillance and management which is readily accomplished by the TERE Service.

THE EMERGING TERE INDUSTRY

Recently, several major and many smaller technology firms have teamed with real estate developers to build into their projects a capability for shared tenant telecommunications services. The emergence of this new industry has been prompted by two factors:

- The interest of real estate developers in being able to better market real estate that has been enhanced by the availability of high-tech telecommunications resources
- The development of microcomputer-managed telephone PBX systems that provide telephone services in many ways superior to those typically offered by telephone company central offices

This trend has been supported by two impinging circumstances:

- The divestiture of AT&T and deregulation of telephone services, making way for the competitive resale of long-distance and other telephone services by many new firms
- Realization by most business managers of a need for professional technology management in order to take advantage of complex PBX and computer systems and the opportunities afforded by the new telecommunications services

An important motivation for the TERE industry has been the difficulty and expense involved in managing and supporting telecommunications, local area networking, office automation, data processing, and business applications technologies. Integrating new technologies in a building presents a mind-boggling array of considerations for businesses. The task requires an integrated approach to building structure, interior design, and space planning both within and beyond a tenant's rented area. Whatever interim reasons developers and technology companies have for meeting in projects today, tomorrow promises to bring an even closer alliance between these two industries.

TERE INDUSTRY EXPANSION

The number of shared tenant businesses in 1984 expanded rapidly—following divestiture—and tapered off in 1986. Development in telecommunications and digital PBX technology is rapidly creating more valuable products for shared services. The fact that shared tenant services are providing attractions for users is demonstrated by the entry of AT&T Information Services, Ameritech, CP National, Continental

Telephone, and the regional Bell operating companies into the multitenant business.

In 1982, there were three entrepreneurs in the shared tenant business. At a meeting of the Multi-Tenant Trade Association (MTTA), a trade association of shared tenant service companies, in May of 1984, the companies represented had commitments to provide service in buildings housing over 50 million square feet of commercial space. It was estimated at this meeting that MTTA members represented less than half of the shared tenant operators in the country. Northern Telecom reports that in 1983 it had installed between 400 and 1000 lines in multitenant service. Two years later, Northern Telecom increased shared tenant lines installed to more than 50,000. NEC, Rolm, and AT&T have all announced new product lines in support of shared tenant services. Both Honeywell and Erickson Corporations have switches in development. United Technologies first purchased a switch manufacturer (Lexar) for STS applications and later formed a coventure with AT&T which was chartered to manage STS operations. This coventure has ended, however, reportedly as the result of a lack of attention to real estate marketing which revealed some facts about the evolution of the STS/TERE industry.

Although there is a potential for profits in the resale of long-distance and point-to-point communications services, shared tenant services must have an effect on commercial real estate development and marketing.

PBX—THE TECHNOLOGICAL BASIS OF TERE OPERATION

The private branch exchange, or PBX, grew out of the manual plug-and-wire switchboard located in a large building to route calls between people in the building without going through the telephone company central office. Prior to the PBX switchboard, every telephone required its own line to the central office. When people in the same office called each other, they would be connected by a remote central office switch. With a PBX, the ratio of lines to central office was reduced to one for each five to ten telephones.

The manual plug boards were eventually replaced by electromechanical switches. When a call came in, instead of manually plugging a wire jack into a socket to make the connection, operators dialed the party being called and electromechanical switches made the connection. Later, crossbar switches stored the dialed number of the incoming call in electrical circuits and made the connection without operator intervention.

Until the U.S. Supreme Court's Carterfone decision in 1968, the telephone company (AT&T) was the only company allowed to make and sell equipment that could connect to the lines of common carriers. Following Carterfone, technology for the PBX progressed rapidly. The computer branch exchange (CBX) was the next evolution after crossbar switches. CBX machines are still manufactured and sold. They use a computer to direct the flow of traffic, connect the switches, and so forth. Their applications are limited, however, since they are still mechanical switch devices, though they are computer-controlled.

The digital branch exchange quickly followed the CBX. The digital switch allocates the use of lines between simultaneous callers through a time division multiplexing technique. Time division multiplexing is accomplished by compressing the signals so that more than one conversation can be carried simultaneously on the same line (see Chapter 4). Voice or data traffic of several conversations is intermittently transmitted in digital form along lines to and from telephone sets. These telephones are intelligent terminals. They are equipped with a computer chip to decode the digital signals and translate them into analog signals. A computer is employed in the digital PBX to control and allocate the line and trunk use and also to provide a variety of features for phone users. These include:

- Automatic least-cost routing service
- Automatic call distribution
- Call detail recording
- Call conferencing
- Call transferring
- Call forwarding and waiting
- Speed dialing and redialing
- Data communications

TECHNOLOGIES OF SHARED TELECOMMUNICATIONS SERVICES

The service and equipment options offered by manufacturers of digital PBX equipment do not vary greatly. There is a continual development of products; after each new product is announced by one manufacturer, the others are soon to follow. One of the greatest values to users of shared tenant services is the advantage of earliest access to new technology. As new products become available, shared service operators are quick to purchase them and further enhance their own ability to compete with the telephone company. Shared tenant operators are rapidly becoming high-volume purchasers of digital PBX equipment.

They are influencing PBX manufacturers to develop many new products designed especially for the shared tenant industry. They are also encouraging more efficient transmission methods, including fiber optics, microwave bypass, and video conferencing equipment.

TERE PROFITABILITY

A TERE business can be profitable for only two reasons: more efficient management of resources, and the provision of more valuable and higher-quality services than are available from the telephone company. It is always in the interest of the shared tenant vendor to stay as far ahead of the telephone company as possible and to incorporate new technologies as rapidly as they can be developed. Several recent additions to the capability of the digital PBX which can now be made available in shared tenant service are:

Voice store and forward. This service, also known as phone mail, allows subscribers to have their phones answered by a computer-driven answering machine, when desired. Instructions can be given from any telephone, by users, as to how to handle messages and what the announcing message should say to callers. Unlike less sophisticated answering machine devices, the computer can be instructed to call the subscriber with messages until he or she is reached.

Message centers. Call screening and receiving centers can provide very efficient management of calls received while the user is out or busy. In message centers equipped with state-of-the-art PBX systems, operators have video display workstations which display a screen of information about the party being called. This information tells the operator where the called party is located, the call-handling preference, how the party wishes the calls to be answered, and how the messages should be forwarded.

Protocol conversion. This is a means of converting data from one machine to a language understandable to another machine. For instance, a client may want to send a document to another person for revision and editing even though the two have noncompatible equipment.

Modem sharing. A modem converts the digital signal coming from a computer to an analog signal that can be sent over public telephone lines.

Bypass. The local telephone company wire network is bypassed so users can go directly to other users' telephones or data terminals. For instance, a TERE service might install a microwave transceiver in the tenant's building. Through the use of transmission facilities supplied by various competitive sources (CATV, telephone company dedicated circuits, etc.), calls can be routed to a receiver in another telephone company exchange district, bypassing the tariff call structure and access charges of the telephone company. A cost is reduced or eliminated, resulting in a discount to the caller.

ACCOUNTING AND BILLING MANAGEMENT

Digital PBX systems make an accurate record of calls made on the system. Since the software for switching calls needs to read a call address to program switching intelligently, all the necessary information is automatically recorded. In addition to recording trunk usage, however, the billing system can be programmed to identify other features of the call, such as the caller's extension number and codes which can be used to charge the call to a particular accounting file for the caller's internal accounting purposes.

Call detail recording can be used for a number of statistical studies valuable to business management. For instance, a business may want to measure the effectiveness and frequency of a telephone sales campaign and compare this with the cost of the required telephony. By comparison, the telephone company's call detail recording serves only one purpose—documentation of bills to customers. In a shared tenant environment, the billing process has functions that can provide amenities for system users.

MAINTENANCE AND OPERATIONS

The day-to-day flow of work involved in installing and operating telecommunications equipment services is transparent to users. What differentiates the shared tenant service from the telephone company service in this regard is the greater stability in a telephone system maintained and managed by people who have a proprietary interest in the system. This is further enhanced by the relationships that shared tenant service personnel have with users. Telephone company customers are used to never seeing the same telephone maintenance person twice. When service is bad or down, it is either tolerated or reported. Typical telephone company service is not known for responsiveness. There does not seem to be anyone who is accountable or any recourse that can be taken. This may also be true in a shared tenant situation, but—in most if not all shared tenant services—the dissatisfied user has the option of reverting to telephone company service. The shared tenant service operator clearly has a vested interest in being known as a solver rather than a maker of problems.

TERE COMPANIES OPERATING AT PRESENT

TERE operators have started up in most urban centers of the country. Here is a list of some prominent service operators:

American Network, Inc.
Portland, Oregon

Electronic Office Centers of America, Inc.
Schaumberg, Illinois

Honeywell, Inc.
Minneapolis, Minnesota

Howard Communications
Denver, Colorado

Lincom
Dallas, Texas

Pacific Telesis
San Francisco, California

Planning Research Corporation
McLean, Virginia

Polaris Network Systems
Costa Mesa, California
Toluca Lake, California
Warner Center, Los Angeles, California

SBS RealCom
McLean, Virginia

ShareCom Tel-Management Corporation
Dallas, Texas

The Teleport
Port Authority of New York and New Jersey

United Business Communications
Atlanta, Georgia

WRC Telecommunications
Seattle, Washington

THE REGULATORY ENVIRONMENT FOR TERE

Telecommunications services are regulated by the Federal Communications Commission, by state public utility commissions, and through franchising of local operations by various local governments. Regulations govern franchised telephone company operations and control tariffs that may be applied by franchisees. The future growth of shared tenant services depends on the regulatory climate. An understanding of the AT&T, the regional Bell, and independent telephone company strategies since divestiture helps to forecast regulatory developments. At this time, carrying services within a building are outside the jurisdiction of federal, state, or local regulation. However, the availability of competitive local and long-distance services is critical for profitability in the TERE business.

Competition is difficult for telephone operating companies. Years of operating without internal financial accountability have resulted in a very large organization with few cost-cutting management controls. In addition, telephone company central office technology has been overdesigned and is now obsolete; physical plant improvements are so expensive that the cost of adding new lines and equipment has been estimated at more than 10 times the cost of maintaining the already installed equipment, line for line.

Divestiture has eliminated a large part of the subsidy for local telephone company operations with long-distance revenues. The Federal Communications Commission has limited this form of subsidization to a monthly charge (called an "access charge") made by the phone company for allowing access through its wire network to long-distance carriers. This charge now amounts to $1.00 per month per telephone line. The telephone operating companies' strategy is to continue filing for increases in prices to customers for extended local area services. Recently, there has been a price-related redistricting of local service areas in most places. Local business and residential customers are feeling the effects of a substantial increase in the cost of calls made to areas close to but outside of their unlimited free access local exchange privileges. The intent of these rate increases is to raise this portion of users' bills to make up for the revenues lost in the separation of long-distance and local services.

BYPASS AND TELEPHONE COMPANY PRICING STRATEGIES

Local bypass is anathema to the telephone companies' pricing strategy. A microwave or private fiber optic circuit can bypass the rising costs of local service by bringing calls from distant areas directly into a local telephone company's wiring network through privately owned microwave, CATV, and other facilities. Microwave, fiber optic, satellite, CATV, and other technologies offer the ability to connect users through direct point-to-point lines more efficiently, more cost effectively, and with greater security than do wires provided by the local telephone company. Video and high-speed data transmissions cannot be offered by standard telephone company services. These services cannot be denied to protect a privileged group of telephone companies. It is the stand of the Justice Department, state and federal legislatures, and local municipal franchising agencies that restricting the application of these technologies is not in the interest of the community, state, or nation.

In the long run, the future augurs well for shared tenant service users because it is so convenient to bypass network TERE-owned and

-operated PBX systems via microwave, shared fixed-service lines, and satellite. TERE operators will therefore find themselves positioned well to take advantage of profitable telecommunications opportunities.

THE ECONOMICS OF BYPASS

Telephone users in the United States traditionally evaluate service, not price. They have had no standard for evaluating the appropriateness of pricing because telephone service costs have always been arbitrated by public utility commissions who needed to consider the costs of subsidizing the local network. Given the complexity of most telephone company rate submissions, the most a concerned business communications user could do to reduce phone costs was to reduce calling or move to another location.

In a recent survey of 35 major corporations conducted by The National Regulatory Research Institute on the bypass issue, virtually every respondent agreed that they would elect a relatively unknown carrier if their savings were to be 10 percent or greater. The advent of equal access and the availability of services such as those provided by MCI-SBS, Express-Tel, GTE-Sprint, ITT, Western Union, Allnet, and others should provide discounts of 10 percent and greater. However, the service rates of these companies vary unpredictably and are subject to change without much notice. Choice of carriers presents yet another costly management problem for the business customer—not to mention the dilemma of selecting telephone instruments, special features, and the management of a PBX facility.

One aspect of the "information age" is an increasing reliance on sophisticated telecommunications. This involves a broad range of services, including video teleconferencing and videotext as well as the use of on-line databases and other computer-driven resources.The prognosis is that people are going to be spending more investment and operations dollars on managing technology services in general and telecommunications in particular.

Recent studies have shown that lowering telephone tariffs has resulted in an increase in the total revenue to long-distance carriers. Conversely, in situations such as hotels, which at present charge inordinately high rates for telephone services, guests have consistently reduced their hotel room phone use as rates increase, so that total hotel telephone revenues have dropped an average of 20 percent.

The choice that shared tenant services brings up for most businesses is economic. There are cost-saving discounts for users who can share the use of WATS and other measured-rate, high-volume trunks and other discounts for every class of user due to more efficient management of digital PBX technology. These important values offered by the shared tenant environment are possibilities which have been previously beyond the reach of all but *Fortune* 1000 companies.

Efficient, automated procedures take the tedium out of most tasks. Computers can make work enjoyable and businesses more profitable when the system is complete and well supported. STS networks offer the potential to make computer assistance an immediate reality for small businesses and professional people. When applied with care for the human element, computers bring a quality of reliability and effortless accomplishment to jobs. Managers, professionals, and employees are freed from laborious information management tasks to apply their expertise in their professions.

CHAPTER 9

Developing the Community

ESTABLISHING CRITERIA FOR DEVELOPMENT

Community development in the United States is traditionally initiated by real estate entrepreneurs who follow the "guidelines" of pro forma investment procedures according to their whims, personal prejudices, interests, and tastes. Sometimes, by chance, the personal criteria of a developer may include consideration for public and community well-being. Problems of traffic congestion, ecological preservation, and other issues are dealt with, or not, as they arise. With few exceptions, the primary and overriding criterion is a focus on commercial value.

This attitude about development in the United States results from the time-honored presumption that land, biological, mineral, and human resources are subject to our technological ability to refine them to our needs. Our current generations are beginning to face the reality that the proper management of land and ecological networks is critical and that they are finite and unreplaceable resources. We are also beginning to comprehend the danger to humanity presented by the possibility of destroying the balance of the planetary ecosystem.

While we have been systematically destroying the environment's ability to function in our nation's domain, others have been hard at work in Europe, Asia, Latin America, and Africa. We are meeting the needs of immediate survival at the cost of destroying important ecological resources that have taken millenia to create. Forested lands are stripped for agriculture; the previously stripped lands are worked into exhaustion and left to become arid wastes. We have begun to learn the cost of such carelessness in terms of environmental destruction. We have not realized the extent of the more costly social problems created by inappropriate development—it is a cost in human lives.

We are beginning to understand that when we develop a human community, we are doing more than erecting buildings; we are building a technology to support synergy of human interaction with the environment. In the words of Winston Churchill, "We shape our environment and then our environment shapes us." There are aspects of a community which affect the way people view themselves and relate to one another.

A community is self-generating; it becomes a resource for the accomplishment of the visions of human lives. Although the potential of this resource is more important than revenues to be had from building, selling, or renting the buildings that support the communal infrastructure, there is no mechanism in the policies of investment and commerce for dealing with long-term issues.

Community is that which creates the *potential* for human productivity, individual and artistic expression, and the solutions or causes of social problems such as hunger, war, and ecological destruction. In order to succeed as a species, with a free enterprise system, we will have to discover how to dynamically control growth and development industries. Our development industry is now organized according to priorities which encourage our people to become a nation of consumers. Our methods of attaching value to and selling real estate also help to sponsor the feelings of separateness that underly the consciousness of ghettos. Our buildings and communities therefore reflect these preoccupations. So do our social problems. Most of our criminals are involved in the acquisition of material by taking property which the criminals perceive as belonging to others with whom they feel no relationship. This is the same psychology underlying the rationale for war.

It is not that the problems of war, famine, crime, and violence are only or directly attributable to unintelligent development. Rather, the point is that the society has needs which can only be addressed in community development and which are systematically not being met. This leads to conditions that foster problems, and our politicians seek ways to diplomatically avoid challenging the powerful investment brokers. The only escape from this situation requires a change in the process of development to provide for consideration of new criteria. This will necessitate much more community participation in the development cycle. The good news is that the implementation of new technologies is forcing us to lean in this direction anyway.

It will facilitate matters if we comprehend that the present system, in which buildings are speculatively developed on the basis of profit pro forma, misses the highest potential value of the financial investment as well as causing social problems. The assertion is that any development will be more profitable if it proceeds in a manner consistent with the growing needs of society. *Inept development is less profitable as well as ecologically damaging.* The side effects of primitive development practices are costly not only to the health and well-being of citizens but also in terms of business development and real estate appreciation. For example, growing crime statistics, especially among youthful citizens, is an index of inappropriate community development. The prevalence of stress-related illnesses, such as heart disease and cancer, is another indicator of the way individuals live their lives and the opportunities which are afforded them by the community. The possibilities for human development are directly related to the physical structure of the community. And business and economic development is obviously affected by the health of individuals in the community.

AESTHETIC CRITERIA

Assuming one wanted to develop buildings which would become a contribution to the well-being of the people who would use them, work in them, and live around them, or who would be otherwise affected by their presence or the activities of the people who used them, what would we have to know to develop wisely? To even consider this question requires some familiarity with the sciences of psychology, sociology, economics, technology, ecology, and so forth. All of these sciences should be involved in determining the aesthetic character of a potential development. It might be argued that the task seems impossible. How could any development project leader be expected to have such arcane and extensive personal knowledge?

Recently, the International Development Research Council (IDRC), an organization that represents corporate real estate planners, announced the availability of new computer software that incorporates thousands of criteria in a program to assist companies with finding the right location in which to build new facilities. By incorporating criteria relevant to community well-being, expert systems can be similarly devised to bring up and consider issues of concern to citizens and communities.

AESTHETICS IN BUILDING DEVELOPMENT

Aesthetic values ("taste") are believed to be subjectively derived—a matter of individual prejudice. The psychology of the individual, the quality of social taboo, and other social norms influence the decisions of individuals making judgments of "taste." If a community has a set of well-thought-out criteria, the taste of a developer can be accountable to and compared with priorities established by the community. In the United States, development of open space in frontier areas has provided a less restrictive environment for entrepreneurism. In places where there are no established communities, there have been no traditions or other criteria to interfere with the profit-oriented concept of proposed developments. The Los Angeles area is an outstanding outcome of development with no criteria at all.

It is probably not going to be possible to train developers to think responsibly about the long-term impact of their activities on others. It is also impossible to make them legally liable for the long-term results of poor planning. They are protected from legal recourse by the "permit" process, which places the blame for problems on the government that issued the permit. That is why the only possibility for change is for those who are responsible for community planning, and for citizens in general, to have the authority to evaluate proposed developments, providing that *all* of the interests in the community are engaged in a forum for the consideration of development criteria. There is at present no forum that inquires about development in unincorporated areas. Although in incorporated towns and cities, the community needs to be better informed and educated about aesthetic criteria by architects and planners who are not beholden to the developers' projects, to do this, we need a common language for discussing *issues*, and the forums for discussion of development issues need to encourage participation of more citizens with a broader range of concerns.

One purpose of this book is to help provide the language for such discussions. A conversation about development criteria must include knowledge about philosophical, psychological, sociological, and economic well-being as well as expertise in the technologies of building, business, and communications. The purpose of this chapter is not to examine the nature of aesthetics, psychology, and economics but to apply knowledge about these subjects to the issue of community development with the intention of creating common understandings about the problem. I request that the reader bear with me as I introduce subjects which might at first blush appear distant from the purpose of this inquiry.

IN GOOD CONSCIENCE

During the 1960s, psychologists and social scientists conducted studies at the Stanford Research Institute to measure the discomfort experienced by individuals involved in conflicts of personal integrity. They developed scientific proof for the folk saying, "Every man has his price." In modern jargon, this is sometimes referred to as an individual's "bottom line." The Stanford project demonstrated that when people were offered the symbols of social acceptance, such as monetary reward, they were willing to violate their own integrity, and that the amount of the reward varied according to the size of the violation. A woman would lie to her husband for one price and to her mother for another. Depending on the amount offered relative to the "crime," every one of the tested subjects was willing to lie, cheat, or steal. The knowledge revealed in this study has been put to use by motivational research professionals in the commercial advertising industry.

The Stanford research project provides valuable insights into the ethics of the development and real estate business, where those involved are often selling and razing natural places of importance to the community which cannot be given a dollar value. In situations like these, there is an inherent conflict of integrity since destructiveness is involved—offset by profitable reward for the entrepreneur.

Ethics versus Integrity

In entrepreneurial activities where the potential profits are huge (and of political consequence because of the dollar value), the concept of personal integrity is proceduralized and relegated to the domain of professional ethics. The word "integrity" has become a virtual taboo in our culture. It does not make for polite cocktail party conversation. The word is a cynical joke in a bureaucracy. It is impossible to place the word anywhere in the public school curriculum. Integrity is considered a risky word to use in advertising copy. To imply that a political opponent lacks integrity is considered redundant. Integrity in a corporation is wholly dependent on the procedures for management and the successful implementation of computer-assisted applications to keep track of the execution of requests and promises.

The most significant revelation of the earlier cited Stanford research project was the reflection that the human being is, by nature, a being possessed of integrity. There would be no conflict or discomfort possible if there were no moral choice—the idea of integrity would not exist. To assist our proclivity for acting with integrity, we have developed ethical systems of behavior. Ethical systems help the individual to deal with contradictions that arise when social demands are in conflict with a sense of personal integrity. In ethical systems, procedures replace the subjective analysis of conscience. If you do your job according to ethical rules, no matter that the outcome is contrary to your own morality, you will be rewarded. Pay scales help ensure that rewards offset the discomfort of bad conscience. As you sell your childhood playground to be developed as an oil refinery, you can be relieved to know that you hired the best environmental consultant to explain the results. It then becomes natural for the individual to violate the agreed-on rules of society as if the rules were not important or the individual is above certain rules because of a moral commitment.

Heading the list of areas in which there are frequent reports of white collar crime, the telling of lies and half-truths, and general cheating are politics and government. However, double-dealing, fraud, and misrepresentation exist just as much in the defense contracting industry, building development, commercial banking, telecommunications, broadcasting, the entertainment industry, the legal and medical industries, petroleum and energy production, securities trading, and generally middle- to upper-level corporate management. Although news reports about drug trafficking, Defense Department cheating, and banking swindles are more sensational, the problem of big rewards for ill-intended acts has also had enormously damaging consequences with regard to the management of our natural, land, and human resources and the intelligent planning of communities.

The problem is that people, including the poor and middle income groups, become involved—through the lure of easy money—in acts that damage the community and the environment. Although such acts may be immoral, they are not usually illegal. This problem applies not only to societies with income-related classes but also to societies such as the Soviet Union and China, where the methods of striving bureaucrats may create similar difficulties.

The short-term rewards for selling the life-support system of the planet and the economic well-being of communities "down the river" of development are very high. The well-being of future generations is consequently being damaged by the practice of short-term-oriented development of land, energy, and mineral resources. The problem of inappropriate development is made greater because it involves wastefulness and promotes gradual bankruptcy of the resources of political states and communities. This situation has been recognized for some time, and we have been at a loss for direction toward appropriate action.

THE POLITICAL BACKGROUND—CUPIDITY AND DEVELOPMENT

Although a developer might well suggest that the politics of the national and global community have nothing to do with a grandiose plan for a new commercial center, the international political climate has much to do with the future of business in every part of the United States. There are few who dispute that the cupidity of the American people, guided by the commercial mass media, has led this resourceful nation into many devastating events, not the least of which, in recent history, was the Vietnam war. No one today is unaffected by the competitive pricing of goods and services imported from foreign lands. We now live in an international marketplace. Acts of international terrorism demonstrate that we live in an international body politic. Communities in America look to the entire world to find markets for products and sources for production. Development is an international as well as a local political issue—there is emerging a new climate of greater political involvement of citizens. The population is growing to realize that solutions to the enduring problems of humanity (starvation, war, pollution, etc.) will be solved not by enlightened leaders but by enlightened personal action. Urban development is a meaningful arena for such action.

END OF THE ERA OF CUPIDITY

For many years, Europeans have associated American culture with the Walt Disney character Mickey Mouse. America has risen as the *enfant terrible* of international law and politics. Militarily and economically powerful, for many years we have virtually held the rest of the world by the throat. Like a good-natured and passionate idiot, we have sought to maintain idealistic principles without a background of refined tradition. The arrogance of this stand has been frustrating for the international community. At the same time, the candor of American goodwill has been a lifesaving grace, and so Americans are honored with toleration though not taken too seriously (like Mickey Mouse). Other societies have other problems. We have the advantage that we can possibly grow out of our problems.

Several events during the past quarter-century are moving us toward a more enlightened relationship with the rest of the world. Following the second world war, commitment to American society gradually became seen as futile. The plays of Eugene O'Neill and Tennessee Williams, and especially Arthur Miller's *Death of a Salesman*, depict the experience of the individual confronted with a society without goals or meaningful ideals.

The wisdom of John F. Kennedy was to inspire the American public with ideals and to point out the difference that our lives can make as a contribution to a world that works. During his administration, arts and education began to flourish and programs were started which began to give Americans a more worldly outlook. Not the least of them was the first step of man into space.

Because of the assassination of John F. Kennedy, followed swiftly by the assassination of the inspiring civil rights leader, Martin Luther King, Jr., the American electorate was effectively disenfranchised. The management of the investigation into these assassinations left many people with misgivings about the complicity of powerful special interests in the assassinations, and the succeeding government lost the atmosphere of inspiration and integrity associated with the Kennedy management team. Certain public welfare programs were stigmatized and lost their good effect. There could be no trust in the democratic process of government when votes of millions could be so easily cancelled by an assassin's bullet. Clearly, if people's lives are to make a difference, it will not be because of their leaders but because of personal responsibility.

The pursuit of the unpopular war in Vietnam by the American government which followed the assassination of John F. Kennedy gave evidence for the idea that our government was not representational, that democracy doesn't work. With the subsequent assassination of the Democratic candidate, Robert Kennedy, anyone who was not already convinced that the democratic process was unworkable could be so persuaded. The American people were deprived of an opposition candidate, leading to the election to the highest public office of a man who had left American politics following disclosures of financial impropriety (in the acceptance of "gifts"), and who had been a leader in the anticommunist witch hunt of the infamous political opportunist, Senator Joseph McCarthy. An attitude of separation from the government arose from these events—the idea became prevalent in America that we are not our government.

A part of our cupidity as Americans is that we have come to regard others as if they have the same philosophy as we do. An examination into the problem areas of the world where American military aid and economic investment are involved reveals that the governments of these places are at a distance from the people they pretend to represent; they include such places as South Africa, the Philippines, and South Vietnam. Meanwhile, we have been at odds with nations where this is less the case, such as China, the Soviet Union, Nicaragua, and North Vietnam. Americans cannot comprehend why Soviet citizens do not protest, demonstrate, and verbally abuse their government. They read this as a sign of suppression of free speech. Soviet people present different evidence; they express themselves as participants in government. They feel they have procedures that make them responsible for the actions of their government and, therefore, their abuse of the government would be abuse of self.

A TURNING POINT

The revelations about the criminal antics of the administration of former President Richard Nixon reached beyond the absurd into the realm of the sublimely ridiculous. Given the possibility of nuclear warfare, exposure of the incompetence at high political levels refined the dominant mood that the government does not represent the people by adding the terror associated with the thought that civilization may not last long enough for anything to matter. People in Europe profited well from the American involvement in the Vietnam war, (a key to Nixon's "successful foreign policy"), and there was little hope of criticism coming from the mainstream media of other parts of the world. What was wrong in America was supported by the establishment in Europe. The laissez-faire morality was perpetuated throughout international society and coincidentally supported unregulated development for profit.

The figurative prosecution of former President Nixon and his associates in 1973 proved to be an act of no small significance. It became a turning point, allowing the possibility of a belief in the eventual return of civilization from the dangers of nuclear warfare and the mismanagement of technology. However, the pursuit of intelligent economic and urban development remains frustrated because we have not yet educated ourselves to understand enough about the nature of technologies, especially regarding the management of new international corporate economics. The technology of government (the form of our political systems) has proven incapable of dealing with the complex economics of independent entrepreneurism. The result has been a cumulative destruction of wildlife and ecological resources, as well as the gradual decay and ruin of older urban neighborhoods.

When seeking solutions, it is useful to define problems accurately—to see what is so and what is not so. Poorly analysed development by Americans is not the fault of the custom of free enterprise. All of the environmentally responsible organizations have been started and supported by entrepreneurial people. Because of the work of these organizations, we know that uncertainty about the welfare of future generations is a common concern wherever people are not preoccupied with the more pressing problems of immediate survival such as hunger and starvation. We also know that government regulation is at best a weak response to development problems since national, regional, and local governments are dominated by economically powerful private interests who support dvelopment. This is especially true where building industry associations, and lobbies representing development interests are highly organized and wealthy relative to the organizations of environmentalists, who do not personally profit from their voluntary service.

LOCAL POLITICS AND THE BUILDING INDUSTRY

The assertion of this book is that major international problems (hunger, war, terrorism) can be at least in part resolved by means arising from a new approach to the local building and development process. The theory is that we can implement technology to intelligently structure development projects which are appropriate to the ecology and society of localities based on criteria which respect the needs of the ecosystem and the lifestyle commitment of the local populations. To move this theory into a practical plan requires dealing with the local politics of development. It will be of little value to try to deal with the problems of the rest of the world while neglecting to manage our own land intelligently.

LOCAL POLITICS AND THE BUILDING INDUSTRY IN AMERICA

A study of local political campaign contribution sources in California, conducted by Common Cause in 1985, revealed that *22 percent* of all campaign contribution dollars were coming from employees of companies that are members of the Building Industry Association (BIA). The BIA is a political action group committed to supporting the interests of developers, builders, and building trades people on issues which are often in conflict with the interests of other parts of society (sometimes including parts of its own membership). The BIA will, for instance, support politicians who favor controversial energy and road development projects because inexpensive sources of electricity and transportation are necessary to development. Because the proximity of a nuclear or petroleum fuel power plant may have negative impact on real estate sought for development, the BIA's stand is sometimes self-contradictory and hard to determine. The BIA has been until recently highly fraternal in nature and, with its inordinate power in local politics, still cannot be said to represent the interests of women as much as those of men.

As an example of its influence in local politics, in 1979 the BIA was behind a movement in California to persuade local governments to adopt regulations about air and water pollution. For any plan to be effective, every local government had to agree to the adoption of an extensive set of complex regulations affecting every individual and business—a seemingly impossible task. The BIA was involved because of the federal Clean Air Act of 1970, which threatened to withhold federal subsidies for water, solid waste disposal, and road improvements from states that could not show how they would achieve certain minimum air quality standards by 1987. Federal subsidies for water, sewer, and road improvements are a direct form of subsidization for the building industry. The status quo of the building industry was thus threatened by federal environmental legislation which ultimately required a form of compliance with new regulatory measures from virtually every business and individual in California. The acceptance of a thick volume of restrictive measures by local governments was achieved by a well-focused campaign, which took less than a year.

News media reported that the BIA was motivated by an interest in preserving the environment. The BIA was actually motivated by an interest in maintaining government road, solid waste disposal, and water improvement subsidies. This may explain why less attention has been paid to the plan's implementation than to the problem of having the plan adopted. Although many of the measures adopted in this plan are of value, no means of funding effective enforcement of regulations has been provided and no new alternatives to development were proposed in the plan to help alleviate future problems. In fact, adopted regulations were very deliberately written to win the support of the BIA, which provides loop holes such as the trade-off allowance wherein development that causes pollution in one area is permitted if the developer pays a fee to clean up a mess somewhere else.

Assuming that we are able to muddle through the management of dangerous technologies like nuclear physics and survive, how do we untangle the complex hegemony and control of local governments by thousands of entrepreneurial, profit-minded building developers and their associated trade unions, investment bankers, and political cronies, not to mention a veritable army of real estate brokers, agents, and upwardly mobile neocapitalists? These appear to be conditions which will not change without a revolutionary change in the economic process of development. And what do we need to change? How do we change?

Aside from the daily reports of terrorism, criminality, and moral turpitude appearing in the media, frequently there is news about land development projects that are upsetting for people. (The press deals in sensationalism—the quality which determines the newsworthiness of a story is its potential for causing upset.) Development has come to be characterized by the bulldozer and concrete mixer looming ominously over a vulnerable verdant forest. It is demoralizing for people to think that we are not able to make a difference about development in our own communities, or that we have to take our attention away from our work and families and struggle with politicians to prevent an obnoxious and opportunistic development enterprise in the community, often to be undertaken by those who live elsewhere and who have no commitment to our community. We look on while our developers build on flood plains and fault lines, and cringe when reading headlines about "natural" disasters due to floods and earthquakes. We sit in cars for hours in freeway traffic jams inhaling carbon monoxide and other gases while along the roadside our developers are continuing to exploit every opportunity to increase profits by increasing density without providing public transportation. We pass by nuclear reactors and cannot help reflecting on the danger of nuclear accidents and the effects of radioactive pollution of rivers and oceans. We pass homeless people in the streets and feel uncomfortably compromised in our complacency. We participate in the folly of misguided development by our silence in the face of these obvious issues and in so doing deny our own responsibility and our rights as citizens.

APPLICATION OF A TECHNOLOGICAL APPROACH TO DEVELOPMENT

I began a study of social psychology and the historical basis of our economic systems, as well as an analysis of the personal psychology which supported these systems. I looked at the traditional practices of real estate development to find new ways of viewing the problem. I noticed that lifestyles have been dramatically affected by the implementation of new technologies. It seemed logical that development could possibly be influenced by the implementation of technologies. With this idea in mind, I became more interested in operation methods of development firms and in their relationships with government.

AN INTELLIGENT BUILDING PILOT PROJECT

In 1981, I began the operation of a new technology-related business, the method of which was to unify emerging technologies with building development. With the help of people at the Xerox Corporation and Northern Telecom International, I installed a network of computers and a state-of-the-art telecommunications facility in a large office building in Los Angeles. The concept was to make it possible for smaller space users in a building, individual tenants and businesses, to have access to technologies that were previously available only to *Fortune*

1000 firms. This business pioneered a new industry within commercial real estate which came to be called "shared tenant services," associated with development of "intelligent" buildings.

In theory, an intelligent building provides for the total needs of a building's tenants. Consequently, the interface of building tenants with people who provide support services for business is a key concern. The term intelligent building grew out of the concept of providing high-technology supported services as a function of urban building management. The ideas motivating shared tenant services emerged from an intention to solve the problem of providing businesses and professionals with access to state-of-the-art technological support, by means of support systems associated with the building. The two ideas merged and influenced each other because of the natural confluence of interest. Both concepts were of concern to building developers and owners and the managers of businesses that located in multitenant buildings.

As a result of the work done on the pilot project, much was revealed about the influence of technologies on business and development as well as on the policies, practices, procedures, and politics of developers and the considerations of commercial real estate tenants.

INDUSTRY AND DEVELOPMENT

Historically, commercial buildings have been an opportunity to lavish great expense on artfully rendered, intricately detailed, and monumental architecture. The interiors and exteriors of many older buildings are often feasts for the eye and imagination. They were frequently the artful expression of partnerships between the wealthy (traditionally the nobility and church and, later, corporate concentrations of wealth) and architects for the purpose of building monuments. Smaller residential buildings were similarly usually the product of local craftspeople and families building for posterity.

A different trend led to the modern-day "town house" or condominium. This kind of development evolved with the growth of large urban centers and factory towns as rows of houses were constructed in European and American cities to permit the concentration of populations for the economics of industrialization. Oriented around mass production of similar, marketable space units, this kind of development is governed by market economies and profit analyses. It has become the dominant influence in urban and commercial development. Because of the savings facilitated by economies of scale when building multiple similar units, most land development now serves the purpose of speculative investment.

In the twentieth century, land development has become an industry called "commercial real estate." Because of the legal distinction involved in classifying land and buildings as real property as opposed to personal property, banks and other financial institutions are able to collateralize loans on "real estate" with ease. With lending institutions as partners, developers can build speculatively rather than building homes or places of business on order. This has an obvious effect on the quality of architecture. The mass development of homogeneous structures with maximum profit as the highest priority has a great effect on the appearance and quality of life in a community. Meanwhile, the shift in purpose from building per request by the user to building for speculation has undermined the intention of land-use law, since legal codes and other methods of land-use regulation are based on practices appropriate at a time prior to speculative industry practices. Specifically, our permit and review process is not appropriate to speculative building or mass production building technologies.

THE BACKGROUND OF COMMERCIAL REAL ESTATE DEVELOPMENT

Speculative real estate investments have made sense in the United States for important reasons:

1. Financial institutions recognize the collateral value of real estate for construction financing loans.
2. Federal tax incentives have provided credit both for depreciating the value of buildings over time and for interest paid on building loans.
3. Megabusiness enterprises had demanded large amounts of inexpensively constructed space. (As these businesses grew, they acquired thousands of employees and occupied relatively enormous spaces in urban buildings.)
4. Taxation has been used as a means of subsidizing the infrastructure necessary to develop open space areas such as roads, energy, and sanitation services.

All of these conditions are now being subjected to radical change. Soaring interest rates coupled with the overbuilding of areas have slowed the availability of financing for speculative projects. Congress is becoming more sensitive to the need for modifying the tax laws because of the cumulative effects of the growing national deficit on the voting constituency. One of the most compelling forces affecting the construction of large commercial buildings is that the growth path of megabusiness has taken a new course due to the design of computer-driven information management and telecommunication technologies. These technologies are changing the ways that business is done so that the need for space is changing rapidly.

Today, as new businesses grow, rather than moving into larger spaces as they did in the past, they are likely to acquire multiple locations of smaller spaces so as to operate more easily over a larger geographic area. They also require less space for the storage, creation, and filing of records. With the miniaturization of microelectronics, they need even less space for the same or greater productivity. Because of the trend toward more professional specialization, the problem of supporting personnel for modern businesses is also changing—businesses are becoming more interested in the quality of space.

DETERMINING AESTHETICS FOR THE HIGH-TECH WORKPLACE

The effect of new technologies on attitudes, behavior, and psychology has surfaced as an issue in building development. Living and working with computer systems has been found to be stressful. When decisions are made by computers, a system of rules is applied to a situation. When decisions are made by people, a system of rules is *interpreted* and a judgment is made. Aesthetic issues are present in the human analysis of problems and the creative synthesis of solutions. Buildings may be designed to efficiently incorporate high-tech systems and still avoid the potential for the workplace to become the highly clinical environment of "modern times." A new synthesis of art and technology is emerging to provide graceful as well as efficient space for human productivity. This synthesis will become an element of design as methods are found which prove more successful in the marketplace for commercial space.

DRIVING THE MARKET FOR COMMERCIAL SPACE

The purpose in building buildings artfully is to make them more inviting habitats and therefore more desirable and valuable for tenants. For the development company that is motivated by a desire for profit, the purpose of creating an intelligent building is to make it more desirable in order to market space. However, unlike the artful adornment of facades and interiors, high technology installed in a building is not a visible improvement and will not, of itself, market the space. In order for the intelligent quality of a building to manifest itself in the form of increased sales, that intelligence needs to become recognized as a virtue by the marketplace. Because buildings are still being erected by investors who are investing in terms of potential cash return per square foot rather than building projects of vital support to people and business, the market can only judge a building by its price tag, its appearance, and its location. The relationship between a building and the people who will use it has been left out of the development pro forma.

In an attempt to solve this problem, some architects and developers have been working to develop more grandiose and better landscaped monuments in concrete, glass, and steel. Some have even begun to incorporate state-of-the-art telecommunications services and other computer-driven technologies. Although a few of these development projects have improved the appearance of areas by redeveloping decaying neighborhoods, the practice has had no impact on the market. Millions of square feet of commercial space are at present under construction while millions more stand empty in many U.S. cities. In some areas, the vacancy factor has risen to 60 percent of available space. Similar figures have been forecast for many places in the United States based on the current rate of development and absorption of space.

The burden of this empty space is ultimately passed on to the middle-class taxpayer in the form of inflation in the economy, higher taxes, and diminishing quality of social services. This burden is a sufficient economic justification for government to formulate a more constructive approach to urban development which involves the entire community in determining what needs to be built and where. This demonstrates the need to replace the current policies of permit review and approval with more constructive planning policies.

THE ENVIRONMENTAL IMPACT REPORT PROCESS

Permit and review were an outgrowth of property laws that also provided the basis in law for the acquisition without compensation of the American continent from the native inhabitants. Very simply stated, these precedents assume that, having obtained the land by purchase or by simply occupying it in defiance of others for a long time, the individual has the right to make the best use possible relative to a personal purpose, with no one having the ability to protest by civil or other action. The problems of this uncivilized approach are obvious. As a result of federal legislation in response to public demands because of environmental degradation, the permit process was recently expanded to include the filing of environmental impact reports (EIRs).

In the EIR process, the land owner or developer submits an independently compiled report describing the possible impact of the development on the surrounding community and ecology. Naturally, the EIR program falls prey to the same politics and methods as the rest of the permit process. It does not create a positive approach to development planning nor does it posit criteria for analyzing projects that are meaningful to the community's needs and problems. The EIR process has led to such practices as the environmental damage trade-off scenario. According to the rules of this game, an environmentally sensitive area in one locality is restored in return for allowing ecological losses in another area. The developer pays a lump sum which provides for the improvement of some previous damage done elsewhere in return for a permit to develop. (The economics of these deals are usually unrealistic given that the community is able by means of taxes, bonds, and assessments to pay for environmental improvements, parks, and other recreational areas, and gains little by relying on speculative developers to be responsible for environmental preservation.)

PUBLIC INITIATIVES AND OTHER ALTERNATIVES

A major problem of the EIR review and permit process is that whereas the developer maintains a paid staff and political consultants to work on several projects simultaneously, the community must organize voluntary citizen actions to fight undesirable developments as they arise. Because of the solidarity and well-organized lobbying of groups like the building Industry Association in California and elsewhere, even when a community organizes sufficiently to pass new regulatory legislation, ongoing, militant, and voluntary action is required on the part of many concerned citizens to have any enduring effect. As the economics of the investment marketplace for real estate development continue to change (for instance by modifications of the federal tax laws) without correlative change in laws about development, citizen initiatives have become necessary to give citizens an opportunity to regulate development in their neighborhoods more directly in order to preserve what is left of our land and other ecological resources.

Ordinances Restricting Development

Recently, in San Francisco, California, an ordinance that absolutely limits development and grants extensive powers to the city planning authority was signed into law. There may be no other way to inhibit the investment and development process and create more local control for the sake of the environment and the health of the community. Northern

California, Oregon, and the state of Washington have long been leaders in the movement toward environmental responsibility.

Moratorium on Development of Infrastructure Services

In one of the older examples of prohibitive regulation of developments which has proved to be successful, the County of Marin, north of San Francisco, placed a moratorium on the issuance of permits for water main and sewer construction and thereby successfully preserved some very rare and special open space.

Community-Sponsored Development

An alternative to a moratorium such as that imposed in Marin County, is community adoption of a plan to constructively attract investment dollars to intelligently planned and successful buildings in locations where they are used, appreciated, and more easily marketed. The state of Virginia recently provided such incentives for the development of a high-technology commercial center.

The Public Land Trust

Another alternative being tried with great success throughout the land is the provision of tax advantages for investment in development which meets sound criteria. The public land trust concept is an indirect application of this technique. In public land trust transactions, land owners are provided with tax credits for donating large portions of their land to a trust for purposes of environmental preservation. Given the tax advantage developers can then develop the remaining land more profitably. The public land trust has been used effectively by citizens of Jackson Hole, Wyoming, to preserve the integrity of their unique natural environment. A national organization, known as The Trust for Public Land, has been privately endowed to support such activities. The land trust concept depends on the willingness of land owners in an area to support open space preservation.

Constructive Involvement

All of the alternatives to simply halting development by local moratoriums, created by voter initiatives, require that communities adopt more complex criteria and more constructive involvement in development. This is taking place in many communities, most notably in areas where tourism is a primary industry related to enjoyment of the natural or traditional appearance of a place rather than the business of civilization. Ultimately, because of the rate of growth in ecologically desirable areas such as coastal regions, unless some form of constructive action is taken, the damages resulting from irresponsible development will leave little to preserve. The question is: How much of the planet's irreplaceable living resources will be destroyed before the situation becomes a threat to survival?

In the logic of commercial real estate, only when a scarcity is created in a commodity does it become more profitable to improve neighborhood environments than to raze natural open space. The investment structure of free enterprise cannot be expected to follow a course of environmental preservation or community well-being. Organizations such as the Sierra Club provide excellent means for people who are activists to meet and strengthen their voices; however, the problem is of such substantial size and great immediate concern that meaningful political action must take place in communities to provide systematic means of control.

CREATING CRITERIA FOR DEVELOPMENT

Since any enduring solution providing for intelligent development requires that communities adopt new criteria for development, the nature of these criteria emerges as the focal issue. We possess the technological ability to make the necessary corrections to the development process. It will help to describe the forces and conditions involved in developing in concert with new technology. An understanding of technologies might make it possible for people to make better choices about how they build or buy a business location or residence and about the way they vote on environmental issues at the polls. The physical and mechanical nature of various technologies has been discussed in the previous chapters of this book; more space is given later to the human relationship to technology as it relates to development.

SUPPORTING AND INFLUENCING CHOICE

In a democratic and free enterprise society, first and foremost, all problems devolve to one of individual choice. A general reappraisal of land-use law, planning, and development policy is critical for the purpose of creating a more informed public opinion to ensure that major land development companies act responsibly. Much land subject to commercial development in the United States is owned by corporations and government agencies. For instance, the railroads have extensive land holdings, as do most state departments of transportation and the United States Department of Defense. The development of most of these lands is subject to speculative enterprise. In addition, in every locality, there are large business concerns (such as the Times-Mirror company in Los Angeles) which have large investments in real estate and which now regard these investments as assets that can be aggrandized through development. The priorities of this investment are not concerned with conflict with community health and well-being.

As an example, for many years several hundred acres of open space in Los Angeles, California, was preserved because of its proximity to a private airport owned by the Hughes Aircraft Company (Summa). Development proceeded around this space so that, over the years, it became more valuable. It has also become the *last remaining open space* in a large area of very high density. When the property's real estate value reached a point greater than the income from its use as an airport, the company owning the airport (Hughes Aircraft) announced its intention to move its operations to Phoenix, Arizona, and also announced its plans to develop the airport and the surrounding open space. This was despite the objections of concerned citizens in the neighborhood of the proposed development, despite the concerns of employees who were to lose employment, despite the absence of open space in an area of very high population density, despite the fact that no desperate need existed for housing, and despite the fact that commercial space was already overbuilt in the area. Even though this area includes part of the last remaining undeveloped wetlands area in a stretch of more than 100 miles, the City of Los Angeles, the California Coastal Commission, and the citizens of Los Angeles are allowing the Summa Corporation (parent to Hughes) to proceed with plans.

That which is preserving the present problems in development operates at the level of individual choice on the part of those responsible for the policies of organizations like Hughes. The task of intelligent development may be impossible without the committed action of people in positions of responsibility. This is a general truth, the reality of which is inescapable; there are not going to be simple, legislative solutions. We have arrived again at the findings of the Stanford Research group. It is money, rather than love, that conquers all.

This issue should not be avoided and treated as an irrevocable condition; an examination into the nature of being in our culture reveals some very helpful directions in dealing with it. Further study brought up these questions: What does it mean to be a person—what motivates the individual? What are the problems and benefits involved in expanding one's choices in life? What are the forces in the community which guide people in determining choice? Especially relevant is the way people are affected and motivated by the environment in which they live and work, and the way this can be influenced by what we build and how we build.

ALIENATION AND THE PSYCHOLOGY OF COMMUNITY

As a group, we in the United States, more than populations elsewhere, spend a lot of time dealing with the experience of separation. By "experience of separation," I mean the thought or feeling that we are alone in the world; that people do not care about each others' welfare; that the world is a difficult, dangerous, and sometimes fearful place in which to keep body and soul together.

In native American groups and other societies that we call "primitive," because of the simplicity of the technologies they employ, the connection between man and the environment is acknowledged in the day-to-day language which is spoken, as well as in forceful rituals and ceremonies. *Our* language also constantly refers to that which we regard as the source of our lives and well-being. But for us, this source appears in an abstract form, seemingly distant from our nature. Our predicament is that our personal power and success in society appear to be results of individual action. We are encouraged by this circumstance to feel isolated and competitive with others, and we are prone to moods of loneliness and often feel separate from friends, family, and larger social groups.

When discussing this problem, psychologists use the word "alienation." As a cultural group, Americans spend an inordinate amount of time and effort trying to avoid the feeling of being separate or trying to resolve the consequences of actions in which we or others were motivated by an attempt to avoid the fear of an alienating experience. As the individual grows more aware of this aspect in social experience, new ways of relating to others appear which are more inclusive and productive, a process that is thought of as growing up. We become able to observe and even predict people's motivations. Studies in social sciences reveal a correlation between this individual evolution and what appears to be an evolution of Western society through an age of alienation.

When the logic of commercial media and advertising are observed, the rootedness of alienation in our language and customs becomes more clear. Either directly or as an assumed background of the obvious, much commercial advertising appeals to fears about alienation and usually offers a product or lifestyle change. The promise of the advertisement is that the product or service will deliver the audience into a relationship with family, lovers, friends, and a world without fear of separation.

The applications and even the forms of many technologies have also been shaped by the logic or psychology of alienation. As an example, most point-of-sale and accounting/auditing technologies have been designed to protect businesses from dishonesty. The source of commercial dishonesty is the perceived relationship between businesses and their clients, employers and their employees, and so forth. The U.S. Department of Defense recently began to require that contractors utilize a computerized system for evaluating and reporting chargeable expenses. This resulted from a history of substantial abuses of trust. Apparently, there is no corporate awareness of responsibility for the success of the government or its agencies. The client, in this case the government, is seen as separate from and even fair prey for the entrepreneurial corporation.

An easy way for an American to experience his or her unconscious attitude of separation from government is to have a conversation with others who do not possess such an attitude. In America, we believe that we have a job. In Japan, one believes that the job is one's life. In America, we believe we have a government. In Russia, one believes one is the government.

The distinction between these two kinds of attitude is very important. Recently, a video conference was held between a group of Soviet citizens in Leningrad and a group of Americans in Seattle, Washington. The 2½-hour videotaped confrontation was telecast in the United States and the Soviet Union. Over and over again, the Americans in a TV studio located in Seattle made statements that presumed they knew more about Russia than did the Russians. Frequently, the Russians pointed out that the world was not as the Americans imagined. Americans who had traveled in the Soviet Union gave evidence that the Russians' point of view was correct and Americans were misinformed. The primary American misconception was that the Russians' attitude toward their government was similar to their own. The Russians, however, expressed themselves as if they were not alienated from their government. The logic of Nikita Kruschev's passionate demonstration at the United Nations many years ago, when confronted with Richard Nixon (when Kruschev hammered with his shoe on the podium of the United Nations General Assembly), becomes extremely clear in the light of this revelation. While Nixon held forth about our ability to provide citizens with color televisions, washing machines, and private automobiles, Kruschev was pointing out that the technologies of our government and its diplomacy appeared primitive to his land. He also pointed out that, in the long run, technologies for sensible human management would prevail, barring, of course, the possibility of human extinction through the mismanagement of industrial or war technologies.

Albeit the Soviets have other problems to solve, the problem of alienation may be better approached by the Soviet form of government than by our own. We would be smart to take a closer look at what has worked in Russia, to see what we might learn to apply here. The expressions of Karl Marx have had a significant impact on the world. How have things turned out, as we near the end of the first century of the life of his ideas? We also could benefit from a better understanding of how things have worked here and how we might use technology to solve social problems.

IMPACT OF TECHNOLOGY ON SOCIAL ISSUES

Technologies have the effect of amplifying or creating new opportunity for human expression. Given the enormous effort of individual human will expressed through technologies of all kinds, it is possible that many social problems and much of the opportunity for social change lie within the domain of technological management. Our culture is defined by our commitment to technologies. We have built our communities in such a way that we depend on technologies for our survival. For this reason, management of technology in the domain of urban and commercial development may be the best place to implement programs that support social and psychological well-being.

INTEGRITY AND ALIENATION—CULTURAL BREAKTHROUGH

A closer review of personal experience with alienation reveals more. Many high-level business, professional, and political interactions are characterized at times by struggles caused by selfishness, greed, and broken promises. When this is so, personal integrity seems to be an issue subordinate to personal or financial success. This does not suggest that lapses in personal integrity are the cause of alienation; rather, it implies that lapses are the result of decisions people make as they go about life operating under the assumption of alienated existence (i.e., assuming they are separate beings living in a competitive world, surviving at each others' expense). Such assumptions also cause stressful inner conflict. Life lived as a separate experience becomes an empty and meaningless exercise devoid of the relationships through which everything we do and become is acknowledged and rewarded. This is one area in which we might benefit from a look at the Russian experience.

It is logical that in order for there to be a fear of being separate and alone, there needs to be a prior assumption—that of not being separate, of having something to fear the loss of. Humanity is defined by this prior assumption about relationship. A person is not able to be another way. This has been a recurring theme in the work of artists through the ages. The poet e. e. cummings evoked this reality about life very powerfully for our age, especially in a book recounting his imprisonment in Spain, called *The Enormous Room.* On the other end of the spectrum, I recall a conversation I had with a plumber in Puerto Rico, in 1968. His father had been an opposition political leader. He had been imprisoned with his father and branded a "communist" at the age of 10. For most of his life this man had been dealing with oppressive practical realities associated with the perceived domination of his political expression by Americans. I asked him why this was a problem for him personally, given that he was resourceful and could make his opportunities in any situation. He replied, "Not to be free, not to decide for myself what I am to do, is not to live like a human being." He could not consider himself potent if he had no voice in the politics of his community. It was an aesthetic problem, not the problem of a criminal.

In any individual case, e.g., in therapy, the interaction of a trusted observer can be used to address and resolve a problem of attitude within the context of any circumstances. There are many therapeutic solutions available for personality problems that arise in individual cases. Here we are concerned with finding ways of interpreting community and defining development in order to eliminate some causes of individual problems so as to create the greatest potential in our communities for the growth of citizens in good health.

Humanity is defined by an ability to comprehend and act in relationship, and we make automatic assumptions about relationship which are similar to our belief in the force of gravity. We do not argue with the reality of such phenomena as gravity, so we invent beliefs about these phenomena. The belief systems that we individually create about ourselves and our relationships with others share a fundamental precept about who and what we think we are. The unspoken but understood precept that we have in common is the assumption of ultimate relationship among all people ("No man is an island") and, in fact, all beings. We hold this kind of idea as an unuttered, unthought-of belief rather than as an intellectual choice that we make. At times, we are overcome by feelings which bring up ideas that are in agreement with the belief and we experience being moved by the ideas. Underlying the belief is knowledge of the relationship between all things. This knowledge exists as a position from which to view things—a set of personal operating criteria. Although we usually are not aware of the way we make decisions and choices, it is easy to see our operating principles in day-to-day conversations, in the basis for a sense of humor, and in meetings that inspire compassion and feelings of companionship.

The assumptions of a common humanity are the context in which the acts of both the criminal and authoritarian personalities are judged by society. Evidence for this line of thinking can be found in phrases from fundamental concepts of every major religion; these include the Christian Golden Rule, the Jewish "I am thou," the Buddhist "Namaiste" ("I greet my self I meet in you"), the existentialist "There is nobody out there" (but myself), the mystic "One with the universe." Whenever we act (or act by omitting an appropriate action) in a way which is not consistent with a sense of belonging to the community of man, we experience a conflict of personal integrity—the uncomfortableness which the Stanford study, earlier referred to, called "cognitive dissonance." The psychological by-product of this inner conflict is the expectation or fear which psychologists call alienation. When our actions are inconsistent with our beliefs (traffic violations, broken promises, unpaid bills, evaded taxes, etc.), they are actions in contradiction to personal integrity and tend to increase feelings of alienation. Conversely, acts which right the wrongs of personal integrity (payment of past due bills, tax returns, apologies, etc.) are accompanied by moods of expansiveness, compassion, and security.

The experience of alienation is imaginary. Since alienation is a physical impossibility, the experience involved can only include the expectation or fear associated with the idea of alienation. When someone is afraid of something that doesn't really exist, we say that the fear is paranoia—the person is "crazy." Survival-oriented behavior is motivated by fears about something that has no basis in reality. Even in real *life-threatening* situations, consistently present for the individual is a commitment to life, as distinct from a threat to or fear about survival.

The result of actions motivated by fears about survival of the individual is inauthenticity in the way we speak, feel, and observe what is around us. Whenever we operate in a manner that is inconsistent with the inner knowledge of relationship, the action we take is used to justify and validate the fear of alienation—to make it real. Rationalizations and justifications are created by the individual to explain why it is acceptable to feel not related or not compassionate toward others. Many of these rationalizations are common to a culture and incorporate specific language the purpose of which is to characterize another. ("He's a———!")

The individual's attitude about human interdependence reflects the values of the community in which the individual was raised. These values are expressed in the way the community is developed. As learned from family, school, friends, and the media, the interpretation of these values shapes the way we view others and act toward them and the world. Our interpretation of situations is set up by cultural and familial conditioning. People can hold contradictory beliefs such as that of apartheid and still believe that they are deeply committed to humane values.

If I were a white South African, it would be logical for me to construe that a human being with brown skin was in a class distinct from and subordinate to one with white skin. It would then be reasonable for me to act as if I were not responsible for the black person's predicament. This condition resembles the attitudes which many German people had about Jewish neighbors during the Nazi pogroms. It is similarly characteristic of the northern European's attitude toward "guest workers" from Turkey, Italy, Algeria, etc., the Californian's view of "undocumented workers" from Mexico, and the eastern American's view of Puerto Ricans. In this way a society may aspire to humanistic values and still persist with inauthentic values and suppress the expression of authenticity in individuals.

BUILDING FOR PEOPLE AND COMMUNITIES

What is the possible effect produced on people by high-security commercial and residential complexes, isolated by gates and guards? The fear of alienation has unmistakable psychological consequences. Since alienation is the thought, feeling, or impression of being not connected to or not a part of that which is going on around one, it is a mood characterized by a feeling of dependence. It is as if the individual lives at the mercy of circumstances over which he or she has no control, about which he or she is powerless to do anything, and for which he or she was not the cause. Situations such as that of the Afrikaner, mentioned above, are characterized to different degrees by feelings of impotence on both sides of the subordinator-subordinatee equation.

The psychology of alienation is confusing because it is validated by what appears to be very logical evidence such as daily reports in the mass media about murder, rape, war, social discrimination, and starvation. It is impossible to be around any urban center and fail to observe scenes of ugly or destructive activity. How can one witness this without feeling a sense of powerlessness? Presumably only by repressing the experience, with the help of appropriate rationalizations. In the process of rationalization, the individual becomes blind to entire areas of vision as if they did not exist. It is difficult for individuals to see themselves as responsible for conditions over which they have no control. They might be considered insane were they to suggest that they are responsible for the acts of murderers and others with whom they have never had anything whatsoever to do. However, given the underlying belief in the ultimate connectedness of all beings, which is an absolute, the responsibility is still felt. It is similar to the identification which occurs between an audience and the characters in a play. One knows that this is just a play, but emotions and associated physical sensations are very real. A similar experience of empathy is evidenced by the fascination people sometimes feel in the presence of macabre accidents or crimes.

At times when the consciousness of an individual is dominated by emotions, the ability to experience is diminished. Depending on the individual and the strength of the emotions, compulsions to which an individual might be prone show up—eating or not eating, smoking tobacco, drinking, or going shopping. To the extent that an individual is compelled by such emotions and not experiencing, to that extent it might be said that there is no experience of life. If this is not being present to life then what is the possibility called being present to life? What exactly is given up in this process called alienation?

ALIENATION AND INTEGRITY

The logic of alienation is convoluted. When one witnesses a criminal act or receives the report of one, the sense that one is responsible for the acts of others supports the thought that one's own integrity is at stake. There is emotion—anger felt toward the perpetrator and frustration with the victim. Unless the individual can acknowledge responsibility for what is witnessed, these emotions are likely to reinforce the illusion of alienation and heighten the mood which cancels experience, leading to inauthentic thought and action.

Each event that is witnessed, whether it be directly or via the media (television, newspapers, etc.), adds substance to the illusion of alienation by indicating yet another part of the universe which it becomes necessary to disavow as something for which the person cannot take responsibility. The more that is witnessed, the easier it becomes to rationalize, in contradiction with beliefs, that we are powerless over most matters, that nothing makes much of a difference, and that ultimately one's life is separate from such realities. The inconsistency between the belief system and the rational process also creates confusion about many choices in life which would otherwise be very simple—choices about the use of drugs, alcohol, and cigarettes; choices about defense spending and unproven nuclear energy technology; choices about urban development and ecological well-being; choices about child raising and child abuse; choices about marriage and sexual behavior.

Actions motivated by this confusion of values are frequently antagonistic toward life (as distinct from acts which are the authentic expressions of a protagonist in life). Antagonism refers to the taking of action in response to and against real or imagined circumstances. This is characteristic of a situation where individuals cannot see themselves as responsible for the circumstances which seem to control opportunities in life. Antagonistic actions are reactive attempts to prevent experience rather than to create experience. The actions of an authentic being, who is open to and feels responsible for the experience at hand, are initiated by a desire to experience rather than to prevent experience as a reaction to circumstances which trigger emotions. For this reason, actions from antagonism lack potency with regard to constructively altering circumstances and usually result in counterreactions. In expressions of anger, the least they achieve is a venting of frustration usually without direction or in irrelevant directions rather than directed toward a constructive attempt to change the cause of the circumstances within the realm of socially acceptable action. The most they achieve is a state of war. Reactive responses include acts of escapism, such as the abuse of drugs and alcohol, as well as a feeling of dullness and incompleteness in relationships.

OPPORTUNITIES FOR RELATIONSHIP IN COMMUNITY

The way in which the community provides opportunity and respect for the interrelatedness of groups and individuals creates the background for antagonistic reactions or authentic action. Either the individual can see the contribution he or she makes to the family or neighborhood group, and the contribution which the group makes in relation to other groups, or the individual cannot. This aspect of individual potency is very deeply associated with the control individuals may feel they have over the process of community development.

The work of American playwrights and novelists of our era (ranging from Eugene O'Neill, William Faulkner, and Ernest Hemingway to John Irving, Tom Robbins, and Kurt Vonnegut) typically depicts the tragedy of situations involving characters having reactive relationships. In the popular media, antagonism as the problematical cause of action is depicted in the crime and adventure melodramas of the American television media and most of the product of the motion picture industry.

Although it is a subject separate from that with which I am dealing, the similarity between the media and the development industry in the way they are dominated by the same motivations provides a useful analogy. In the commercial media industry, writers and directors commonly build dramatic situations around relationships motivated by antagonistic ways of viewing life. The difference between good and evil characters engaged in bickering disputes over money, sex, and personal power has to do with the style with which each plays out an antagonistic viewpoint. The underlying antagonistic premise of this kind of media product can easily be distinguished from works of *pro*tagonistic art.

In light of this, the role of the commercial media in manipulating the public by selectively providing witness to acts of criminality presents a critical issue, which suggests that social and psychological scientists (rather than dramatists and businesspeople) should be employed as news editors. Most acts of crime, especially those committed by youth (according to national statistics youth are responsible for more than 80 percent of the crimes perpetrated in the United States), are the antagonistic acts of people acting without particular direction, guided only by a general sense of frustration that directs them against symbols in which they perceive the cause of their frustration. The conditioning of those who become criminals has been provided by the public media and public educational institutions as distinct from a more socializing education which might occur in communities where there was opportunity for responsible relationships to be expressed and acknowledged. (Juvenile gangs have become the only opportunity for many young people to find a meaningful setting for relationship.)

Although awareness about antagonistic motivation and reaction is valuable, no one has ever claimed that it is possible to do anything about changing antagonistic reactions in others. Only a commitment from the individual will permit the experiential transformation of the individual's habits of speech, thought, and behavior which might be required. Customs of antagonistic reaction are securely imbedded in our personal modes of expression. They are entrenched in the semantics of business, professions, and politics. Although it is possible for a committed person to struggle through a process of revolutionary self-education, the mechanisms of society (its customs, traditional ways of acting, and taboo subjects) are antithetical to revolutionary thinking.

There are few big rewards available for pioneering in the field of free expression. There is a risk of being thought crazy, especially among those who are unaware of their own survival-oriented mannerisms. It is more comfortable for an individual to "go with the flow." Besides, it is healthy for people to want to be the way they think society wants and needs them to be. This presents a problem for youth because—although society appears to need revolutionary, thinking beings who act from commitment—the mechanisms of social organization require the suppression of contradictory thoughts and feelings. The contribution of youthful revolutionary attitudes and energy is then left without a constructive outlet and is lost to society.

The urgency of the planetary ecological situation and statistics about stress-related illnesses indicate that the time has come to create some tolerance for and awareness of the contribution of revolutionary ideas. The old ideas are failing; medical science has not been able to cure stress-related illnesses and only deals with the symptoms. We are able to build instruments to carve out or destroy cancerous tissue and to replace organs with artificial technology, but we are making slow progress in the *prevention* of heart disease and cancer. Even as we announce cures for some long-standing medical problems, new forms of illness arise from the same source—stressful living habits. It could be that the major killers of our time, such as heart disease, can be eliminated through stress reduction related to the way we plan and develop our communities.

THE FUNCTION OF COMMUNITY DEVELOPMENT

It is paradoxical that the improvement of human well-being does not require that we do anything about symptoms such as crime and illness. (This would be more reaction to circumstances.) Instead, we need to create public understanding of the causes of the condition and to provide opportunities for alternatives. This is the function of community development. A person can only see his or her own alienation and antagonistic acts in the context of that which is not antagonistic—the context of the protagonist. Development needs to proceed in the direction of creating this context. Through the recognition of antagonistic acts, one can see the cause of consequences in personal and professional relationships that could be avoided. Besides being disruptive, these consequences reinforce the mood of alienation and provoke thoughts that one is alone in the world and that the world is a place of antagonism and struggle.

THE SEARCH FOR APPROPRIATE ACTION

I experimented with this thought by operating on the principle that antagonistic actions are analogous in meaning to the idea of sins we commit in life. The awareness of this principle, in considering and guiding action, is not a new idea. It is the fundamental ethical principle of Christianity, Judaism, the Islamic faith, and most other socializing belief systems. In American society, the socioeconomic systems of capitalism and free enterprise have so influenced the individual's psychological needs, through the alienating effects of self-centered individualism and competitiveness, that most people live with major contradictions to their own ethical values as a corollary to financial success. They allow their competitive striving to overwhelm other values, and they compromise their experience to an ideal of economic success. Unfortunately, most people don't discover the cost of this until they survive a heart attack or other major calamity.

For those who are trapped in the cycle of capital accumulation and consumerism, there is little satisfaction found in life until they learn to put the principle of protagonistic action ahead of the large rewards for antagonistic self-interest. The statistics of health and longevity in women would seem to indicate that the feminine point of view in community development might be worth consulting. It is the female *point of view* that needs to be consulted. When women have played by the rules of male-dominated activities, they eventually become as strident as their male role model and are subject to similar fallacies.

ALIENATION AS A MEASURE OF COMMUNITY DEVELOPMENT

Karl Marx thought that the experience of alienation and reactions of antagonism are appropriate to a certain condition, a stage in the evolution of humanity, leading to the creation of a new social order, beyond capitalism and communism—one that inspires protagonistic behavior.

Societal evolution involves the adaptation of society over time to changing circumstances. As the human individual changes, her or his wants, needs, and desires are altered. This alteration is reflected in a parallel evolution in society. This happens because of the consequential change that must occur in the rules, policies, and procedures (customs) which govern interpersonal transactions within the society. Through the established institutions of family, government, and commerce, the newly evolving social scheme then shapes the new generation of individuals.

If alienation is a stage through which the individual must evolve in order to live creatively in constructive relationship with others and to coexist on the planet with other forms of life (whales, trees, etc.), it is also true that society may need to grow through a similar set of experiences. Nazism and World War II might have been unnecessary had people at that time been able to comprehend their relationship as the clue to their survival.

Since evolution aims at survival by progressive adaptation to changing circumstances, if the human race is to survive, it is clear that we will do so by becoming aware of the nature of alienation and how it motivates our acts of antagonism. Awareness follows experience. Our purpose in this conversation is to create an awareness through media, rather than by way of experiences of war, economic depression, and ecological destruction. The result of higher awareness will be seen in a change in the participation of people in social groups committed to meaningful action.

In becoming aware of relationship, the individual learns the importance of commitment to the well-being of the community. Because of the nature of our technology, this commitment must expand the concept of community from a local, group, or national unit to at least a planetary group. This is essential to our survival as a species inasmuch as biosphere ecologists now claim that our survival as a species does depend on how well we comprehend and act appropriate to our interdependence on each other and all other forms of life on the planet. Driving the process of this evolution is the development of technology that has given us ultimate power over life and death in the biosphere. The broad power of our technologies has literally made us custodians of the well-being of the ecosystem that supports all life, perhaps for all time.

THE USE OF TECHNOLOGY FOR COMMUNITY AWARENESS

Modern technologies lend enormous power to the expression of human acts, whether they are authentic or not. A positive example of this is to be seen in the emergence of such social groups as the International Hunger Project. The Hunger Project represents a planetwide, apolitical, and voluntary group of individuals, at present numbering more than 4½ million, who are committed to the end of starvation on the planet. The Hunger Project has been cited by an association of world hunger organizations as being the primary organization responsible for ending a condition of famine in southeast Asia following the Vietnam war. The Hunger Project is now focusing on a situation in Somalia, West Africa. Never before have people accomplished such a feat on behalf of others without being prompted by a self-concerned political strategy or by the condition of war, and never before has a famine been ended anywhere by act of human will. The activity of the Hunger Project has been made possible by the commitment of individual people through modern technological resources of communication, production, and transportation, through the facilities these technologies can lend to ad hoc hunger organizations.

It is most significant that the Hunger Project was organized by volunteers as a form of expression requiring participants to assume self-defined roles in the organization out of their personal commitment to end hunger. Their actions take a form consitent with their own well-being—the acts of protagonists in life. *This in itself represents an evolution in what it means to be human.* In the context of community development, this evolution changes our thoughts about those for whom we need to develop, whom we are serving. Through the utilization of available technologies, the individual today has enormous potential power for expression and action.

TECHNOLOGY AND HISTORY

When the role of alienation in the evolutionary process of the individual and society is understood, reexamining the nature and applications of technology provides a new mastery of its uses and effects. When new technologies are developed and implemented, an array of unthought-of applications, effects, and uses shows up, accompanied on occasion by catastrophic disasters.

Technologies are always invented for particular purposes and usually have some unpredictable side effects. Sometimes, the real nature and value of a technology is not known to its inventors. They are frequently focused on solving a particular problem and see only a limited aspect of the tool they discover or invent. Again because of the concurrence of ritual effect, a good example of this can be seen in mass media technology, including radio, television, motion pictures, and printed media. It would be very helpful for the reader to see the physical community as a kind of medium for expression, as if the community were no more than the sets and props in which the action of life takes place, providing the circumstances and forces that influence all relationships.

As in building and community development, the most important aspects of electronic media technology don't exist in the thoughts of most of its engineering designers or most of those involved in the commercial production and broadcast industries. The situation is similar to that created by the speculative development of commercial real estate. Media professionals live with illusions that obscure the philosophic premise of their work. They are encouraged by society to see the value of the media relative to a career ambition or related to jobs for which they need to use mass communication such as commercial or dramatic art rather than the contribution that their work is to others. The parallel between media and development is important. The distinction being created in drawing this parallel is the key to understanding the power of Churchill's statement: "We shape our buildings and then our buildings shape us." In other words, we need to look at development as the medium for the *committed* expression of human life. What a being sees as possible shows up for the individual in the social and physical environment we call community.

MEDIA—THE CREATION OF HISTORY

The power of mass communications technology, including the applications of all kinds of media, is that it operates directly in the realm of social evolution. It operates through the creation of history. Just as the technology of a highway creates the potential for transportation, the technology of mass media creates the potential within a social group for the common understanding of history. History, in this sense, is myth—the way in which individuals look to see who and what they are, as individuals and as members of groups, families, communities, nations, and races. Society uses history in formal education to shape the minds and hearts of children and citizens. This mind shaping is the application of history as a technology. The product and potential of the application of history is social evolution. The speed with which the history-making process occurs today, owing to applications of electronic media recording, editing, and transmission, increases the pace at which evolution can occur to a rate which makes social evolution a real-time science.

Today, a cultural group numbering in the billions can be motivated within a few minutes to new ways of thinking, feeling, and acting through the use of mass media. This has presented new problems for psychologists and social scientists. It is becoming increasingly difficult to establish social norms—they have become a moving target.

The way things were in Freud's time, the social character of the individual (those traits which the individual shares in common with other members of a society) caused the individual to want to do what he or she had to do based on what the society needed done. A good example of this is the so-called "work ethic." Unless the worker in an industrial society clearly saw fulfillment in getting up every morning and working diligently all day at a specialized task, there would have been no industrial society. Social character is a product of family, school, and other social conditioning. When a society evolves or is radically restructured, as has been the case in France, Russia, and China after their respective revolutions, a period of instability follows until the new structure is again supported by the individual's voluntary commitment to his or her social role—the modern social character.

Mass media and telecommunications technologies have accelerated this process. The youth of well-knit, long-evolving societies are receiving, from the commercial broadcast media, conditioning that is in conflict with what is wanted and needed by the traditional structure of their society. This brings up problems, including antisocial and neurotic behavior, individual confusion about identity, and an increasing societal reliance on symbolic gratification and vicarious experience (money, sex, and drugs) to buy compliance of individuals, in place of a genuine engagement in life and the communal process.

George Orwell had foreseen these events and used them as a background for his famous science fiction novel, *1984*. He projected a situation in which people were dominated by the absolute values of machines and had become a human resource. The possibility for using mass media technology to manipulate behavior as Orwell predicted was practically demonstrated by early radio broadcasts—most notably the address of Charles Lindbergh in New York after the transAtlantic flight, and also the public reaction to Orson Welles' radio drama, *War of the Worlds*. Because of the reality which Welles' production evoked, many listeners thought the planet had really been invaded by "aliens" from another planet. Today, the masters of consumer marketing and commercial motion picture production are making the most of this possibility of mass media technology. Hardly a week goes by that does not see an orchestrated shift of consumer buying habits due to the manipulation of public taste by commercial television, radio, and other media. In the United States, we have elected an actor to the highest office of the land.

The effectiveness of contemporary mass media technology is such that, along with its destructive exploitational effects, it creates a possibility that we can evolve a new expression of a common humanity. This evolution is essential if we are to intelligently manage the resources of the planet and to control technologies that are potentially dangerous to life such as atomic energy. Despite the *historical* impotence of our international political organizations, there is a possibility now for a powerful transformation in international communication, owing to recent advances in the development of fiber optic cable and satellite transmission of data, radio signals, and television signals. The range of media programming alternatives available to viewers is growing rapidly and will continue to do so.

Programs sponsored by the producers and performers of contemporary music, because of the powerful place they hold in the estimation of their youthful audiences, have the opportunity to present subjects which have previously been taboo in many societies. These performers speak through music compellingly, uncompromisingly, and inspiringly to the youth of the world, a population group with a vested interest. This audience is committed to listening and has no reason not to be interested in finding ways to resolve the contradictions of alienation and integrity it sees everywhere. This audience is hungry for explanations for the expressions of alienation which it senses in home, school, and community situations. Moreover, the youth of various nations, by aspiring to common feelings, customs, and traditions expressed through music, are acquiring an international culture.

A similar transformation is occurring among other generations as well as through the growth of international professional societies in fields such as medicine and biotechnologies, finance, telecommunications, and engineering technologies. In each case, an opportunity has been created for expanding the experience of relationship in the planetary community and for providing individuals with an arena in which they can have an impact on the course of vital events.

This aspect of human development expands the context of community into a global issue. It affects the development of the local community because many business and social services and products are now being provided and supported by international networks.

THE EVOLUTIONARY GESTATION RATE

I have spent a great deal of time in this chapter discussing individual psychology and growth because it is this with which we are dealing when we measure the height of ceilings and the allocation of parks, theaters, and wildlife preserves. Although we discuss alienation as if it were a social phenomenon, it occurs only in the individual's experience and its solution is in individual awareness of relationship with others. In the evolution of society, the experience of alienation is like an amniotic fluid into which the child is born after it recognizes its existence separate from the mother. The length of gestation in the amniosis of alienation varies for each person depending on the nature of early childhood conditioning and the context of the social situation into which the child later grows. Everything we do in building our communities has an impact on the quality of this conditioning and the consequent length of gestation. It would be of little importance to try to teach about the interdependent relationships of people in schools, for instance, when the child experiences separation in the relationships at home. The political philosophy of schools is also involved. How is the student to internalize the concept of relationship with Canadians but not with Mexicans, Russians, or Ethiopians?

To develop facilities in the community consistent with an intention to manage planetwide resources implies that we recognize our relationship with others across geopolitical boundaries and biological diversities. We need to address management of local ecology and community resources as part of a wider context. At the threshold of this is the level, expressed in participation with others of the individual's experience of commitment in the community versus the experience of alienation. If we were to consistently develop the community to support the growth of individuals, presumably this problem would be solved and we could go on to some new, perhaps more interesting, problems. This statement is not idealistic philosophy, but a reporting of the news.

Because of the strength of the labor unions, fair employment practice codes, and growing professionalism in all fields of work, modern business operations demand that workplace environments represent the value and equality of all members of the organization. In developing commercial space, we need designs that better reflect this idea. Because of the service-client relationship between businesses, this idea must extend to a consideration of the entire community.

THE SUPPORT OF RELEVANT VALUES

The criteria emerging from this conversation appear now to be about buildings that enhance the experience of belonging, group, and community yet reinforce the concept of individual choice. When we are aware of our connectedness with others and with nature, alienation subsides and acts of inauthenticity become easier to recognize. Depending on the complexity of the civilization in which one is raised and the number of contradictions involved in the society; authenticity is more or less natural. The integrity of a bushman may be more simply defined for him and his relationship with genuine values more clear than that of a member of a high-technology society. Consequently, in evaluating a development, we need to take into account the practices of the local culture.

PROVIDING FOR GROWTH AND FLEXIBILITY

Experience matures awareness. As one grows more aware in any system of rules and consequences, smaller infractions bring consequences which seem more distinct. Thus in planning community development, we need to allow for the growth of community awareness which will take place in the community, probably in an accelerating fashion. When the ability to distinguish the cause of actions is refined, the problem-solving ability is strengthened. In human relationships, this frequently entails communication that needs to be made about previously unuttered thoughts or fears, promises one failed to keep or withdraw, or effects produced out of acts of ignorance, carelessness, or apathy. To manage around the diversified habits of individuals, access to information, opportunities for quick and easy communication, and environments which remind the individual of the experience of relationships are all required.

To support the "growth" of the culture, the technologies that enhance opportunities for communication need to be easily modifiable. The process of increasing awareness becomes more refined as more actions become authentic. There is an analogy to this situation in music: The more capable the musician, the more obvious are faults in intonation. So it is with the practice of personal integrity. Fessinger's work revealed that a side effect of rewarding lapses of integrity was erosion of the individual's ability to recognize such acts. The subjects he studied would accept lower rewards for repeating "wrong" acts and eventually were satisfied with no reward, acting wrongly today in order to be consistent with and justify a previous action.

Activities such as the compulsive habit of cigarette smoking follow this kind of logic. Cigarette advertising has sometimes appealed to this psychology, as in the billboard illustrations depicting healthy young men and women enjoying the pleasures of smoking a cigarette in an inspiringly beautiful fresh air environment. The repetition of such "wrongful" acts and development of destructive habits (compulsive behavior) results in the individual's gradual loss of ability to experience relationship authentically. This situation is analogous to a musician's losing the ability to hear. Living is experienced through relationship. In relinquishing one's ability to experience relationship, one loses the time of one's life.

TECHNOLOGY AND ART IN DEVELOPMENT

The inquiry thus continues with an analysis of practical development technologies. The question is this: How do we utilize technologies in community development to enhance the individual's experience of relationship and to support the values of personal integrity? Technology is not inherently qualified with regard to integrity, though a particular application of technology may be said to have integrity. Technology is characterized by its effect. Technology works by creating the potential for the accomplishment of some purpose. It works on things by making them into a resource. As mentioned in the first chapter of this book, I discovered this valuable distinction in the writings of Martin Heidegger. As he explained it, the essence of technology is that it creates "standing reserves." A technology emerges as distinct from mere things as a result of its function. A hammer ceases to be a hammer when the handle breaks and recedes into the "thingness" of its constituent parts—wood, iron, etc. In its function, a technology creates a potential of some other thing or things in the way that a gasoline motor makes of petroleum a standing reserve. Without the technology which uses petroleum, it would exist not as potential energy but simply as unqualified material—black, sticky stuff, a thing.

Art, as distinct from technology, is characterized by its evocative nature. Like technology, art is invented and brought into existence by humans. It is not, however, defined by a function, nor does it exist because of its making of something else into a usable resource. Art brings its audience into relationship with a world, experienced as an idea, feeling, or emotion. Through art, we experience ourselves in dimensions of the world. Heidegger qualifies art by suggesting that "art worlds the world." In other words, art makes a context called "world" by evoking the experience of a relationship between things. He gives the example of the Greek temple, which by its presence creates the context for the hills, grass, trees, sky, and the observer around it.

In its essence, art is not technology, though many expressions of art use technologies and exist in the form of or use material objects. (This is distinct from the art associated with Zen Buddhism, which is an artful way of being. It is possible to think of yoga, meditation, and other disciplines which are artful ways of being as technologies that create the potential for transcendant ways of thinking, being, and acting.) When forms of art utilize technologies, the technologies become tools of art. Technology may become art under certain circumstances.

Technology does not need to be artful to achieve its ends; however, technologies increase in our estimation when they possess aesthetic qualities. The evidence for this in the consumer marketplace indicates that artfully employed technologies are ultimately more commercially successful than technologies that are, relatively speaking, artless. An explanation of this is that we are fascinated by, and form aesthetic judgments about, technologies, especially the more dramatic examples such as projects in architecture and aeronautics. For people who possess abstract intellectual interests, there are computer programs and mathematical formulas which are regarded as being elegant and artful. There are instances of highways, bridges, automobiles, and other machines in virtually every category of product or process that some will regard as beautiful and inspiring.

These technologies appear artful and fascinating to us because of the integrity with which they appear to interact with nature. This is experienced as hearing or seeing truth in terms of the design and construction process (how well the technology is executed). Gravity and hydraulic phenomena, for instance, are the standards that allow us to experience the quality of an airplane design. In the marketing of a commercial building development, the aesthetic quality of a building is as important to commercial success as are the efficiency and reliability of the construction techniques and the choice of materials.

HIGH TECHNOLOGY

In the contemporary vernacular, we use the term "high technology" to distinguish between technologies which are highly evolved (fiber optic communications) and those which are less sophisticated (hammers). In architecture and industrial and environmental design, the words high technology are used for designs which display rather than mask the elements of technology. The term is also used in talking about structures which are necessary to support state-of-the-art technologies, ranging from blimp hangars and refineries to microwave dish clusters and local area networks.

State of the art is an aesthetic judgment: Technologies appeal to us as elegant because of the relationship of form to purpose, function, a natural force (gravity, thermodynamics, etc.), or environment. This is associated with the awe and excitement we feel in the presence of blimps, airports, jetliners, computer systems, and automobiles. The relationship of this aesthetic judgment with integrity and the concept of alienation provides an insight into planning urban development and implementing technologies in the workplace.

Inconsistencies in the design process of sophisticated technologies show up as unworkability. The more sophisticated the technology, the greater are the negative effects of small errors on what is to be produced. In computer programs, the effects of errors tend to be absolute. A bug that disempowers a computer program may be a single circuit that is closed instead of open, producing a 1 instead of a 0 in a program consisting of a sequence of billions of 1s and 0s. Everything that follows from such an error will be invalid, continuing to a place in the program where a smart programmer has placed a reference for the computer to check a place in the program ahead of the error.

In Denmark, north of Copenhagen, I was once shown a place where a major highway had been diverted around a huge concrete overpass bridge and intersection that were crumbling due to a minor error made in the mixing of concrete during construction. The unused bridge stands as an enormous monument to the mistake. In Los Angeles, a large federal office building was built with its rear entrance facing the street because the plans were viewed in reverse by the contractor who built the forms for the foundations. Recently, an interior concrete bridge spanning the lobby of a hotel collapsed at the opening of a new construction in Atlanta, with tragic loss of life and limb. In Bhopal, India, in excess of 2000 human lives were lost as the immediate result of a minor technological error at a chemical refining plant. We have not begun to question what technological process led to the fact that the September 1985 earthquake in Mexico City caused such a catastrophic disaster. Nor are we completely aware of the actual cause or extent of the nuclear disaster at Chernobyl.

The great effect of small actions, amplified by powerful technologies, has been the motivation for the latest breakthrough in computer science—the development of expert systems, machines that make decisions, and control systems that allow the human mind and body to control processes which are otherwise too immense or too fast to comprehend and manage. Such systems, which are capable of making billions of decisions every second, are being used to facilitate nuclear engineering science. They are producing calculations it would take tens of thousands of years to compute by any other means available.

A mundane example of less sophisticated use of similar technology is presented by the control systems involved in the multiplexing, transmission, and interpretation of light-wave signals. Although the concepts involved are relatively simple, these operations require a level of precision beyond what the human sense and intellect can perceive. In mundane applications of computer science, very simple computer programs created for large organizations keep track of expense allocations involving millions of transactions each day.

On the frontier of computer science is "artificial intelligence," an outgrowth of the technology developed to control other processes and technologies. The computer industry is moving toward the extensive use of artificial intelligence. "Expert systems" programs have been developed and are used in fields ranging from medicine and psychology to petroleum exploration, as well as the generation of new levels of programming ability. An essential part of an expert system is the human interface, the part which people use to command, question, and otherwise control the machine. State-of-the-art expert systems allow people to communicate with computer programs in human languages such as English, French, German, or Japanese. These systems use programs called "natural language processors" to translate the human language instructions into machine instructions. The machine is able to monitor minute and rapidly fluctuating conditions (such as the nanosecond-interval activities of computers) and to control such processes in real time, where humans would otherwise not be able to observe, let alone have time to act. Expert systems can provide the ability to manage businesses with absolute procedures, removing the possibility of human subjectivity or subversion. Questions arise around the problem of implementing such systems into established office or business social structures. These questions are of practical concern to anyone who has the task of implementing information management technologies.

To the extent that a technology is harmonious with nature (including compatibility with humans), it becomes an artful expression of human commitment to life. A technology so implemented is authentically appreciated by those who are affected by it. This process is identical with the product or behavior that we call art. This does not imply that technology ever is art but states that it can become artful in application as a consequence of the flawless nature of its design and application. For a technology to be flawless, it must be consistent with fundamentals of physical law and human aesthetics, taking into account social and psychological qualities of human beings such as respect, trust, admiration, and acknowledgment. This technology will thus be true to nature, and in the expression of that truth it will express a kind of authenticity which is a reflection of a relationship with nature.

When we observe the integrity of good design, we recognize a quality that qualifies the world and ourselves. Such technology operates in a way that is appropriate to life and to the world over which it has dominion or influence. This way of being, which is considerate of life and the part of the world it influences, allows the technology to become married to life in the way that an object of art, such as a painting or sculpture, is married to life. In the case of the art object, the artist who created it intended such a purpose. There are aesthetics, therefore, of windmills, airplanes, lighthouses, and ships—even of the song of a buoy in a seaway. The product of the technology (that which the technology acts on, makes possible, or produces) may be artless.

AVOWEDLY DESTRUCTIVE TECHNOLOGIES—WAR MATERIALS

Unfortunately, some technologies are intended to cause destruction. The technology may be flawlessly conceived and well-executed relative to this purpose. However, implicit in the design is the destructive potential. Awesome as the technology may be, to the extent that the individual is aware of the destructive potential, it will at best inspire only intellectual reaction to its antagonistically motivated purpose. This reaction will usually be expressed as a rationalization to justify macabre interest. Such technologies appeal to the logic of rationalizations used in support and justification of alienation.

There are also technologies developed for avowedly constructive purpose which have had destructive side effects or are put to destructive use. A technology put to a destructive use, or applied carelessly with destructive effect, is qualified by the effect produced and will tend to inspire a mood of alienation. This is especially noticeable in the history of the nuclear power industry, the telecommunications monopoly, and in the fall from grace of the chemicals manufacturing industry. It will be seen in each of these cases that the destructiveness always resulted from carelessness or compromise in design or construction attributable to a prior interest which subordinated the community well-being to the motive of personal or corporate survival at the expense of others—the paradigm of alienation.

SHAPING THE ENVIRONMENT

In examining the values of particular technologies, it is easy to identify those which are artful and those which are not. Sometimes while awestruck by the monumental effect of a building, for example, the Transamerica tower in San Francisco or the World Trade Center in New York City, we may also be aware of the building's self-serving quality as a real estate development. This quality detracts from our appreciation of the aesthetic architectural value. The building seems to rise above and even stand on the shoulders of an urban landscape characterized by the struggle for economic survival, crime, pollution, poverty, and other symptoms of alienation.

If the purpose of building is to create a productive community, committed to the well-being and life of the citizens, then this inconsistency is a technical flaw relative to this purpose. The contrast of the building with the life around it accentuates the powerlessness of the tiny individual in the face of an enormous economic machine. This is not a flaw in the technology of building design and construction. It cannot be corrected by changing the design or construction of the building. Nor is it a flaw in the scale of the building, though reducing the building's size could make the flaw less noticeable. The alienating motivation would still be present, though the symptoms might not be as expressive. The flaw in this case occurs in the technology of the economic system involved in the development process. This includes the science of community government administration and planning, which unites what we know of personal and social psychology, ecological planning, communications, economics, architecture, and so forth. This points to a flaw in the development procedures in the lack of a forum wherein proposed community development can be debated in the light of social issues as well as short-term return on investment capital.

Because what we build becomes a part of history—just as much as or more than what we print, speak, or record with film or other techniques—our buildings reflect what we have been as well as shape what we may become. The realization of this concept provides an opening through which we can observe reality differently and learn to act more responsibly with powerful development technologies in order to create constructive change.

Consider the practicality of developing with consideration of social issues, with the intention of creating environments which have built into them the potential for periodic change and evolution. To achieve such flexibility will require application of technologies in revolutionary ways and consideration of individual, family, and community goals and commercial interests. It will require that developers maintain an ongoing involvement in the operation and redesign of buildings. (Such a practice discourages absentee or disinterested ownership—which is at the core of most current speculative real estate development.) It will require community involvement in determining the nature and direction of development.

The availability of new telecommunications and other computer-driven technologies is providing the opportunity for more people to become involved in the development process. Cable television coverage of political events and legislative hearings provides the public with ear-to-the-ground awareness of planning and entrepreneurial action.

Two-way cable transmission of television signals makes possible the instant polling of a community regarding minor but relevant development issues and provides for public forums to take place about new development with relative ease. It should be possible for a developer to present a development plan and solicit community approval for a project prior to expenditure of any planning resources.

Expert systems for evaluating complex traffic and other needs make it easier to understand the analysis with which planners evaluate the effect of proposed developments relative to the community's long-term needs and short-term problems.

THE MOMENTUM OF THE MARKET

The wisdom of developing for long-term benefit has been recognized for many years by people in planning and development agencies. The introduction of new technologies is having an effect on the economy and organization of business that adversely affects the commercial real estate market; this is causing developers and investors to seek new ways of building. Many developers of commercial space, who are paying the mortgages on mostly empty buildings, are looking for ways to change in the direction of more intelligent building. They are systematically unwilling to incur expense for design or technology or to compromise their present positions in the community-planning process. Their investment pro formas will not support such activities. They can build only on the basis of actual or projected demand for raw space. They have learned to provide for security, climate controls, elevators, and other sophisticated mechanical systems as they emerge and become factors of consideration in the marketplace.

Because most developers in the United States have graduated from being building contractors, and are not architects or urban planners, they may never comprehend ways of building to better support communities of people and businesses using sophisticated technologies for information management and communication.

Businesses are becoming more interested in locating in communities that provide qualities which attract and keep good personnel. As human productivity becomes more crucial to high technology processes, issues of human well-being can no longer be separated from profitability, as they have been in the past. Eventually, the successful developer will be the builder who designs and builds in a manner that is consistent with the total needs of the human being and the community. The fact that to some this may seem a long way off should not be discouraging. For the first time in history, we can see the light at the end of the tunnel. Technological sophistication in the development of commercial real estate has become an important part of the process through which society is growing out of alienation into a civilization of healthy and sustaining value for the individual.

Many aspects of the development issue which I have only touched on in this chapter should be addressed as part of a community development planning process; these include such issues as transportation, recreation, telecommunications, educational facilities, the polling process, and ecological well-being. It should be possible to address all of the technologies of civilized development with the same criteria relative to human well-being.

The technology of transportation is a useful example. Transportation planning is an issue that obviously cannot be separated from building development planning. It has become clear that the automobile has been an interim and frivolous solution to public transportation and one which creates serious environmental problems. In addressing this issue with criteria other than automotive industry profits in mind, the community can plan transportation scenarios that permit radically different urban development planning.

THE LANGUAGE OF DEVELOPMENT CRITERIA

The fundamental problem with respect to dealing with all of these issues is that of building the common linguistic and scientific understanding that enables people from various cultures and disciplines to converse with one another in situations where people now speak different technoprofessional languages. Today's development, technology, land-use, city planning, and political professionals need to better understand each other, the language and needs of modern businesses, and the concerns of social science. How else can they begin to create environments that promote healthy community relationships? A conversant knowledge of the principles of information management technology is also essential for any serious planning or development professional.

FACTORS CREATING CHANGE

People are rapidly becoming more knowledgeable about and comfortable with technologies. In a study conducted by the Associated Press during the summer of 1985, 80 percent of respondents declared that they were comfortable with computers; 35 percent used them every day; 17 percent used them at home. Less than 5 years ago, computer programming was considered by most people to be a weird and esoteric science.

The effect of technologies on the marketplace is driving a few developers to self-education about technologies.

Investment pro forma analyses now take into account much longer periods of vacancy for new buildings. However, as long as it is profitable for foreign and other investors to invest relatively low cash amounts for the sake of high asset value and depreciation allowances, many communities may soon find it necessary to grant more regulatory powers to governmental agencies, perhaps requiring an appropriate educational qualification and licensing of development professionals.

VOX POPULI

At the time of this writing, the Mayor of San Francisco, Diane Feinstein, announced that she had signed into law an ordinance restricting future development in the city to 950,000 square feet over the next *3* years. The ordinance grants to city planners new powers to choose which large office buildings will be erected, where they will be placed, and how they will look.

In the state of California, a legislative measure can be placed on the ballot of any regularly scheduled election provided that a petition is received within a certain time prior to the election which petition is signed by a substantial percentage of the voters registered for that election. The city and county of San Diego are experiencing one of the highest rates of growth in the nation. Frequently, developers in San Diego have appealed to the city council for specific variations from approved growth plans for the area, in order to exploit a land development scheme. This has so alarmed many citizens who are concerned about destruction of the environmental quality and lifestyle of the area that a public initiative measure, which was signed by more than 80,000 voters, was placed on the ballot and was passed in a general election by an overwhelming majority of San Diego voters. It requires a public vote before the city council could allow any divergence from the established community growth plan which has set aside green belts and an urban reserve. At present, 25 cities in California have already enacted or placed managed growth initiatives on the ballot for forthcoming elections. A similar petition is now being circulated in Los Angeles, the largest city in the state.

In the tiny, conservative, suburban town of Del Mar, California, where I reside, citizens have passed an initiative which requires a public vote on *any* future downtown development project. Another initiative on the same ballot asked voters to approve a specific zoning change to allow the development of a hotel in an area at present restricted to residential use. It failed resoundingly.

Aside from the impact of local political changes and the potential benefits to environmental preservation, these actions of grass roots initiative represent a new community trend to take control of the development and planning process. Provided that we create more opportunity for public education about building healthful community environments, we can look forward to more community involvement in the development process. At first, this may be seen as a restriction in commercial development. Regrettably, some development companies will look for less restrictive political environments rather than adjust to new conditions. Those who do continue will need to adopt new procedures and better methods for working with the community to plan and evaluate projects.

A Glossary of Selected Terms

ABOVE 890 DECISION: The Federal Communications Commission (FCC) decision of 1959 concerning domestic allocation of frequencies in the spectrum above 890 megahertz, generally referred to as microwave. Establishes that private point-to-point operations are allowed frequencies in this spectrum, thus creating the possibility for alternatives to the telecommunications common carrier services and providing the basis for competition in long-distance telephone service.

ACCESS: Ability to connect to a network for telecommunications services or to log on to a data information network.

ACCESS CHARGE: A tariff charged by an exchange carrier to an interexchange carrier for the use of its local exchange facilities.

ALLOCATION: The assignment of a specific range of frequencies for use by particular users or elements of a network.

ALPHANUMERIC CHARACTERS: Both alphabetical and numerical symbols.

AMERICAN TELEPHONE AND TELEGRAPH 1956 CONSENT DECREE: A judicial settlement ending the federal government's 1949 antitrust suit against AT&T and Western Electric. Among the provisions was a restriction that the Bell System engage only in the manufacture of equipment and the provision of services related to the regulated common carrier telecommunication services and those services incidental to the provision of such services.

AMERICAN TELEPHONE AND TELEGRAPH 1982 CONSENT DECREE: A judicial settlement ending the federal government's 1974 antitrust suit against AT&T, Bell Laboratories, and Western Electric. Among the provisions agreed to were the divestiture of the local exchange service and access functions of the 22 Bell operating companies as well as the modification of the AT&T 1956 Consent Decree so that the remaining Bell System may enter into unregulated markets.

ANALOG SIGNAL: The proportional electrical equivalent of an original form of communication. When a person speaks into a telephone, the telephone generates and transmits an electrical signal that represents the voice. The electrical signal is proportional in intensity and frequency to the soundwaves striking the telephone mouthpiece.

ASCII: Acronym for American Standard Code for Information Interchange. The ASCII code is a widely established and accepted code which uses the numbers 0 to 127 to represent alphanumeric characters.

APPLICATION: A purpose for which a computer system is implemented. Word processing, for instance, is an application.

APPLICATION SPECIFIC INTEGRATED CIRCUIT (ASPIC): An integrated circuit chip which contains most or all of the necessary logic and software elements for a specific and usually very complex application.

ASYNCHRONOUS: Not synchronized to a clock pulse; description of a method of data transmission.

AT&T COMMUNICATIONS: The division of AT&T which operates, manages, and sells AT&T long-distance network telephone services and other services available through access to this network.

AT&T INFORMATION SYSTEMS (ATTIS): The division of AT&T which manufactures and sells hardware and software for telecommunications and computer applications. The lines of telephone central office equipment, PBX systems, telephone sets, and computers sold by AT&T are produced, maintained, and sold by this division.

AT&T TECHNOLOGIES: Formerly Bell Laboratories; this division of AT&T develops new technologies.

ATTENUATION: Decrease in signal strength due to absorption by a medium through which the signal is being transmitted.

BANDWIDTH: The frequency range that a component, circuit, or system can pass. Voice transmission by telephone uses a bandwidth of about 3000 hertz (3 kHz). A television channel occupies a bandwidth of 6 million hertz (6 MHz). CATV cable systems use between 5 MHz and 300 or 400 MHz of the electromagnetic spectrum. Currently available optical fibers have usable bandwidths of up to 3.3 billion hertz (3.3 GHz).

BASEBAND: A telecommunications transmission technique which uses the entire available bandwidth on a single physical transmission medium such as a coaxial cable. Baseband signals are not modulated onto a carrier signal, they remain in their original, unmodulated form. When transmitted, they reside at the base of the channel bandwidth. Baseband technology is predominantly used for data transmission because of the high volume and high speed at which baseband can transmit signals.

BASIC TELECOMMUNICATIONS SERVICES: The Federal Communications Commission's definition of common carrier transmission services which result only in the movement of information and do not involve the manipulation or restructuring of such information. (See also ENHANCED TELECOMMUNICATIONS SERVICES.)

BAUD RATE: The speed, in bits per second, at which data is transmitted.

BELL OPERATING COMPANY: One of the 22 regional or local telephone companies formerly within the Bell System which at present provide local and intrastate telephone service.

BELL SYSTEM: AT&T and its subsidiaries. Before divestiture, this included the Bell operating companies, the major providers of the nation's local and intrastate telephone service; AT&T Long Lines, the largest interstate telephone network; Western Electric, the leading manufacturer of telecommunications equipment; Bell Laboratories, a provider of research and development service which is jointly owned by AT&T and Western Electric; and AT&T International, the international arm which markets Bell System products and services outside the United States. The AT&T 1982 consent decree calls for the divestiture of parts of the Bell System into several economically separate companies.

BINARY SYSTEM: A numerical system using base 2. There are only two digits in the binary base system, 0 and 1. Data is encoded using the binary values 0 and 1, which represent the *on* or *off* states of the switches that compose a computer's internal memory.

BIT: A contraction of the words "binary digit"; the smallest unit of computer memory, represented by a binary digit (0 or 1). Information in digital code is represented in binary form by 0 or 1, and a bit refers to a single digit.

BOC: Acronym for Bell operating company.

BOOT: A vernacular term for the function which clears the computer and reloads a program into active memory storage.

BRANCH: An intermediate cable distribution line in a broadband or CATV network that feeds or is fed into a main trunk.

BROADBAND: CATV, local area network, or other telecommunications systems which can carry signals that use a large portion of electromagnetic spectrum. The spectrum is divided into segments which may be allocated for specific purposes such as television, voice, data, and other services.

BROADCASTING SATELLITE SERVICE (BSS): A radiocommunications service which transmits or retransmits signals via orbiting satellites for direct reception by the general public, direct broadcast satellite service.

BROADCASTS: Over-the-air transmissions of programs intended to be received by the general public, as differentiated from transmissions intended for specific addresses, e.g., point-to-point common carrier transmissions.

BUFFER: A storage area. Associated with a computer telecommunications device, the buffer stores an incoming or outgoing message in order to balance the activity of the computer with the telecommunications system or the device with which a machine is in communication.

BUNDLED RATES: Telecommunications utility rates in which the various rate elements comprising the service are consolidated into a single tariff.

BYTE: Usually, 8 bits of information in a sequence, forming a "word." The byte has become a standard means of expressing the memory capacity of a computer.

In ASCII coding, each character of the alphabet and number is represented by a byte. The byte "00000111" represents the number 7.

CABLECASTS: Transmissions of programs intended to be received only by cable system subscribers, as differentiated from over the air broadcasts or point-to-point transmissions to specific addresses.

CABLE FRANCHISE: An agreement by which a cable television company contracts with a local government for the right to provide cable communications services for the community.

CABLE LOSS: The amount of attenuation (signal loss) created by a given length of a particular cable. Cables attenuate higher frequencies more than lower ones. These losses may be calculated and corrected for by amplification.

CABLE TV (CATV): Community antenna television. A communication system which simultaneously distributes several different channels of broadcast programs and other information via a coaxial cable.

CARRIER SENSE MULTIPLE ACCESS/COLLISION DETECTION (CSMA/CD): A telecommunications technology controlling access to the medium, usually baseband, that allows many transceivers to share a single channel. All units monitor the channel and do not attempt transmission if a signal is sensed (carrier sense). When the channel is idle, any unit can begin transmission (multiple access). If two or more units begin transmitting at the same time, the energy level on the line is sensed as a collision (collision detection), and a set of procedures is followed by each node so that one of the nodes begins transmitting before any other, thus avoiding the possibility of a collision. The procedure is based on the distance each node is from the termination point of the network.

CARTERFONE DECISION: The United States Supreme Court decision, in 1966 to 1968, and subsequent FCC regulatory decision which allowed the Carterfone company to sell and install telephone equipment to connect with the AT&T telephone network. This established the legal rights of telephone subscribers to attach privately owned instruments to telephone company lines if this does not adversely affect the telephone system.

CATV: Community antenna television (*see* Cable TV).

CCITT: International Telegraph and Telephone Consultative Committee. The permanent organ of the International Telecommunications Union where member nations and recognized operating agents formulate recommendations concerning technical, operational, and tariff aspects of international telegraph and telephone systems.

CELLULAR MOBILE RADIO: A form of portable telephone service technology which allows mobile radio telephones to initiate and receive calls with private line quality. A metropolitan area is divided into geographical cells, each served by a low-power transmitter which is linked to other transmitters by an intelligent system utilizing computers.

CENTRAL RETRANSMISSION FACILITY (CRF): The location for the equipment that processes radio frequency signals for network retransmission in a broadband network; also called the head end.

CHANNEL: A specific range of frequencies for transmission of signals.

CHARACTER: Any symbol used to represent a digit, letter, punctuation mark, or mathematical or other operand.

CHIP: A silicon or other crystal wafer on which an integrated circuit has been printed by photomechanical means. Chips are used for such purposes as data storage, microprocessors, and managing various routines which a computer system needs to do regularly and routinely.

CIRCUIT: A connection between two or more points allowing continuous electrical signal communication between connected points.

CIRCUIT BOARD: A thin board on which a set of wiring circuits has been printed by a photomechanical process. In computer-operated systems, circuit boards have mounting plugs for the pins of chips which provide memory and other utilities.

CIRCUIT SWITCHING: The process by which continuous communication channels are established by switching circuits together between a call initiator and a receiver. Once the channel is established in circuit switching, it is maintained until the call is completed and disconnected.

COAXIAL CABLE: A single cable with two conductors having a common longitudinal axis separated by an insulating dielectric such as nylon. The center conductor carries information signals; the outer conductor acts as a shield and is connected to ground to prevent interference from unwanted signal frequencies. The shield is often made of a flexible foil, braided wire, or solid aluminum.

CODEC: Acronym for coder-decoder, a device which is used to translate digital signals to analog signals, for example, for transmission on the analog public voice telephone network.

COMMON CARRIER: A supplier of telecommunications services to the public subject to state and federal regulation.

COMMUNICATIONS SATELLITE: An orbiting space satellite station that receives video, audio, data, and other transmissions from uplinks and retransmits them to downlinks.

COMMUNICATIONS SATELLITE CORPORATION (COMSAT): A private corporation created by the Communications Satellite Act of 1962. COMSAT is the United States participant in the International Telecommunications Satellite Organization and the provider of international satellite services for communications between the United States and foreign countries. Comsat is also the United States Representative to the International Maritime Satellite Organization and provides a variety of domestic satellite communications facilities and services. Three out of fifteen members of the Board of Directors are appointed by the President with the advice and consent of the Senate.

COMMUNITY ANTENNA TELEVISION: CATV; the name for cable television services which originated by providing the service of transmitting over the air broadcast signals in areas of poor reception.

COMPUTER II: The regulatory decision of the FCC (also known as the Second Computer Inquiry) which amended the regulatory scheme governing provision of regulated telecommunications services. The FCC abandoned its previous regulatory scheme, which was based on distinguishing between "communications services" (regulated) and "data-processing services" (not regulated). The Computer II regulatory scheme went into effect on January 1, 1983. It differentiates "basic transmission services" (regulated) from "enhanced services" and customer premises equipment (CPE) (not regulated). The FCC required that CPE charges be unbundled and that equipment be sold separately. AT&T, the dominant carrier, was permitted to sell competitive services (enhanced services and CPE) only through separate subsidiaries. All carriers were required to prevent cross subsidization between the two.

CONNECTOR: A cable end device of a standard design for interfacing cables with equipment and with other cables.

CONTINUOUS FORM PAPER: A continuous stock of paper for computer printing purposes which has been perforated to allow the paper to be easily torn into sheets after printing. Most paper of this kind is provided with standard perforated edge strips for printers equipped with "tractor" devices that help to feed the paper correctly into and out of the printer.

CONTROL CODES: Codes reserved for communication management purposes, such as the codes that are part of the ASCII character set which allow a printer to control the output of the computer.

CPI: Acronym for characters per inch, referring to the number of characters which will fit into a columnar inch in a horizontal line.

CPS: Acronym for characters per second, referring to the number of characters a printer will print in the duration of one second. Line and high-speed laser printers will print at the rate of thousands of characters per second.

CPU: Acronym for central processing unit, referring to the part of the computer which manages the computations and keeps track of the location of information being processed by a system.

CROSS SUBSIDIZATION: The use of revenues or facilities of one service to allay the costs of another product or service.

CSMA/CD: *See* Carrier sense multiple access/collision detection.

CUSTOMER PREMISES EQUIPMENT: CPE; the telecommunications-related equipment located on a customer's premises which is connected to telephone company facilities to terminate or adapt that facility for customer use.

DAISYWHEEL: A print element having the characters placed on petal-like spokes surrounding a hub. The element is mounted so that it can be spun to select the character to be printed and can be hit by an electromagnet-controlled hammer at the appropriate moment. Daisywheel printers are relatively inexpensive, produce high-quality text, may use hundreds of different character sets, and can print at the rate of 25 to 45 characters per second (25 to 45 cps).

DATA: Information that has been encoded in a formal, standard manner, making it usable by a computer.

DATABASE: A collection of information organized for a purpose.

DATABASE MANAGEMENT: The task of organizing a database.

DATA COMMUNICATIONS EQUIPMENT (DCE): Equipment that links a user's data terminal equipment to a common carrier's line.

DATA RATE: The rate of information transfer, expressed in number of bits per second (b/s).

DATA TERMINAL EQUIPMENT (DTE): Equipment that is the ultimate source or destination of data transmission.

dB: *See* Decibel.

DEC: Digital Equipment Corporation.

DECIBEL: A unit used to express the ratio between two power or other signal values.

DETECTORS: Elements of a fiber optic transmission system which detect the light signal and translate the signal into an electromagnetic signal.

DIGITAL: Referring to the use of binary form for encoding, processing, and communication of data.

DIGITAL EQUIPMENT CORPORATION: The primary manufacturer of mini-computer systems.

DIGITAL SIGNAL: Discrete signals consisting of a choice between two possible states, representing 1 or 0. The presence or absence of an electrical signal (*on* or *off*) or two different electrical signal levels can be used to represent 0 or 1.

DIP SWITCH: Acronym for dual in-line package switch, a set of small switches designed and manufactured as a package by a method resembling that for an integrated circuit. It is used to preset control parameters for computer-related devices and peripherals.

DISTRIBUTED PROCESSING: A method by which computing resources are placed in a number of different locations which are interconnected, usually by means of a local area network. The processing load may then be distributed among a number of machines, each one of which may be assigned a certain range of specialized tasks.

DISTRIBUTION AMPLIFIER: An amplifier used to increase radio frequency (RF) signal levels to overcome cable and other signal losses.

DOMESTIC SATELLITE CARRIER: A carrier which provides intercity communications services within the United States via a domestic communications satellite.

DOMSAT DECISION: *See* Open skies decision.

DOWNLINK: A unidirectional transmission path from a communications satellite to an earth station.

EARTH STATION: An antenna that is electronically equipped to receive signals from satellites and/or to transmit signals to satellites. Television receiver only

(TVRO) satellite dishes are commonly used by cable companies and others; they only receive signals.

ECHO: Secondary signals caused by the collisions of the transmitted signal with structures or objects in its path. Echoes can occur in a cable system by impedance mismatches and cable discontinuities or irregularities.

EIA: Electronics Industry Association

EIA RS232C: Standard adopted by the Electronics Industry Association for a 25-pin physical connector for connecting computers and computer-driven devices and peripherals. The standard establishes the shape and dimensions of a 25-contact connecting plug and socket, which can be wired according to a manufacturer's or user's wish.

EIA RS422 and 423: Standard adopted by the Electronics Industry Association for a 16-pin physical connector for connecting computers and computer-driven devices and peripherals.

ELECTRONIC MESSAGE SYSTEM: An electronic message service; any computer-managed message service such as electronic mail or electronic funds transfer.

ELECTRONIC NOISE: Random electrical interference that a computer or peripheral device could interpret as signals or data, causing anomalies in data or information or erratic performance by a system.

ENHANCED TELECOMMUNICATIONS SERVICES: The FCC definition of common carrier transmission services which involve the manipulation or alteration of basic telecommunication service offerings, for example, protocol conversion.

EQUAL ACCESS: A provision, ordered by the FCC, that local telephone companies must provide telephone customers with equal ease of access to all common carriers of long-distance signals.

EQUALIZATION: Technique used to modify the frequency response of an amplifier or network to compensate for distortions in the communication channel. The ideal is to achieve a flat response. Slope compensation is usually done automatically by a module within an amplifier enclosure.

ESTABLISHED CARRIERS: Common carrier firms which provide the nation's telecommunications services under regulation; AT&T Communications, the Bell operating companies, and the independent telephone companies.

ETHERNET: The product name for a set of specifications for a baseband local area network technology jointly developed by Xerox, DEC, and Intel.

EXCHANGE ACCESS: The connection of interexchange carriers to the local exchange carrier's telecommunications network.

EXCHANGE CARRIER: A provider of telecommunications exchange service.

EXCHANGE SERVICE: Telephone service within a geographic area established by a regulated operation which provides customers with the ability to originate calls within that local area, to receive incoming calls, and to obtain access to the message toll network; under the terms of the AT&T 1982 consent decree, service provided by a divested Bell operating company which remains with a local access and transport area.

EXECUNET DECISIONS: Two decisions of the District of Columbia Court of Appeals which approved competition in the long-distance telephone market. The first decision remanded and reversed the FCC decision not to approve tariffs filed by MCI for its Execunet service. Execunet provided an alternative long-distance network for subscribers by allowing them to interconnect over public telephone lines with an MCI microwave link through which they could reconnect into the public telephone network of a distant city. In the second decision, the court required AT&T to provide local physical interconnection with its network for MCI, which was essential to provision of end-to-end service.

FCC: *See* Federal Communications Commission.

F CONNECTOR: A standard, inexpensive, 75-ohm connector used in the CATV industry to interconnect coaxial cable to equipment.

FDM: *See* Frequency division multiplexing.

FEDERAL COMMUNICATIONS COMMISSION (FCC): The United States federal agency which regulates the use of radio frequencies for broadcast communications and the operations of firms in the mass media and telecommunications fields.

FIBER OPTIC CABLE: A signal transmission medium that uses frequencies in the visible light spectrum to transmit signals.

FIBER OPTICS: Technology for transmitting light in thin glass or plastic fibers. This technique is used to carry large volumes of information quickly over long distances.

FILE SERVER: A node on a local area network that consists of software for storing and providing access to data files which have been stored by users of the network.

FLAT WIRE: Cable manufactured in a flat cross section, like a ribbon, allowing the placement of wiring under carpeting.

FRAME: A term used in token passing and other packetizing techniques for local area networks. The parameters of the frame are bits which may be set to indicate the source and destination of the message. Space within the frame is reserved for a volume of data which is to be the actual message.

FREQUENCY: The number of times a periodic signal repeats itself in a unit of time, typically 1 second, usually expressed in hertz. Frequency is the measure of the number of waves that pass a given point in a given time period. One hertz (1 Hz) means one cycle per second. One kilohertz (1 kHz) is 1000 cycles per second. One megahertz (1 MHz) is 1 million cycles per second. One gigahertz (1 GHz) is 1 billion cycles per second.

FREQUENCY DIVISION MULTIPLEXING (FDM): A multiplexing technique which divides a communication channel's total bandwidth into several subchannels with different carrier frequencies. Each subchannel can carry separate data signals, in either direction.

FREQUENCY RESPONSE: Change of a parameter (such as signal amplitude) with frequency.

GATEWAY SERVER: A node on a local area network which consists of software for carrying transmissions into and out of the network. A gateway device could, for instance, automatically route a message intended for a remote destination out of the LAN into the public telephone system, to a remote network gateway server which would receive the transmission and pass it along to the destination on that network. This particular process is known as automatic internetwork routing.

GEOSTATIONARY ORBIT: *See* Geosynchronous orbit.

GEOSYNCHRONOUS ORBIT: An orbital path at an altitude of 22,300 miles above the Earth's equator. Satellites in geosynchronous orbit complete one revolution of the Earth at the same rate as the Earth makes one revolution on its axis. They therefore stay at the same point relative to any point on Earth.

GIGABIT (Gb): 1,000,000,000 (1 billion) bits per second.

GIGAFLOP (Gf): 1,000,000,000 (1 billion) decisions per second.

GIGAHERTZ (GHz): 1,000,000,000 (1 billion) cycles per second.

GTE: General Telephone and Electronics.

GTE-SPRINT: GTE long-haul telecommunications service.

GTE-SPRINT TELENET: GTE public packet-switching network.

HANDSHAKING: Term used to refer to the establishing of communications between computers and between a computer and peripheral.

HARD COPY: Text or other data printed or plotted on paper from data generated by a computer system.

HEAD END: The facility that contains a cable system's electronic control center. In a CATV system, it usually includes antennas, preamplifiers, frequency converters, demodulators, modulators, and other equipment to monitor, amplify, filter, and convert broadcast signals to cable system channels. In broadband local area network systems, the head end includes a frequency translator and possibly a host computer system.

HERTZ: Unit of measurement of frequency; equal to 1 cycle per second. *See* Frequency.

HEXADECIMAL SYSTEM: Numbering system and data encoding technique using a base-16 numbering system. The units in the hex system are 1, 2, 3, 4, 5, 6, 7, 8, 9, A, B, C, D, E, F, 0.

HIGH FREQUENCIES: Frequencies allocated for transmission in the forward direction in a midsplit broadband system; approximately 160 to 400 MHz.

HIGHSPLIT: A frequency division scheme for broadband data communications networks which permits two-way traffic on a single cable. Reverse path signals travel to the head end or hub on frequencies of 5 to 174 MHz; forward path signals are sent from the head end on frequencies of between 232 and 400 MHz. No signals are permitted between 174 and 232 MHz to achieve reliable signal separation.

HP: Hewlett Packard Corporation.

HUB: The head end for bidirectional networks such as broadband local area networks.

IBM: International Business Machines.

IBM 3270: A data terminal product series manufactured by IBM. The protocols for communication between the IBM 3270 series workstations and host computers have been generally adopted as a standard in the industry.

IBM SNA: IBM Systems Network Architecture. A set of specifications for establishing a local area network compatible with IBM systems.

IMPLEMENTATION: The process of installing a computer system and software on the job, including the training of personnel and management procedural changes that may be required.

INBOUND CABLE: The cable carrying signals from nodes in a broadband local area network to the head end in a dual cable system.

INDEPENDENT TELEPHONE COMPANY: A firm which is not part of the Bell System or Bell operating companies and which is the designated established carrier for telecommunications common carrier services within a geographic area. There are about 1500 independent telephone companies in the United States which provide less than 20 percent of the nation's telephone service. The other 80% is provided by Bell operating companies

INFORMATION: The interpretation of data.

INITIALIZED STATE: The preset operational parameters for a computer or computer-driven machine that are automatically assumed when the machine is powered up. In a computer printer, for instance, this would include settings for margins and tabs and the positioning of the print head, print element, etc.

INSERTION LOSS: Loss of signal level in a cable caused by the insertion into the signal path of passive devices.

INSTALLATION: The process of setting the parameters of software, such as an application program, so that the program will communicate with the peripheral devices on the system, such as printers.

INTEGRATED CIRCUIT: A wiring plan, usually printed by a photomechanical process onto a board or chip. The circuit contains several elements of a system in an integrated plan. An integrated circuit is often a single piece of silicon on which a number of electronic modifiers are directly etched along with the connections between them. This allows for whole sections of a computer's functions, such as logic or memory components, to be contained within one chip.

INTEGRATED SERVICES DIGITAL NETWORK (ISDN): A telecommunications network which permits the simultaneous transmission of signals that carry voice, data, and video signals. The signaling method of the ISDN is digital, which means that analog signals (such as voice and video signals) must be coded in digital form for transmission and decoded to an analog form when received (*see* CODEC).

INTERACTIVE CABLE SYSTEM: A cable television system capable of transmitting signals in both directions, allowing viewer response or participation.

INTEREXCHANGE CARRIER: A provider of telecommunications interexchange service.

INTEREXCHANGE SERVICE: Telephone service between points located in one exchange area and points located in other areas—under the AT&T 1982 consent decree, service provided between local access and transport areas or service between a local access and transport area and a point outside that area.

INTERFACE: The physical connection between computers and between a computer and a peripheral.

INTERLATA: Communication between local area transport networks.

INTERNATIONAL TELECOMMUNICATIONS SATELLITE ORGANIZATION (INTELSAT): The international organization which owns and operates the global satellite communications system. It was established in 1964, and there are now 106 member nations.

INTERNATIONAL TELECOMMUNICATIONS UNION (ITU): The United Nations organization that coordinates international telecommunications operations, including the management of spectrum assignment. It has 150 member nations at this time.

INTRALATA: Communication within a local area transport network.

I/O: Input/output.

I/O BUS: A specialized communications technology optimized for computer communications over very short distances. Used for communications within a computer system to connect the dependent components of one system and between a computer and peripherals.

ISDN: *See* Integrated services digital network.

ISOLATION LOSS: The amount of signal attenuation of a passive device from outlet port to tap outlet port.

ITT: International Telephone and Telegraph.

LAN: *See* Local area network.

LASER: Device for light amplification by stimulated emission of radiation. A laser utilizes the natural oscillations of atoms or molecules between energy levels to generate coherent electromagnetic radiation in the ultraviolet, infrared, or visible light spectrum. This produces a tightly packed, highly concentrated, narrow beam of light formed by the emission of high-energy molecules.

LOCAL ACCESS AND TRANSPORT AREAS (LATAs): Geographic regions which represent the postdivestiture service areas of the 22 Bell operating companies and independent telephone companies. All telephone service within a LATA is defined as exchange service, while service between LATAs is defined as interexchange service.

LOCAL AREA NETWORK (LAN): A broad variety of technologies for efficient, high-speed, high-volume communications over limited distances; usually a private network. LANs typically allow a great number and variety of machines to exchange large amounts of information at high speed over limited distances.

LOCAL BYPASS: The use of an alternative telecommunications system instead of the local established carrier to gain direct access to customers inside a local exchange service.

LOCAL LOOP: A circuit that connects equipment to a switching facility or distribution point of the LATA.

LONG-HAUL COMMUNICATIONS: Communications over distances that range between a few miles and several thousand miles.

LOW FREQUENCIES: Frequencies allocated for transmission in the return direction in a midsplit broadband system; between 5 MHz and 116 MHz.

MAIN TRUNK: In a CATV or broadband system, the major cable link from the head end or hub to downstream branches.

MCI: Microwave Communications Incorporated.

MEASURED LOCAL SERVICE: Telephone service incorporating a method of pricing based on the time of day and the number, duration, and distance of calls within the local exchange area instead of by a flat rate.

MEGABIT: 1,000,000 bits.

MEGACOMPUTER: A supercomputer capable of operating at levels in excess of 10 gigaflops per second.

MEGAHERTZ: 1,000,000 cycles per second.

MESSAGE SWITCHING: The technique of receiving a message, storing it until the proper outgoing line is available, and then transmitting it.

MESSAGE TOLL SERVICE: A nonprivate line intrastate and interstate long-distance telephone service which permits local subscribers to establish two-way service on a message by message basis.

MICROCOMPUTER: An 8-, 16-, or 32-bit machine which can be used as a stand-alone intelligent terminal or computer system.

MICROPROCESSOR: The component in a microprocessor computer which does the computations and keeps track of the location of information during processing. An integrated circuit chip which contains the electronic circuits of a central processing unit.

MICROWAVE: Short electromagnetic waves in the radio frequency spectrum at 1000 megahertz or greater. Any form of signals can be transmitted at these frequencies between line-of-sight points.

MIDBAND: The part of the electromagnetic frequency spectrum, between television channels 6 and 7, reserved by the FCC for mobile units, FM radio, and aeronautical and maritime navigation. This frequency band, between 108 and

174 MHz, may be used to provide additional channels on cable television systems.

MINICOMPUTER: A relatively small, general purpose computer typically used for dedicated applications.

MODEM: Modulator/demodulator. The modem is used to convert the digital signals of a computer to or from analog form for transmission on analog networks such as the public telephone network. The modulator codes information in digital form onto an analog carrier signal by varying the amplitude, frequency, or phase of the carrier. The demodulator reconverts information from a modified analog carrier.

MULTIPLEXING: A method by which a single channel is divided into many channels in order to transmit a number of independent signals simultaneously. When signals are multiplexed onto one channel, capacity of the medium is increased and more users can be served.

MULTITAP: A tap into a broadband, CATV, or baseband network medium composed of a directional coupler and a splitter with two or more output connections.

NATURAL MONOPOLY: A market situation in which government public utility regulators have deemed it more efficient and economical for a product or service to be provided by a single firm under regulation than by two or more competing firms. The provision of telecommunications services was originally considered to be a natural monopoly market situation.

NETWORK: A system for communications, with established standards and procedures for common access by a number of users.

NETWORK ADMINISTRATOR: An individual in an organization responsible for the maintenance of the communications link and the assignment of access privileges.

NETWORK MANAGER: Software that is part of the network technology for managing use, regulating access, and monitoring system effectiveness.

NODE: Any device with access to the network, such as a user workstation, print server, file server, host computer, or network manager device.

NOISE: Undesired signal in a communication system.

NOISE FIGURE: Measure of the amount of noise contributed to a system by an amplifier.

NOISE FLOOR: Minimum noise level possible on a system.

NORTHERN TELECOM INTERNATIONAL (NTI): Subsidiary of Bell Canada; the primary manufacturer of PBX equipment in North America.

NTI: *See* Northern Telecom International.

OPEN SKIES DECISION: Also known as the Domsat Decision, the FCC decision which allows any non-federal-government entity to construct and operate communications satellite facilities for domestic use

OPTICAL FIBERS: Continuous glass or plastic filaments which carry the optical signal (light) in a fiber optic communications system. They are produced in varying thicknesses and densities, based on intended use, and are sheathed in an opaque material to prevent loss of the light signal and entrance of outside light noise. Higher performance is obtained from glass than from plastic.

OTHER COMMON CARRIER (OCC): A carrier authorized by the FCC to provide telecommunications services in competition with the established carriers (includes domestic satellite carriers and specialized common carriers).

OUTBOUND CABLE: The cable carrying signals from the head end or hub in a dual cable system.

OUTLET: A connector used to provide access to a network or source of power. In a broadband or CATV system, for instance, a type F connector port is used as a means of attaching drop cables to devices or TV receivers.

PACKET: A part of a whole message. In packet communications systems, whole messages are divided into discrete units of data, of fixed or variable length. Each packet contains bits for synchronization, control information, message number in the series being sent, number of the current and last packet, destination and source addresses, acknowledgment and error checking, and the data.

PACKET COMMUNICATIONS UNIT (PCU): Device that connects a terminal or computer to a broadband packet-switched network.

PACKET SWITCHING: The process by which packets are placed on a communications channel and by which they travel across to their destination.

PACKET-SWITCHING NETWORK: A communications system for the routing of packets among locations which may be very widespread; a data communications switching and transmission system whereby an input data stream is broken into uniform packets to which are appended addressing information, sequence counts, and error controls. Each packet is transmitted independently through the network so as to maximize the utilization of transmission facilities, and at the receiving end the individual packets are resequenced and combined as necessary into the output data stream.

PAD: Passive attenuation device used to reduce a signal's amplitude.

PARALLEL INTERFACE: The multipin physical connection which allows parallel transmission.

PARALLEL TRANSMISSION: A method of data communication wherein a number of wires are used to simultaneously send parts of a message. In parallel transmission, the whole words of a message are sent at one time, rather than in a serial stream of bits.

PARITY: Method of checking for errors in data transmission. The system determines that an error has been made when the number of bits received is odd or even, depending on the setting of the system.

PBX: *See* Private branch exchange.

PERIPHERALS: Devices that may be used or driven by a computer including printers, disk or tape drives, plotters, scanners, and monitors.

PORT: Software-supported connection between a computer and a peripheral device.

POWER SUPPLY: Component of a computer or computer-driven device that provides a continuous and uniform source of electrical power. It may also convert current from one form to another.

PRINT SERVER: Node on a local area network which performs the task of producing hard copies (paper copies) from data files.

PRIVATE BRANCH EXCHANGE (PBX): Device developed initially as a means of connecting calls between parties on the same premises and switching calls between the premises and the outside telephone network.

PROTOCOL: Set of procedures controlling the way data is transmitted between a computer and peripherals.

PUBLIC SWITCHED NETWORK: The local public telephone network, formerly the Bell System network.

QUERY: Formulation of an inquiry into a database according to a previously established form.

RADIO FREQUENCY SPECTRUM: Frequencies between the audio and visual spectra in which electromagnetic impulses can be radiated through space. This range is utilized for services such as communications, radar, earth resources sensing, and commercial radio and television.

RBOC: Regional Bell Operating Company.

RECEIVER: A radio frequency receiver.

RECEIVER ISOLATION: The attenuation between any two receivers connected to a cable system.

REFLECTION: *See* Echo.

RESALE CARRIER: A telecommunications service carrier which leases circuits from a telecommunications common carrier and resells them to individual users for a profit.

RESET: To resume from a stopped position; for instance, in the case of computer-driven printers, to resume printing after the printer has paused for ribbon or paper insertion.

RETURN PATH: Reverse direction in a broadband system, toward the head end.

RF: Radio frequency.

RIBBON ARRAY CABLE: An array of fiber optic cables arranged horizontally in the form of a ribbon. Ribbon array cables are premanufactured with connectors to allow the rapid installation of a system according to a previous plan.

ROUTING SERVER: Node on a local area network which routes communications between the network and external networks.

RS232C: *See* EIA RS232C.

SATELLITE, ARTIFICIAL EARTH: A manmade object in Earth orbit; includes a number of different types for telecommunications, broadcasting, weather research and conditions reporting, geodetic survey, navigation, security reconnaisance and scientific experimentation.

SATELLITE MASTER ANTENNA TELEVISION (SMATV): Television signal-carrying systems that provide services similar to CATV but only provide services to a private premises, such as an apartment building or condominium complex. SMATV operators contract with property owners, as opposed to securing franchises from local governments to supply service by stringing cable alongside or under public thoroughfares.

SATELLITE SYSTEM: A telecommunications system using one or more Earth satellites.

SBS: Satellite Business Systems.

SBS/REALCOM: Satellite Business Systems division for operating shared telecommunications systems in large office buildings.

SEMICONDUCTOR: A solid with an electrical conductivity that lies between the relatively high conductivity of metals and the relatively low conductivity of insulators. Semiconductor elements include crystal diodes, transistors, and integrated circuit chips.

SERIAL: Refers to the method of transmitting data in a serial stream of bits, one after the other.

SERIAL INTERFACE: A physical connection for serial data transmission.

SHARED USER: A user of telecommunications services who with other users subscribes to a private line service of an established carrier, in order to share the cost of obtaining that service in a collective nonprofit arrangement.

SIGNAL: Electromagnetic energy used to convey information; an interpretable variation of electromagnetic or light waves which can be transmitted and received.

SIGNAL LEVEL: The voltage measured at the peak of an RF signal, usually expressed in microvolts referred to an impedance of 75 ohms or in dBmV.

SLOPE: The difference between signal levels at the highest frequency and at the lowest frequency in a cable system.

SPECIALIZED COMMON CARRIER (SCC): A carrier which provides intercity private line service in competition with established carriers.

SPECTRUM FEE: A proposed fee to be charged to users of the radio frequency spectrum, either in proportion to the frequency space occupied or based on a percentage of profits realized. Proposals for use of such a fee or tax have been previously viewed as methods for reimbursing the government for associated regulatory costs and for funding public interest broadcasting. Spectrum assignment and fees have been proposed in this book as a means of regulating telecommunication services in a competitive environment.

SPRINT: A specialized common carrier. *See* GTE-Sprint.

STOP BITS: Bits of data used for error checking in the transmission of data between computers and between computers and peripherals such as printers.

STROBE: A signal transmitted over a parallel interface that tells the computer when data can be sampled on the interface. When the strobe signal is not set, the data lines of the interface are in an uncertain state.

SUBSPLIT: A frequency division scheme for broadband that allows two-way traffic on a single cable. Reverse path signals transmit at 5 to 30 MHz and forward path signals (from head end) at 54 to 400 MHz. No signals may be present between 30 and 54 MHz, to provide channel isolation.

SUPERCOMPUTER: *See* Megacomputer.

SURGE ARRESTOR: A device that protects electronic equipment against surge voltage and transient signals of trunk and distribution lines and power sources.

SYNCHRONOUS: Refers to a method of data communication whereby data transmission is synchronized to (brought into phase with) a clock pulse. The clock pulse is transmitted through the interface with the data.

TAP: In baseband local area networks, a passive device to provide physical connection to a cable. In broadband, a tap is normally installed in a feeder cable to remove a portion of the signal power from the distribution line and deliver it to the drop line.

TAP OUTLET: In broadband, a type F connector port on a tap used to attach a drop cable. The information signal is carried through this port.

TARIFF: A statement filed by a telecommunications common carrier with the appropriate public regulatory agency which describes the service it offers and lists a schedule of charges for the use of that regulated telecommunications service.

TELECOMMUNICATIONS: The transmission of signals of any kind by wire, radio, optical, or other electromagnetic system.

TELETEXT: A one-way information system in which textual and graphic material is generally conveyed as part of the television broadcast signal or over cable.

TERMINAL EQUIPMENT: Equipment for sending or receiving information over a telecommunications channel and using that channel for mechanical (computer/PBX) or human voice communications.

TERMINATION: In broadband technology, a 75-ohm resistor that terminates the end of a cable or an unused tap port with its characteristic impedance to minimize reflections.

TIME DIVISION MULTIPLEXING (TDM): Method of allowing several users to share a common communications channel by giving each user access to the channel for a defined length of time, according to a preset, repeated sequence.

TIME-SHARING: Method of allowing a number of users to share a computer system through allocation of time between them.

TRANSISTOR: A sandwich of semiconducting materials which arranges the semiconductor crystals so that they act like switches, controlling the flow of current throughout. Silicon crystals are the materials most commonly used.

TRANSLATOR: The device in a broadband local area network which receives signals at the head end at one frequency level and converts the signal to a frequency level for retransmission to the recipient's receiver.

TRUNK: In telephone PBX technology, a dedicated line to the local telephone company providing a specific range of local or long-distance calling services.

TRUNK AMPLIFIER: A low-distortion amplifier that amplifies RF signals for long-distance transport.

TRUNK CABLE: Coaxial cable used for distribution of RF signals over long-distance through a cable system; usually the largest cable in the system.

TRUNK LINE: The major cable links from the head end or hub in a broadband system to downstream branches.

ULTRAHIGH-FREQUENCY (UHF): Refers to the frequencies in the 300 to 3000 megahertz band.

UNBUNDLED RATES: Telephone service rates in which the various rate elements comprising the service are separately calculated, making it possible to identify the charge for each component of the service.

UPLINK: A unidirectional transmission path from an earth station to a communications satellite.

USAGE SENSITIVE PRICING: Charges for telephone service based on usage measurement (duration and total number of calls per month) in contrast to a flat fee charge (*see* Measured local service).

VALUE-ADDED CARRIER: A carrier which leases circuits from telecommunications common carriers and then adds special services, such as computer-oriented services, before retailing the use of the circuits to a final user.

VALUE-ADDED RESELLER: A packager of computer equipment and software which purchases the hardware and operating system software elements from manufacturers and then assembles these elements, adding industry specific applications software to produce a total system for a particular kind of business or vertical market.

VAX SYSTEM: A minicomputer system manufactured by DEC which supports the DEC VAX operating system and any software designed to run on a VAX operating system.

VERY HIGH FREQUENCY (VHF): Refers to frequencies between 30 and 300 megahertz.

VERY LARGE SCALE INTEGRATION (VLSI): The technology of imprinting more than 5000 separate logic circuits or more than 16,000 memory units on a single chip.

VIDEODISK: A disk which stores large amounts of data, audio, and/or video information in digital form. The writing and reading of the information employs laser technologies.

VIDEOTEX: Generic term for computer-driven information retrieval systems which display graphics and text on a video screen; includes the concept of teletext (one-way retrieval) and videotext (interactive retrieval).

VIDEOTEXT: Two-way, computer-driven information retrieval and exchange system in which the user is connected to the database by telephone line or cable. The system is interactive; users can send messages or perform transactions in addition to receiving information.

WIDE-AREA TELEPHONE SERVICE (WATS): A telephone service which allows a subscriber to make calls to specific geographic areas for a rate based on volume and time of day at rates substantially less than those charged for message toll service. An 800 WATS service allows inbound calls to be received from specific areas with no charge to the caller.

XEROX: The Xerox Corporation; the Xerox process for photomechanical reproduction of documents.

X.25: The CCITT paragraph containing the standards for international packet communications.

Index